Mystic Voyage

Mystic Voyage

A Journey of Spiritual Mastership

Elizabeth MacDonald Burrows

SEABOARD PRESS

AN IMPRINT OF J. A. ROCK & CO., PUBLISHERS

Mystic Voyage: A Journey of Spiritual Mastership
by Elizabeth MacDonald Burrows

SEABOARD PRESS

is an imprint of James A. Rock & Company, Publishers

Mystic Voyage: A Journey of Spiritual Mastership
copyright © 2006, 2007, 2008, 2010 by Elizabeth MacDonald Burrows

Formerly published as *To Walk With God: Autobiography of a Christian Mystic*

Special contents of this edition copyright ©2010 by Seaboard Press

Address comments and inquiries to:
SEABOARD PRESS
900 South Irby Street, #508
Florence, SC 29501
E-mail:
jrock@rockpublishing.com   lrock@rockpublishing.com
Internet URL: www.rockpublishing.com

Trade Paperback
ISBN-13/EAN: 978-1-59663-527-2

Library of Congress Control Number: 2006931631

Printed in the United States of America

First Edition: 2010

Dedicated to

He

Who is the voyage through

both Shadow and the Light

ACKNOWLEDGEMENTS

My Gratitude to those whose
tireless effort have made this book possible.

Mr. Santosh Kumas Boddikuri

Dr. Michelle Dossett

Rev. & Mrs. Benjamin Godair

Mr. Peter Hiatt

Dr. Tom Holloway

Rev. Don Jacobs

Rev. Gordon James

Ms. Cheryl McLaine

Miss Mary Ransdale

Dr. & Mrs. Ralph Sand III

Mr. Michael Shemet

Miss Cheryl Watkins

Dr. Keith Wong

TABLE OF CONTENTS

Yes, she is all the things described about her, I would discover, and so much more. It comes frustratingly close to being impossible to describe her in simple terms. It is certain, however, after spending time in the presence of Elizabeth Burrows, that she walks her path on Earth in grace and in a light so blinding, it spellbinds.

—Paula Dion, *Las Vegas Sun*

FOREWORD

While a study of mysticism, or even esotericism, may be helpful for most people, it is always difficult to find a genuine source of wisdom. So often we are flooded with different understandings, perspectives and interpretations, and we become lost in an ocean of speculation. This state of confusion is frustrating and often leads to cynicism. While many writings claim to contain a great deal of wisdom, at times they seem to offer little. We may hear much about the "secrets of the spiritual life," it is not often we can actually find them. Yes, a book here and there can offer fragments of the truth, but so often they are mixed in such a high ratio of truth packaging that the end result is a short spurt of inspiration followed by a return to the search.

My own experience was much as I have described. I had spent years reading, studying, compiling, and practicing a little here and some there, but I was slowly sliding into cynicism, as there was little coherence in the overall picture. Even within esotericism I found a lack of continuity and a definite lack of vision. This experience was transformed as I began to study the work of Elizabeth MacDonald Burrows. Now, this is not meant to be a coming to a "Guru" story, as so many of these are an insult to the intelligence of their readers. What it is meant to be is an honest reflection of my own experience. Elizabeth has been given an amazing gift, for she has experienced the Living Christ. This experience, this mystical exaltation, permeates her work. Although she is certainly an impressive scholar with a great mastery of both traditional mystical literature and that of the Essenes and Gnostics, she brings to these a sense of one who has truly experienced what she writes about. What impresses me about her work is her depth of vision; she has penetrated deeply into the nature of divinity and is able to map the journey for us

Robert Ledgewidge, Editor
Living Traditions, Australia

INTRODUCTION

In the worlds of psychiatry and psychology, words such as paranoia, aggrandizement, schizophrenia, psychosis, and many other terms are used to describe what some consider "abnormal" behavior. I have spent almost a quarter of a century piercing the inner planes of the human psyche. The borderline between mental illness and true transcendental experience appears similar at first; however, one very important difference exists. The mentally ill have lost their way along the inroads of the self and are unable to return or function in the natural world. The transcendentalist, on the other hand, maneuvers at all levels of consciousness safely and functions lucidly and effectively on Earth. As Jesus once said, "I live in this world, but I am not of it."

It is impossible to know how many people might have been placed in mental institutions, given shock treatments, or received high potency medication, in order to suppress a completely normal process of transformation. Any who become centered on a path to God, who participate in an intense devotion to a master such as Jesus, or who search into the mystery of life, as Carl Jung did, are prime candidates for a rendezvous with the "dark night of the soul". This process includes people from all walks of life: religious, scientific, and philosophical. In the Buddhist religion it is, I believe, defined as the "Period of Confusion". In India it is called by its more familiar name, "Dark Night of the Soul," while Christianity gives it several names, among these, "the Crucifixion of the Soul," "Armageddon," "Dark Night of the Soul." "War with Lucifer," and "Walk of Fire."

This dark night is a metamorphosis, like the growth of an embryo in the womb of a woman. A cluster of cells develops into a fetus and is born as a human child. The child is never closer to its mother than when it is in the fetal cocoon within its mother's body; yet the darkness that prevails over the fetus is as night, for no light shines upon it. When at last it is fully developed, it bursts from the womb into the light of Earth. Now its own body separates it from the very darkness that molded it.

As it is with the embryo, so it is with the soul. In the soul's search for God, its love and devotion does not go unnoticed.

In time, His Spirit is drawn by mutual attraction and encompasses the soul to affect a divine metamorphosis that changes it from human to divine. During this transformation, the soul does not behold light, for it is now in the womb of God. It remains in darkness until it is no longer bound by its earthly nature but is of the Light itself. This transformation is destined to descend on every human being someday. God designed it that way in the beginning of creation to assure every soul a moment of greatness in the winds of destiny. Each human life bears this portent seed of angelic birth, just as the embryo bears the seed of human life. The mystery of this metamorphosis is the core of all religions. It is also explained in philosophy and observed through scientific research.

Masonry defines this process as a philosophical death. Albert Pike wrote in his book, *Morals and Dogma:*

> Thus the scientific theories of the ancients, expounded in the Mysteries, as to the origin of the soul, its descent, its sojourn here below and its return, were not a mere barren contemplation of the nature of the world, and of the intelligent beings existing there. They were not an idle speculation as to the order of the world, and about the soul, but a study of the means for arriving at the great object proposed — the perfecting of the soul. To them, this Earth was not the soul's home, but its place of exile. Heaven was its home and there was its birthplace.

How many individuals have reached the high planes of spiritual mastery through Masonry will never be known, for it is a secret order. As a brotherhood, the Masons help each other to not only understand this process of change, but also to circumnavigate it. Christianity, in its early years, was also a secret organization. The Pope, Cardinals, and Bishops were sworn to secrecy, for such sublime mysteries were not given into the hands of the masses. In the East these mysteries were and still are secret in many ways, for they are generally passed down from teacher to disciple.

Why has this metamorphosis been kept so secret? I am afraid there is no single answer, but several. The primary reason is concern that instead of enticing people to walk this sublime path of transformation, knowledge of the dark night might frighten them away. On the other hand, those who have managed to traverse its deep waters successfully know that all people will enter one day and that when they do, the mysteries will be revealed. Therefore, much more time has been spent in teaching people how to walk the path than preparing them for it.

One example of this oversight is the science of meditation. It is a fact, that people from all walks of life rush to learn meditation because they seek a world of transcendentalism. Although there is nothing wrong with this, it does open portals into realms we cannot perceive through our human senses. Meditation is not designed simply to give its participants a psychic or mystical experience, but it also purifies. However, many who teach meditation do not inform their students about the effects of this practice. In time mental indigestion, depression, and many other psychological subtleties begin to surface, particularly if meditation is focused on reaching a higher state of consciousness, such as finding God or meeting with the higher Angelic beings. Who or what then picks up the pieces of this mental turmoil: institutions, medication, or suicide?

Several psychiatrists and psychologists have traversed this inner road of the soul, such as Jung and Fromm, but these are few. However, sometime in tomorrow's world, this transformation from human to angel will touch every human being. Each year, as more and more organizations are established to teach the deeper mysteries, more and more people will enter. I have had to ask myself many times, "Are we really prepared for this?"

True greatness and the ability to commune with God and his angels are the common rights of every individual. In our fear to open this secret doorway to these mysteries, we are denying ourselves the opportunity of a better life and, someday, world peace. I am one who has taught this divine metamorphosis openly, both its difficulties and its magnificence, and have given my life to help prepare the human race for this world of tomorrow and to help them to understand it; yet numerous times I have been told that I have set myself higher than other people and crowned myself with sainthood. This offends me deeply, because what I have experienced will in time become the experience of every human.

These realms we cannot see are as real as the Earth on which we live, perhaps more real, for Earth is not the true home of the soul. The soul descends and enters into a dense body for the purpose of growth. When it wears out a body, it discards it and returns to its true state. The process is both simple and reasonable to the senses. What separates these two worlds is nothing other than the difference in vibratory frequency. We hear at a human level, but as we refine our sense layers, the mind, and the subconscious, we become more what we are when not in embodiment, making it possible to see and hear in both worlds. What now may seem an unexplainable phenomenon to most people will be quite commonplace in our world yet to come.

Albert Pike writes in his book:

Most glorious is this capacity! A power to commune with God and His Angels; a reflection of the Uncreated Light; a mirror that can collect and concentrate upon itself all the moral splendors of the Universe. It is the soul alone that gives value to the things of this world, and it is only by raising the soul to its just elevation above all the other things, that we can look rightly upon the purpose of this Earth.

With this in mind, perhaps it will be easier to understand the unusual circumstances that have governed my life for so many years.

—Elizabeth. MacDonald Burrows

CHAPTER I

Into The Light

*I*f someone were to ask, "When does life really begin?" I would have to answer that life begins at different times for different people. For some it is the moment of birth. For others, it begins in grade school, high school, college, or with career changes. I feel that my own life began June 6, 1971 at 10:00 a.m., when my mind suddenly merged with the consciousness of the Infinite. Nothing prior to that day really seems worth mentioning, because a doorway opened into heretofore-unknown worlds. Thereafter it was impossible to return to the narrow confines and unknowing of my once finite limitations. In one single moment I was not only born anew, but also began to die — not as the body dies, but as the ages past have died.

Doctor R. M. Bucke wrote in his book, *Cosmic Consciousness*:

The simple truth is that there has lived on earth, appearing at intervals, for thousands of years among ordinary men the first faint beginnings of another race; walking the earth and breathing the air with us, but at the same time walking another earth and breathing another air. This new race is in the act of being born from us, and in the near future it will occupy and possess the earth.

The story preceding the events of my transformation began on an August day in the early seventies, when one of those periods of despondency which plague all humans at one time or another, fell upon me. Like most people who reach forty, the phantom of middle age had swooped down like a vulture upon a piece of cast away flesh. Suddenly there it was; a crevasse of past memories and little to show for years of living. This period is usually referred to as a mid-life crisis, when both men and woman look back on their accomplishments and chastise themselves because they feel they have not left their mark upon the world. That all people are of great importance and one cannot travel through life without touching those they love and the work they do, was not within the parameters of my understanding. Yet, like others, it was impossible not to speculate what might have happened if I had possessed both the will and courage to follow my dreams. My dream had been to be lawyer, but now here I was, neither a saint nor a villain facing the shadows of what might have been.

With unrestrained furor this mid-life crises seemed to beat upon my mind and heart with the wanton wings of a giant albatross. Little did I realize then, that when this muted ghost had passed, I would discover our deepest sorrow and grief often lays the groundwork for our greatest victories. Without these struggles of human life, it would be impossible to discover the road that leads homeward, and to partake of that one special journey which every human will take one day.

For me, the greatest adventure which can embrace any human began in Portland, Oregon, the land of my human birth. It was here that the first faint flutter of a new life, yet unknown, knocked upon my door. In this state of legends, myths and historical wonders I had been born to an unmarried woman during the latter years of the "Great Depression." It was certainly not a very auspicious beginning, for illegitimacy was looked upon as a terrible enigma — one that would most assuredly cast my soul into the fiery flames of perdition. Thus, in the eyes of the relatives I was considered conceived in evil lust and born without the saving grace of the Church. At that time, all children bearing such an unfortunate disgrace were looked upon as *the lost* children, and it was believed they could never amount to anything.

According to my birth information, my arrival into human existence took place in the White Shield Home in Portland, a Salvation Army retreat for unwed mothers. My mother's family considered their seventeen-year-old daughter, Ruth, who was unable to marry the man whose spark had created me, an outcast. Although a man's seed had given me existence, the family saw me as being quite fatherless. Fortunately for Ruth, and unfortunately for me, she was quite comely and soon attracted another man. Shortly thereafter they were married and before long the birth of a half-sister followed. With my half-sister Barbara's arrival, my presence in my mother's life was no longer wanted.

One day, when Barbara was about six months old, my new stepfather took me to the Portland bus depot to see to my departure. As a castaway, I found myself alone; too small to see the passing scenery through the nearby bus window. I have a fleeting remembrance of sitting on a huge seat with my coarse brown stocking legs stretched out in front of me and looking at my feet encased in a pair of black shoes with a single strap across the ankle.

This early part of my sojourn in the corporeal world is not spoken about with self-pity or excuses, but in an effort to help every human being understand that one's past cannot hold them imprisoned, nor stop the seed of greatness that will be born from them. As I was to overcome these childhood sorrows of mortality, so is the doorway to a greater tomorrow open to all people. Narrow would be a God who picks and chooses, giving wealth to one and poverty to another, illness to one and a strong body to another. If our allocation with destiny were really confined within the narrow roads of human life, then our hopes and dreams would be but fragments with no real destination. It seems, however, that these particles of human dust have sought exploration into outer space, created great symphonies and captured the hearts of the people with poetry and stories. Each tiny bundle of tears that is born with hope and dreams also bears an unrevealed self.

As I rode along there was no knowledge of the yet unopened doorway and glorious future which would one day reveal itself, for through my child eyes I simply saw scuffed black shoes. At the time, I was three and one-half years old and bound for a bleak dot on the map called Burley, Idaho. Burley had two main streets which crossed at an intersection in the middle of the town. It was a typical cattle and farming area, with dusty streets, hot summers and cold winters, and plagued by the constant ravages of the famous Idaho wind. It was said that the wind in Idaho could blow straw through a telephone pole.

My final destination appeared to be desolate farmhouse, located about four miles outside of Burley. This was a farm belonging to my great grandparents and even bleaker than the nearby towns. It stood in the middle of a flat wasteland of sand. When the wind blew newly planted crops were torn out in wanton fury, leaving despair instead of hope. There are memories of my new parents bent against the wind and the sand blowing in their faces, as they hoed, or plowed, trying to encourage a small pittance of survival from the desolation.

The farm held one saving grace. In the southern section of the property was an old Indian burial ground. It was a mysterious piece of land, which was never farmed and therefore remained untouched and solitary. Large clumps of sagebrush grew there, raising their spiny limbs amid knolls of leather-colored sand. This particular piece of land was sacred to the Indians, for it was an Indian burial ground. My great grandfather chose to honor their sacred tradition and allowed this particular remnant of sagebrush desolation to remain pristine, with only the melancholy song of wind to keep it company. It was here I came to seek comfort, throwing myself down in the sand and sobbing with inconsolable grief because of my terrible loneliness.

The one bright spot amid these solitary years of my early youth was the "prophecy." Great-grandmother, although a devout Christian, nevertheless had a fascination for the future and believed to some degree in the divination of tea leaves. When she heard that astrologers were doing astrological forecasts over a radio station in Twin Falls, Idaho, a town about fifty miles away, she sent my birth information in. I was now four years old. Although I had no memory of anything that was said, I was to hear the story of the "prophecy" many times while growing up.

According to great-grandmother, the astrologers whistled when they came to my birth information. They predicted that I would become some kind of a religious leader and build more churches than Aimee Semple McPherson, a controversial Canadian-born American evangelist who founded the International Church of Foursquare Gospel. Her colorful background included the opening of a 5000-seat Angelus Temple where she preached for twenty years. Although the prophecy never really bore fruit, the prediction of the astrologers overshadowed the early years of my life.

Immediately following the prophetic declaration, my great-grandmother began taking necessary steps to prepare me for my destiny. At the age of four I was introduced to elocution lessons. The elocution teacher lived twenty-two miles away in a small town called Rupert. Each week my new mother drove me to my lessons, paying for them with a dozen eggs or a chicken from the hen house. Before long my teacher decided that I possessed a talent for public speaking, as well as a measure of enjoyment for both audiences and acting.

By the age of five, I was in constant demand by organizations such as the Ladies Aid, Granges, farm organizations and churches to give recitations over the state of Idaho. These recitations called "readings," were actually short one act plays in which the presenter acted all of the different characters. Some of these roles still stand out in my memory, such as "The Cornhusk Doll." The play was about seventeen minutes long and had three major characters, Carlotta Camelot, a screen star, Katie, her maid, and a newspaper reporter. It was full of drama, and possessed a climatic ending of emotional beauty. My presentation often left most of the audience in tears.

In many ways, my youthful performances increased the burden of childhood because I was not allowed to play very often. Besides chores, there was the constant necessity to practice elocution. Elocution training in those days was a great art, and those who studied it were trained in a similar manner to opera singers. There were no microphones and one's voice had to reach the back of an auditorium, regardless of its size. Thus it was necessary to practice special breathing exercises to strengthen one's speaking capability, along with mountains of memory work. Unfortunately, Great-grandmother was liberal with the willow switch if I did not adhere to faithful practice. Once she even met me at the end of the half-mile lane leading to our old dilapidated farm house and soundly attacked the back of my leg with the switch all the way home.

As soon as possible I left the desolation of the barren farm with its frugal existence and vowed to never return. Its years of loneliness and hardship had created a deep hatred for the farm and the life it had imposed upon me. Free now to search for new adventure my steps took me from the country into the city. If any tendency toward homesickness spawned a shadow across my heart, the pain of my childhood quickly barred my temptation to return. Neither have I spoken of those years often. Instead, it seemed fitting to allow the mournful desert wind to bury the years of my youth in the half-forgotten abyss of the subconscious.

Two decades had passed since leaving the farm when I found myself back in Portland, Oregon, the same city that had given me human life. Somehow it seemed prophetic that one should face the first labor pains of a new birth in a place that brought them into human existence. As the summer heat parched the earth during these amber days of that August, it also brought a bout of mid-life crises to my soul. It was not a forlornness that could be explained at the time. In retrospect, of course, it is now possible to understand the emptiness of the soul when it has not found its' true purpose. In the words of Omar Khayyam, "The Vine had struck a Fibre; which about it clings my Being; of my Base Metal may be filed a Key that shall unlock the Door he howls without."

Destiny and the world yet to come was a closed door on this late summer day as I reached one of the lower points of my discontent. There were even vague thoughts about ending my life prancing like ghostly shadows through my mind. As the days passed during that August, my anxiety seemed to intensify and I found myself struggling desperately to hang on to some slender thread of life's importance. Although I may have prayed a thousand times there is no memory of any prayers, for I had separated myself from the church years before because I could not live up to the somewhat mechanical idealism it imposed upon me. Facing this battle of encroaching night with its moving phantoms of pain, brought no awareness that I was being prepared for a long and arduous journey which would take me beyond the boundaries of mortality and open a gateway to a world most people have never known.

There is no regret when looking back upon the days of my youth, for my eyes are no longer bound by the self-concepts that once held me to a world of sorrow. This haunting flurry of discontent is a part of almost every human life. If there were no difficulties, one would not seek the inner road to find something more to life and find that sacred spark which will one day burst forth as a morning sun. During this period of introspect, however, such knowledge was hidden from me in the dark mist of unknowing which covers the eyes of those who are encased in mat-

ter. On occasion, however, despair over my *sins* seemed to burn
like an ever-consuming flame, and the haunting words of my relatives, that "*I would never amount to anything*," lingered in the distant Idaho Winds.

One morning, as some indefinable specter held me in its
dogged grip, she came. I do not remember her name and this is
perhaps sad, because her arrival heralded the beginning to the end
of the human world I had always known. As we sat together beneath the early morning sun, shaded by a low-hung roof over the
front porch of the home my husband and I were currently renting, she listened quietly as I talked. It was as though floodgates
had been opened and the story of my discontent flowed out of me
like a rampant river. When the torrent of words had abated somewhat, she asked if I would go to church with her that night and hear
an evangelist who had just arrived in town. Immediately I declined,
for my childhood concept of the church's belief that all human beings
are sinners still clung to me like barnacles to an old ship.

As we talked the day began to wane. Eventually she asked me
if I had a Bible. My answer shot out like a sudden bolt of light-
ning, and the words spoken then are as clear today as though they
had been spoken but a moment ago. "No," I said rather vehemently, "And what is more, I will not buy one. If God intended
for me to read the Bible, He would give me one."

Ah, the sublime innocence of mortality that believes in a God
who sits upon a great throne somewhere in the sky and does not
heed our existence except through prayer and penitence. How
confounded I, or any person, would have been to learn that these
words reverberated through the silent ether world and floated into
the consciousness of God. He had not only heard me, but He
would soon challenge my ignorance.

Although my newly found friend did not push the subject of
church any further, for some inexplicable reason I eventually agreed
to go with her. If there was any apprehension, as I stepped beyond
the locked doors of my heart and into the open doors of the church,

I do not remember. There remains only the memory of a building and an evangelist, not what either one looked like. The subsequent events, however, are etched as though in stone within the corridors of my mind.

The evangelist had been speaking for quite some time, when suddenly his eyes fell upon me. He stopped. For one long and silent moment, he gazed into my eyes. Then, speaking directly to me he asked, "Young lady — do you have a Bible?"

Stunned, I shook my head.

Looking out at the crowd of people who had gathered in the church to hear him, he inquired, "Does anyone have a Bible to give to this young lady? She is going to need it."

A woman rose from a seat in the back row, and came forward with a Bible. I would never know her name either, but I have not forgotten her. Her gift opened a doorway to heretofore-unknown worlds that would never close again. The evangelist took the proffered Bible in his hands and blessed it, and then he passed it on to me. I stared at it in disbelief. The words uttered earlier that afternoon flashed through my mind, *if God intended for me have a Bible, He would give me one.* Tears began falling down my cheeks, for I felt that I had just received this gift direct from God. With this realization, my soul rose from its deep abyss and my previous discontent passed away like a thundercloud departs after the rain.

In spite of my apparent miracle, I did not seek out any churches to further my search for God. There were too many questions which the churches could not answer, such as, who created God? Why did science tell us that our world was millions of years old, when it was taught that earth had been formed in seven-week days? Where was Hell? Why was man a sinner? Because I sought answers to these questions I defied tradition and started the search for God on my own. He had given me a gift and I felt the answers must lie therein. I did not know that I was embarking on a great adventure which would fascinate me for the remainder of my life.

After receiving the Bible, the days passed on the wings of the wind. My gift often lay open before me and, because Old Testament appeared confusing, I perused the pages of the New Testament. Jesus had been a part of my early life in the church and it seemed easier to relate to him. In fact my favorite song during those church years had been "In the Garden." Now it came to life, for it was easy to imagine myself walking in the Garden with Master.

The joy I was experiencing continued as the summer gave birth to fall and the leaves on the trees took on a colorful garnet and ocherous cloak. My husband, Chris, and I decided to leave Portland, Oregon and move to Spokane, Washington. There was no pre-warning that Spokane would become a cocoon for my new birth, or that when this wind of change had passed I would never be the same.

Before Chris and I departed from Portland, however, two extraordinary and mystical events occurred, both of which ultimately created profound changes in both my life and in my beliefs. Each was instrumental in laying the foundation of the new world, which would encapsulate me during the years that followed. The first came to pass a short time after I received the Bible. It was late afternoon, and as I read Matthew, Chapter 10, verses 37-39 a ray of light pierced my soul. This caused me to meander into a line of thinking not previously considered. Suddenly I was possessed with a strong urge to depart from everything I possessed. I wondered, "How could anyone understand the true meaning of these words the Master had spoken if they did not do as he had instructed?"

The idea of such a renunciation did not seem to frighten me at that moment, for I had already experienced the bitter dregs of human life, and had learned to love passionately through pain and heartbreak. Now this love was being born anew, albeit it was still an intangible love, tenuous and nebulous. Nevertheless, the power of this new devotion for Jesus, for God and heaven, created a desire in me to break the shackles of my errant ways and live a more perfect life. As thoughts of departing wandered through the shadowed corridors of my soul, I succumbed to a few brief periods of ecstatic reverie before human logic cast its illusive doubts across my heart. I mused, "How could I leave everything and chase after some intangible future I could not fathom?"

Yet a mighty war had broken out in me. One part hungered for the touch of some intangible road not yet traveled, and the other sought the familiar security of the corporeal life. In the decades to follow I would see this same call to arms within many of my students. When this occurred, they were asked to resolve their dilemma as I had my own, by walking upon Earth for one single day as Jesus had walked. They, as I, would travel without food or money and God would be their only companion, the sun as their friend and the trees their shelter.

My temporary departure from mortality occurred in the late summer of my awakening, although the days were still warm. The leaves rose in colored splendor along the corridor of concrete roadways, heralding the approach of a new season filled with pewter skies and mystic rains. Having risen early I left my home to follow the call of my soul, abiding by Jesus' instructions (Mark 6:8) to take nothing for my journey, neither food nor money. As I walked a powerful invisible force seemed to lift me from the restraints of my corporeal form. It was as though I was floating between two worlds, my feet no longer merely touching the Earth where mortals walked. Although it is hard to define this higher consciousness which now permeated my being, it was as though I became less dense and more weightless. The world seemed surreal, and people passing by seemed to live in one world, while I lived in another. As they meandered on the streets, however, they smiled and stepped aside as I passed.

Throughout the day I moved in a state of exaltation, without hunger or thirst. Then, just as the day began to wane and the sun started its descent into the waiting arms of dusk, I wandered into a religious bookstore. There was no apparent reason for my being there, for I had brought no money. Browsing through the isles, somewhat perplexed over the events that had happened that day,

I suddenly felt someone, or something, staring at me. Turning, I found myself looking directly into the eyes of a painting called *The Eyes of Christ*. The eyes seemed to pierce my soul as a sword cuts through rice paper.

Quickly, turning away I moved to another part of the store, for the sensation was one of unreality and even frightening. There was no escape; the eyes in the painting still seemed to follow me everywhere. Realizing that there was no alternative but to buy the painting, I approached the cashier and asked if she would hold it for me it until the next day.

Departing from the store, still in a transcendental state, I turned homeward. As soon as I had stepped up to the entrance of the house and placed the key in the door lock, the power which had elevated me throughout the day departed. Once more I found myself relegated to the world of corporeal forms and senses. Everything seemed normal, although my acceptance of this normalcy was awkward and I felt almost as though it shouldn't exist.

The next day I returned to the store for *The Eyes of Christ*. Immediately on returning home, the picture was given an honorable place on the wall, where it successfully haunted my inappropriate actions for many days to come. In time, of course, a day-to-day preoccupation took over and the memory of my walk in the footsteps of the Christ lessened.

There is a power greater than human will. About the time I began to seep back into the ways of humanness another set of scriptures entranced me. These would overshadow me for the remainder of my life, and assist in leading me through a doorway of an unimaginable splendor. Certainly, I little realized that destiny was about to carry me into the heights of mystical ecstasy, as well as into the deepest core of a sleeping dragon, the self we do not know. Yet, from the moment I read these verses they reached out and captured my heart. Their words have never left me. They are sufficient for a world not yet born, and they could, if all would but live by them, forever abolish all religious, scientific, and philosophical differences. Wars would cease, hatred would flee on the wings of a golden dawn, and the world would walk in silent peace as brothers. They are such simple words.

"Master, which is the greatest commandment in the law?"

Jesus said unto him, "Thou shalt love the Lord thy God with all thy heart, and with all thy soul, and with all thy mind.

"This is the first and great commandment.

"And the second is like unto it. Thou shalt love thy neighbor as thyself.

"On these two commandments hang all the law and the prophets."

The words hit me like rays of a golden sun shining through the ocean mist. I knew that I must now do as Jesus taught, seek God and learn to love mankind. It was here that religion, as it was taught in the churches and my new world differed, for the church emphasized that a simple human could not directly approach the Creator of the universe. Rather they must go through some intermediate. Such a privilege as direct contact with God was relegated only to holy people and no one, including myself, could look upon me as such. At that moment, however, I had no direct affiliation with any specific church and was simply trying to follow the teachings of Jesus. If he said one must love God and this was his first commandment, then it was obvious these words must be of paramount importance. Fortunately, there was no one to say that direct contact with God was impossible.

It never occurred to me to ask anyone how to go about seeking God, and I soon found myself exploring every avenue of potentiality. Neither did I know exactly what one was supposed to find, if and when, they were successful. At the time it seemed easier to perceive Him as a deity who had a very long white beard, who wore long white robes and sat upon a great golden throne. Thus, my approach to Him was full of naïveté and almost childlike. A smile fleetingly touches my mind when I remember my simple perception of God at the time, for on what planet or on what distant sun in the millions of galaxies would one find such a Ruler?

In days of old, as a lonely child sobbing out my pain on the sagebrush mounds of Idaho, I had allowed myself periods of pleasure by creating a world of introspects and pretense. The ability to focus my consciousness and live in my make believe world had enabled me to dwell beyond sorrows of my lonely life. This talent to concentrate now served me well. The perseverance and dreams of love that had once haunted my life developed a power in me to transcend the corporeal world, and love the infinite and unseen with the collected passion of all my worldly loves combined. Soon, worldly possessions and attractions became less important than finding God. In the months that followed I left no stone unturned in my search for Him.

On arriving in Spokane I obtained a good job as a loan closer for a prestigious mortgage company, while Chris assumed the position of Land Title Engineer with another mortgage company just a few blocks away. During the summers, however, Chris served as an instructor for Military Intelligence. This took him away from the doldrums of routine work and provided both of us with long and wonderful semi-vacations.

A rather nice looking and talented man, my husband possessed a pleasing personality, which afforded him a bevy of friends. He did have one obsession, for he decreed that all churches were hypocritical and that God, at least as he believed most people perceived God, did not exist. Occasionally, he would admit that he believed in something, although I never knew him to define that something very well.

My husband's concept of God did not halt my own pursuit, and love gathered itself from all my journeys and experiences of the past to culminate into one great all-consuming fire. It was a love not woven from the fabric of pretense, nor resting in the shadows of desire, but one that transcended time and space. It alone proved sufficient to break the haunting chains of human attachments. Never would I ever regret having known the struggles of human love, for it now wove a power which carried me beyond the portals of mortality.

At last, I, a simple human, reached the consciousness of God. Kahlil Gibran wrote in his book *The Prophet*:

> For even as love crowns you so shall he crucify you. Even as he is for your growth so is he for your pruning. He threshes you to make you naked. He sifts you to free you from your husks. And then he assigns you to his sacred fire, that you may become sacred bread for God's sacred feast.

Unlike desires born from enticements of the corporeal world, I expected nothing from God. My wish was simply to see Him, although by this time I no longer believed that He was of solid form such as those who walked upon the Earth. Nonetheless, I still hungered to give him something to show my deep devotion and soon began to heap gifts upon Him. These were built in the silence of my mind from creative thoughts, and originated from the unrequited longing deep within my soul. This intense love was not the love of a woman for a man, or the love of a child for its father, although I sought Him with a childlike belief. To me He was the master, the teacher, the father, the friend, and the brother I had never had. My love for God filled all the empty spaces of my heart.

This new relationship with God did not diminish my great love for Jesus, or later for the other greats who had devoted their lives during the passing ages to enlighten mankind. I felt that the Master's words had led me to the feet of God. Nevertheless, I no longer read the Bible to worship Jesus, but to seek out everything he had said about God. All around me I saw dissension and hatred stemming from religious differences, and eventually I reached the conclusion that Jesus had died in vain. His death had brought war, not peace. Crying one night I flung myself down by the side of my bed and fervently prayed, "Please God send Jesus back to earth. We need him now. Don't let him have died in vain." Then I added, "And if you are not going to send him back now, let me help carry his cross."

There was no expectation on my part that my prayer would be answered, nor was one immediately forthcoming. Nevertheless, as God had once heard my comments about a Bible, He had now heard my supplication to help carry Jesus' cross. And, He was about grant me something millions of people have dreamed about – a meeting with Jesus.

By this time it was early fall and the evenings were touched by the frosty breath of approaching winter. One night, when darkness had overtaken day and my hours were steeped in slumber, an angel came to guide me to some unknown destination. Soon, fully awakened, and in a state of conscious awareness, I found myself separated from the flesh that claimed my soul by day. Moving through the intangible ether under angelic escort I was taken to the realms where we dwell when we are no longer imprisoned by the human sheath. My soul body seemed comprised of a semi-light, semi-material substance, and as I walked with the great angelic presence I realized we never died. This body I was now wearing did not seem to differ much from those that housed a soul on Earth, except that it was less dense. Comprised of ether it was a much higher vibratory frequency, one that would have been invisible to human eyes.

In this remarkable invisible realm beyond mortality it also seemed to be of little importance whether one had been rich or poor during life on earth. Rather, heavenly emphasis was placed on those things we could take with us, such as love, understanding, tolerance and wisdom. After being shown these things, I was then put aboard an aerial car, similar to a chair lift one might find at a ski resort. It ascended through the starlit night without sound or sense of flight, until it came to rest at the entrance of a small room. On entering, I noticed that the room had no glass windows, but open places where windows would have been. Without any sense of solid obstruction, I could overlook the panorama of the heavens — greatly awed by its magnificent beauty. Never had I been so close to touching the stars.

Then he came. He bounded up the steps and entered the room as though he had done so a thousand times. In his hands he carried a large pair of black boots, which I have since learned, signifies the soul's merger into corporeality and unknowing. As I stood looking at Jesus his eyes seemed to pierce the very depth of my soul, and for what seemed to be a second, or an eternity, I found myself bound by silence. Within me was a world of words, but seemingly no lips to speak them. At last, when my muted tongue unlocked, I asked him a single question, the one paramount on my mind; "Is your Father coming?"

I will always remember how Jesus' eyes fell upon me with tender amusement and how a subtle shadow of mirth seemed to dance around the corners of his lips as he replied, "My Father will come later."

Then he was gone.

Shortly thereafter I returned to my dense human body, and left to puzzle over this mysterious rendezvous. Many weeks would pass before I fully understood that Jesus had brought the boots for me to wear. It seemed that those who seek the greater mysteries of God must try to walk in the Master's footsteps. As he, and others after him, had journeyed through the black unknowing of mortality, so must I who had prayed to help carry his cross. Little did I realize this would ultimately require the surrender of my personal life, and that I would be asked to work for the betterment of mankind. At that moment this part of my future was sealed behind a closed door.

For a period after meeting Jesus I walked in happiness and greeted the waning days of fall and early days of winter with a contentment I had never known. By this time my heart was deeply entrenched in the search for God, although I no longer sought Him in the pages of a book. Rather I now sought Him in the morning sun and the stars at night, and in my mind I traveled to the heavens to expand the boundaries of my search. In spite of all this, I, the huntress who combed the sky for a vision of God during the early winter, was but a shadow of the huntress who would greet the coming spring.

CHAPTER II

Merger With The Infinite

*T*he winter of the great awakening created a necessity in me to look into the deeper meaning of life. Everything took on a surreal magic that corporeal eyes alone never really see, although its beauty and wonder infiltrates earth at all times. Sunrises now became a reenactment of creation. Sunsets became a hand that tucks the world into bed, and the splendor of the stars revealed a universe which so many pay little heed. Mounds of snow glittered like diamonds under the morning sun, and this winter wonderland seemed wrought upon the looms of heaven. For the first time I loved without boundaries, without fear of rejection, and without expectation of return. It was a selfless love that lived only to give. Beethoven wrote in his letter to Archduke Rudolph in 1823, "There is no loftier mission than to approach the Divinity nearer than other men, and to disseminate the divine rays among mankind."

As 1970 closed its portals, another door was also closing. My years of wandering in the desert of human life were coming to an end. For a brief moment, while looking upon the magnificent splendor of the winter snow I seemed to peer through the silent portals of the future. There was now a knowing that I would one day teach after the manner of the great Master who had help to open the portals of this new life being born in me. Even as this new life was stirring within the womb of my soul I was beginning to understand that it would also be born in all people, and that one day every human being would come to live in this same mystical splendor that was now beginning to hold me within its embrace. Admittedly, I still had little understanding as to why this strange and remarkable metamorphosis was occurring, or why such an apparent miracle was throwing open the doors to a new world of undiscovered immortality.

The early part of the New Year came and went, passing swiftly in the pewter-colored dawns of winter's days. In some instances the rare early morning sun would catch the light of the snow-covered land, turning it into a glistening phantasm of towers and mounds. During this period I took another major step toward my new world. It is one that every person will take some day when they are ready to change their lives and fulfill their destiny. It is called meditation.

It began during the early part of November. I met a woman named Dell, a tall sparse woman in her fifties, who was teaching small Spokane groups and also managing one of the local books stores. She suggested that I learn to meditate, although the term was foreign to me. From what she said, it seemed that meditation held a great deal of fascination for many people. Because I had been living in devotional isolation I knew little about spiritual practices outside of those the Church endorses, such as prayer, song and scripture reading.

Inquiring as to what meditation was; Dell replied that it meant *to think*.

"What should I think about?" I asked.

"Think about Jesus, Buddha, some saint, or some great philosopher" she said.

From that day on, as the cold days of January passed I reached for the stars, soaring through the inner consciousness like a seagull on the wind. I had been presented with a new way to reach God and wasted no time. Nonetheless, being much more familiar with Jesus, I first selected the master as a focal point of inspiration. In my mind's eye, I visualized Jesus and traveled via the road of thought to visit him. Nothing could be easier, and fortunately there was no one to tell me if I was meditating incorrectly or to suggest that what I was doing wouldn't work. Therefore I had no difficulty approaching Jesus, and later God, through the doorway of my heart and the wings of my mind.

With meditation came numerous other devotions. I prayed, as well as meditated, and even selected clothing to reflect the new beauty that seemed to surround me everywhere. While I could not see God, at least as I still conceptualized him, I never doubted that He could see me. By this time, the world most people are familiar with was gradually disappearing, dissolving into a sea of change. Suddenly, unbelievable phenomena were becoming the dessert of the day.

In one instance after purchasing a white hat made of straw-looking material, I looked up at the heavens, as one often does when talking to God, and said, "I have bought this hat for you and I know that you will never rain on it."

Thereafter a day could be ominous and thunder floating in a low, throated sound across a pewter sky, but it seemed to pass away when I stepped forth in the hat. Now I knew Jesus' great secret. The love between man and God forms a link more powerful than the winds and stronger than the sea. Through this personal contact, if mankind but realized it, rests the strength to overcome every obstacle in human life. Now I knew that it was not only Jesus, who possessed the consciousness and power of God, but it was, and is, the heritage of the human race. Moreover, the first step toward this magnificent obsession and great power is so easy. The Master of Galilee left it in a simple teaching; *love God,* to show the way.

By mid-February the meditations had not only deepened, but they had become a priority. I allowed nothing to interfere with them, for they were now the tools that enabled me to come to the feet of the Master of all Masters. One morning, on entering the inner world where the color of violet mixes with ebony shadows, I floated past the myriad of stark white faces that haunt the deeper regions of the subconscious. Abruptly, one of these stopped before spoke, saying, "I am Okaji. I am here to teach you the mysteries of the East."

Although the word "Okaji" is an Egyptian word meaning "of the sun," it was not my Angelic Teacher's true name. Over the years I learned that these great beings from the higher angelic realms do not usually reveal the name they had when they lived upon Earth, because they prefer to work with a measure of humbleness and servitude. Although some, who were more familiar with angels and masters than I was at the time, might have been pleased at the arrival of such a teacher, I was not. Okaji was dressed in mideastern attire and seemed to be of stern countenance. In the past I had never worked well with employers of this nature. Thus, following my meditation I knelt by the side of my bed and prayed, *"Please God, take him back and send me a nice one."*

Immediately I received a message indicating that it was in my best interest to learn to work with him. Peering upward, but with great reservation, I accepted, thinking that it would most assuredly be a difficult ordeal.

During the days following Okaji's arrival, he went with me everywhere. This included work. As he had not been closely associated with anyone on Earth for several hundred years, he had to be indoctrinated into a strange new world. And because my new teacher had not lived on Earth for such a long time it was necessary to explain every detail about this world so familiar to humans, but so foreign to those who have never seen a car or an airplane. Although our conversations were intended to take place at the mental level, this presented a measure of difficulty at first.

Therefore I would find myself walking down some street and talking to someone who could not be seen. It was fortunate that no
one saw me do this, thereby averting any harmful aftermath that
might have ensued.

It did not take long for my teacher to adapt to our world, and
communication became much easier. To accomplish this meant
raising my sense of hearing beyond the heavier vibration of human conversation, as he lowered his frequency to more closely
correspond with those of earth. Eventually, the inner hearing developed to such a degree I could hear him speak as well as I could
hear any human being. As I continued to develop, it became possible to also communicate with other Angelic Teachers, who came
from time to time to teach, discipline, guide, and protect during
my journey toward God. It was well that such guidance prevailed,
because I would soon discover that it could have been harmful for
me to enter the unseen realms beyond both vision and hearing
without such guidance.

With the coming of my Angelic Teacher, the world I once
knew began to disintegrate even more rapidly. Many things I had
always enjoyed now became millstones. My new teacher taught
that one should not take the life of any creature, unless his or her
own life was in jeopardy. He explained that the right to exist is
given to all creatures by a just and loving God. Any excess became
waste, and usually when I turned toward some extravagance, my
Angelic Teacher reminded me of the homeless, the hungry, and
the oppressed.

To replace these things which humanity takes so much for
granted, Okaji taught that knowledge is the doorway to wisdom;
great poetry and classical music are a solace; and honesty, a necessary building block for every expression of life from friendship to
business. Although these concepts may sound easy at first, they
are hard lessons because human tendencies are all too often governed by the senses. It is simply more entertaining to read a novel
than to read the stories of ancient wisdom. And it is more exciting

to ride a roller coaster than to go for an early morning stroll. However, whenever enticed by the delights of my earlier life, my teacher brought me back with a sharp reprimand. Okaji, although kind and beneficent, could be a relentless taskmaster.

The winter days of February passed, and in early March, my husband and I moved into, what was my first real home. The house had been owned by an astronomer and was everything I had dreamed. Quickly I named it "The Keep," for the term "Keep" signified a castle, or fortress. It even had a hidden passageway leading to an observatory. Outside of the observatory were two nice offices with windows that overlooked an imposing yard edged with multi-colored flowers.

Early one morning during the first month in our new home, just as the sun rose to warm the Earth and unlock the tightly pressed blossoms on the delicate flowers, there came an ominous shadow to disturb the beauty of the day. As I wandered about the yard, enjoying the beautiful colors and fragrances of the flowers, a sudden realization assailed me. In that instant, I knew that "The Keep" would never be my home.

Looking up at the azure sky, I spoke. "God, you are not going to let me keep this are you? This is the lull before the storm."

To say that I understood the reason for such feelings, or accepted this premonition, would not be exactly true. Some kind of darkness had descended, which seemed to foreshadow events yet to come. Had this occurred before the pangs of this new birth I now seemed to be undergoing, its disturbance might have brought me great despondency. Instead there was an intuitive sense that these feelings had something to do with God and destiny. Certainly, there was no knowledge as to when, where, or how this would come about.

Within a short time, after our new home had finally been put in order, my Angelic Teacher began getting me up at five o'clock each morning to pull weeds. I complained mightily, but to no avail. Early morning rising was not a habit, for my inclination was to sleep late on the days I did not have to work and just as late as possible on the days that I did. Now, with the early morning chill still in the air, and heavy moisture clinging to the blades of grass, I found myself on hands and knees, working diligently to create a beautiful yard.

As I worked, Okaji taught me about the ways of the mind. He said that the mind was like a garden. It constantly needed weeding, fertilizing, and tender care. As weeds grow in a garden, they also grow in the mind in the form of doubts, junk mail, and hopeless dreams. Left alone, these impure thoughts can ultimately destroy the beautiful and leave behind a deserted and empty wasteland. At the same time, however, while I relished learning, there was certainly no rejoicing over the fact that these lessons were taught as the cold Earth numbed my fingers and my body rebelled at the early morning chill.

About this same time my studies began in "Ancient Wisdom." These were comprised of the teachings of the greatest religionists, philosophers and scientists throughout the ages. Before long there rose a conflict in my soul over the difference between the two different paths — spirituality versus religion. At first glance, these two directions appear the same, and in some ways they are. However, the full spiritual path expands itself over the universe like a restless wind and searches for truth and God. Embracing all religions, sciences, and philosophies, it leaves the narrow confines of limitation behind. Like the nautilus, which moves from each small chamber of its shell to build a larger chamber, so must the soul build new mansions and enter new worlds of understanding.

Religion, in many instances, is relegated to the primary aspect of mankind's devotion. Sometimes it also becomes secular, so that one may experience a sense of isolation from those who believe differently. In addition, some people often restrict themselves from studying the whole of the universe because of rules imposed upon them by independent denominational and biblical interpretations.

The answer pertaining to the differences between religion and spirituality came about abruptly and magnificently, as my lull before the storm came to an end.

On June 4th, I took my husband to the airport. Chris was flying to San Pedro, California and would spend the summer working as an instructor at one of the Military Intelligence schools. After dropping him off in front of the airport and turning the car toward home, a somewhat lonely feeling enveloped me. I decided to submerge myself in housework to pass the time away.

Not long after arriving back at "The Keep" and getting the house in order, a powerful angelic force made his presence known. He flowed through the morning like a mighty river, as though waiting for a time when I would be alone. He did not introduce himself by name as others had done when they came, yet he was one of the most wondrous presences I have ever experienced. He arrived just as the hour hand reached the ten thirty mark, his consciousness holding me captive and leaving me immobile and entranced. His great power and beauty flowing through me like the soft wind of a summer's breeze. Within the embrace of such entrancement, I could do little except to sit silently on the living room couch in ecstatic reverie.

Although this great Angelic presence did not speak, he indicated that he preferred I play some music. Obviously the vibration of Earth was too dense for his comfort, and I soon realized that music would not only assist in raising the vibratory frequency of the surroundings, but also my own consciousness. I rose, walked over to the stereo and put a recording of classical music on the turntable and then returned to the couch to await any disclosure regarding the nature of his visit. None was forthcoming.

The memory of that morning still returns clear and untarnished by the passing years. As the beautiful strains of Rimsky-Korsakov's "Scheherazade" flowed through "The Keep," my visitor held me in a heightened state of consciousness. During this time, there was no awareness of anything other than his presence. His instructions regarding music had been given in unspoken words, created through the expansion and contraction of the subtle either to form comprehensible patterns in my mind. Yet I understood them perfectly.

A half hour later he departed.

Following his passing I returned to the routine of everyday life, and left to ponder the events of the morning.

The next morning dawned bright and clear. As yet I still had no clear explanation as to the purpose of my mysterious stranger's visit. After completing breakfast I proceeded to perform some light household chores, aware of the emptiness due to Chris's departure. It seemed unlikely that such a high being would grace me with a second visit, but to my astonishment, he came again at precisely ten-thirty. Just as he had on the previous day, he indicated that some classical music should be played. Almost instantly the high state of consciousness that possessed my soul on the preceding day again took over.

There was little one could do in such a situation, but to bask in the glorious presence of this great master. He possessed magnificence so far beyond that of human that I had no inclination to move or speak, only to sit motionless. At no time during this period did he attempt to communicate with me, other than to make known his wishes pertaining to the music. I found myself even void of the chaotic thoughts that usually ran rampant in my mind. Under normal circumstances, I would have been filled with questions about who he was, where he came from, and what his purpose was.

One-half hour later, just as on the previous day, he departed. I did not know that he would return once more, and that when he did, the impending storm of change that had been hovering over me for weeks would break like a violent wind stirring a motionless sea. While millions of people await the coming of the end of the world, the world, as I knew it, would end the following morning.

On June 6th, the sun again rose against a cloudless and azure sky. It was a bright and sunny day filled with the fragrance of various flowers. Among these was the white narcissus, which had been dedicated to Okaji. Their blossoms were as white as the diamond-like snow of Mt. Spokane, now standing tall and magnificent against the eastern horizon. Their fragrance was unique, light, and unfathomable, like the subtle ether world existing beyond the boundaries of the senses. My teacher was of that subtle world of ether, and just as unfathomable and beautiful.

When Okaji awakened me on this golden-hued morning in early June, there was a certain naïve expectation that the day would probably be somewhat like the others. Of course, it would have been impossible to not be filled with a sense of curiosity, and to wonder if my mysterious visitor would come again. In the event he did, however, I decided to bathe, dress neatly, and complete the household tasks early. Certainly, during those early morning hours there was no way of knowing that before the day was out, a tidal wave would sweep me into the sea of no return, and by nightfall the person I was then would never exist again.

One cannot help but wonder what might go through his or her mind, if they were forewarned that everything they were, everything they considered human life, and the everyday practices of complacency were to change in a single instant. Yet, as it happened to me, it will happen to every person on earth. It is a wise God who has temporarily blinded us to that exact moment in time when the shutters of unknowing will fall away like the dead petals of a flower. Perchance if one was told, one would be consumed with self-doubts, unworthiness, fear or impatience. Nonetheless, it has been predestined that each will awaken from throes of darkness and will know what they really are and what they will become. Then, in that one single blaze of lighted magnificence, their lives will change.

Unknowing as to what the day would bring and my mind filled with unanswered questions, I automatically followed the same routine as on the preceding two days and began playing classical music shortly before ten o'clock. My wait was not long, for the great Angelic presence came precisely on the half-hour. Once again "The Keep" was filled with his powerful consciousness. This time for some reason I did not sit down when I sensed his presence, but walked over to the window and looked up at the sky as I had so many times when I spoke to God.

Suddenly something very unusual occurred. It felt like electrodes were being placed on each side of my temples. This was not frightening, perhaps because it had occurred so quickly and unexpectedly. Within seconds my mind began to meld into the azure sky, until it merged with a light existing beyond the boundaries of the known universe. Before there was time to question what was happening, all awareness of individual existence dissipated and my mind became one with the consciousness of the universe. At last my dream, and the dream of every human being was fulfilled; I came face to face with God. He was not the God of human perception, but a magnificence that contains the creative light of the universe within Him, and yet each of us is part of Him, a pulsating cell of life in His body.

During these passing moments, as my mind rode the winds of creation, God revealed His Divine Plan for all life — including the final destiny of the human race. It was a beauty so intense and magnificent that my physical heart constricted, causing a spasm. There stood humanity as it would be one day in a semi-light, semi-material body, an advanced civilization taking its place in the universe of the stars. They were beautiful angelic beings of peace, working together for the common good of all life. I knew then, that this human planet upon which we live would one day have the peace it prayed for and, oh, so much more.

If there was any room remaining for a single feeling or emotion, it was the knowledge that one could not live long like this. A person would die from prolonged exposure to such perfection and beauty. But, then, just as suddenly as it had occurred, the clamp-like feeling pressing on the temples was removed and my mind returned to the world of mortality. From that moment on my life would never be the same, for it was as if a large computer had downloaded its knowledge into a small computer. My mind now contained the knowledge of the creation of the universe. Neither would I ever again be completely separated from God.

CHAPTER III

Journey Beyond Mortality

s the years passed, this link with the Consciousness of God became a never-ceasing spring of knowledge. Everything became easier to understand than it had been before, and every book more comprehensible. After my entry into God, or Cosmic Consciousness, as it is known in today's world, a doorway of mental acceleration opened and I feared no area of study. This included all religions, major philosophies, psychology, and the sciences. Having witnessed the Divine Plan, there was now a clear understanding of the basic foundation for everything that had ever been written or taught.

Some of these things revealed would not discovered by science until the latter part of the 1980's and early 1990's. By then astronomers had traced the origin of the universe back to ten to the minus forty-three seconds, or a fraction of a second after it began. However, they still have not pierced the mystery behind that final fraction of a second. And when they do, they will be very surprised to learn that the answer is so simple and beautiful that it would take volumes to

31

explain it. What is the answer? Why, of course, that minute fraction of a second proves the existence of God, and that He is the single underlying intelligence governing the universe.

From the very hour of this remarkable awakening, my life changed. Where once I had walked in darkness and unknowing, bound by senses of a corporeal world, I had now come face to face with the Infinite, not as a deity, but as the causation of the universe. Where once I had strongly believed that death was the end of everything, now there was a knowing that death did not exist. The mind had been accelerated and knowledge that would have taken years of research and study had become mine in that instant fusion with all knowledge.

The next morning I awoke to find that everything had taken on a different perspective, for there was now a deeper clarity and understanding concerning all living things. Everything visible, even the ethereal world beyond, is a part of a living, breathing organism called Earth. This planet is not just an inert piece of matter floating through space, but a living presence and a part of a pre-designed and pre-destined universe. Perhaps some will be astonished to find that God's Divine Plan contains the ultimate perfection of this universe, and thus the ultimate perfection of mankind. The prototype for every human has been created equally and perfectly, and mankind's potentiality has existed even before the universe was ever formed

In the years that followed, I began to study the writings and teachings of some of the greatest illumined people who have ever lived. Each one is a link in the continuity of truth, passed on from generation to generation for millions of years. And this chain will yet continue to grow through ages to come. Each moment of the past has been an integral stepping-stone to an enlightened future, and one only now beginning its sunrise over the whole of Earth. One by one, every man, woman, and child will experience the Light, and then they will cast away unknowing and step out of this night of dreams and shadows to fulfill their greatness upon the earth.

Having awakened the sleeper, God deemed that my eyes should turn away from the corporeal world and that my footsteps should now travel where the greats once traveled, in word, in deed and in thought. I must now learn to walk as they had once walked and learn to serve the world as they had once served. The road map for this monumental journey is etched in the wisdom and lives of the immortals who have strolled across the centuries.

Two days later, on June 8th, on awaking, there was a knowing that it would not only be necessary to leave my new home, but also renounce a personal life. My heart was with God, and my mind had now traveled too far into the interior of a new and strange universe to find satisfaction again in the unknowing of a corporeal world. This is not intended to imply that all people who reach this illumined state of consciousness will leave their families and homes. For me, however, it was the only way. I could not remain a soul torn apart between the enticements of human life and the great magnificence of the spiritual world. My desire was to serve only God and that there was now an obligation to help the world toward its greatness in whatever way possible.

Departure for California was imminent. The last fragments of my human life could only be discarded by saying goodbye to the man who had been my husband. Certainly Chris had some forewarning, for during our many telephone conversations throughout the preceding days he had expressed a fear that he was losing me. Carefully I tried to explain the events that were consuming my life, but he was unable to understand. It was natural that for a time, in the beginning, I hoped that Chris would be drawn to this wondrous path. Sadly, however, his pre-concepts about God and church soon abolished all hope of this.

During the next few days following illumination I packed my personal possessions, such as clothing and books. I also destroyed any picture of the personal life that Chris and I had once shared, as there was no desire to bring pain to my husband by leaving personal reminders behind. Even while preparing for my departure to California many remarkable mystical experiences continued to fill the hours of my life. These went on day and night, leaving little time for doubts to creep in. It seemed that even my own dire prediction of childhood was being fulfilled, "that I would never live past the age of forty." The old began to die, not as the body dies, but as all things must die to become something else.

Because it was summer, the nights were magnificently filled with the mystery of our undiscovered universe. The city of Spokane was edged by the customary flatness of the western desert standing free from the dense clouds of the coast. Nightly it lay under a panorama of lighted stars, which could only be regarded as the splendor of God's night attire. If there was any pain over leaving my first real home I paid it no heed, for who can measure the cup of unknowing against a fountain of eternal enlightenment.

One night, a short time after experiencing unity with the consciousness of God, I turned out the lights as usual and prepared to sleep. My mind was filled with the events of early June. New and constant knowledge still whipped across me like a restless wind blowing over an arid desert. As it blew it brought forth new ideas, concepts, and new understandings pertaining to God and the universe, and it stirred my mind like a powerful hurricane. Shortly after becoming involved in such contemplation, the room began to fill up with minuscule light particles. They had the appearance of miniature stars and shone just as radiantly as those now adorning the sky over Spokane. I watched with fascination as they descended and entered into, what seemed every cell of my body. Then a strange new energy moved within me, moving as though it was trying to adjust to the confines of a now human form. While I had no understanding over what was taking place I felt no fear. Had I known, I would have believed myself to be one of the most fortunate people on Earth. Every human waits, albeit unknowingly, for this mystic moment when God endows them with His divine spirit. Through His descent to dwell with me, I would never again know loneliness, nor would the fear of sickness, old age, and death ever confine the perimeter of my soul.

Somehow I fell asleep for a brief time after that, but when I awoke I could still feel His Spirit moving within my body. It seemed strange and foreign for we are not accustomed to any consciousness but our own, but from that time on the Spirit of God, not only watched over, but also shared in everything that I did. He became the comforter during sadness and rewarded me in beautiful ways when I did something noble. Yet, He also disciplined when some task was not done as perfectly as it should have been. While my Angelic Teacher was a perfectionist, the Spirit was even more so, and He overlooked no error. At the same time His lessons were administered with justice and mercy.

When I had completed packing for my departure to California I took my suitcases to the car. Then I returned to lock the door of my new home for the last time. I would never return.

While traveling southward, there were several near-accidents. This did not seem particularly unusual, for there was still a false concept that I was meant to die as mortality dies and subsequently leave Earth. Because that year had now passed, in which I had predicted that I would die, I was somewhat confident this auspicious event would occur while en route to California. It was not yet possible to comprehend that this impending death did not represent the death of the body, but the death of the human world with its senses and desires. Rabindranath Tagore once wrote: "Birth is from the mystery of night into the greater mystery of day."

If this expectation of dying had formed from some death wish deep in the subterranean recess of my mind, it did not transpire. God's Divine Spirit protected and watched over me like a parent taking a child to school for the first time. I arrived in San Pedro without harm, knowing that the time had come for me to break the bonds that kept me from following my heart. My old world had been shaken and reshaped into a new beginning by the powerful hands that had created the universe. A huge gulf had grown between Chris and me during our four weeks of separation and now this gulf was vast as a mighty sea, a sea so wide that my husband would never be able to cross it. Neither would he choose to try.

The subject of separation did not come up immediately, for each of us seemed intent on postponing the inevitable. I could not quite bring myself to tell Chris that I was leaving him, more because I did not wish to cause pain to someone who had been good and kind, rather than from sentiment. Chris chose not to mention the subject either. I know that he was loath to think that our marriage was over, although deep down I believe he knew that it was.

On the night of my arrival we went to a party sponsored by the military. While observing the mortality of a world that I had so recently been a part of, it became obvious that we human beings all too often possess little appreciation for this precious gift of life. Somehow, and for some reason, we have a tendency to seek the road of temporal pleasures at the cost of both health and mind. Even so, as I watched the people drinking, dancing and making merry, it seemed that I loved every man and woman present as much as my husband. Evidently His Spirit, which now abided with me, wanted me to experience the love He held for all people, an unconditional love without partiality.

During the ensuing days it was my intent to imbibe in the same things that had occupied me during the preceding summer, to read, swim and lie in the sun. However, Okaji did not allow the corporeal world to penetrate too deeply. He, along with the now indwelling Spirit, consumed my time with a variety of mental contemplations, meditations, and continued mystical experiences.

Not long after arriving in San Pedro, and just having gone to bed, two lights appeared. One was white, the other black. They began to war. Soon a struggle ensured between these two forces and a voice began quoting scriptures from St. John's Revelation. As it spoke, I started to experience the great drama of Armageddon, not only occurring outside, but also within. When the voice said: *And she being with child cried, travailing in birth, and pained to be delivered.* (Rev: 12-2) I felt my stomach swell and light contractions inundate my body. As these contractions lessened, new scriptures were spoken, and with them came new images.

The battle continued throughout the entire night, and by morning I possessed the master keys to the interpretation of St. John's Revelation. As dawn broke across the already hot California morning there came with it, a knowing. The great Battle of Armageddon would not be fought in the outside world, but that it would be a powerful inner war, which would transform human into divine. Many months would pass before all of the pieces of my experience would be put together and I would be able to fully comprehend its true meaning. At that time, I had no knowledge that there were hidden Christian mysteries pertaining to a sublime transformation or, as it is perhaps better known, the Resurrection of the Dead. It is unlikely that many Christians have. Neither did I dream that such a transformation from human to divine was possible for mere mortals, or that this transformation signified the true prophetic end of the world and every human would attain it.

By this time, my relationship with God was full of wonder and delight. It consumed my waking hours and lived in my heart like a giant flame. As yet it was still difficult to accept the fact that God dwelled with me, for I adored Him as ruler of the heavens. One time I even stopped my car by the side of a road and beat my hands on the steering wheel, sobbing "I will not have you in me. I want you up in the heavens where you belong." Somehow it was difficult to fully understand that one cannot experience the unity of all things, except that His Spirit dwells in you.

Only a night or two had passed after the revelation of the Great Battle, before I was again called upon to depart from the familiar patterns of human existence and partake of another mystical adventure. It was eleven o'clock in the evening. Chris and I were involved in one of our long discussions pertaining to the experiences now shaking my world. Although he tried to be understanding and patient, it was too little avail. Suddenly a presence from the Angelic Kingdom interjected and said, "You must leave this place. You are to take nothing with you, and this means no money or belongings. You must leave now."

There was a sense of great urgency welling up inside of me. I somehow knew that I must leave immediately. Looking at Chris, I said, "I have just been instructed that I must leave immediately and cannot take anything with me. I do not know if I will ever return." Although my husband urged me to take some money, I declined, for my instructions had been quite specific.

Quickly I exited the apartment and descended to the bottom of the stairs. Just before I passed through the security door leading outside, the voice spoke to me again. "Follow the pillar of Light. Do not follow the stars."

As I stepped into the warm summer night, I beheld stars dancing along the street to my left. They seemed to move playfully under the numerous lamps lining the sidewalks, as though they were beguiling me to follow. Had my instructions not been so definite I might have been greatly tempted, for the pillar of Light, which appeared on my right was heading in the direction of the dark, unlit side streets. Unlike the stars, it seemed intent upon melding in to the blackness of the opaque night. There seemed little recourse, but to do as I was bid.

Stepping into the night, a powerful force, the same that had taken possession of my soul a number of days before, enfolded me like a giant cloak. The weight of His Spirit almost caused me to stagger to my knees. Nonetheless, I continued to follow the pillar of light like an obedient child, without comprehending or understanding its reasons.

As I walked, the pillar was a beacon before me. Sometimes it felt as though death was waited on the black streets. Other times a massive weight seemed to push me to the earth, while all around the blackness of approaching midnight spread its enveloping darkness into every crevice. Strangely, I, who had always been afraid of the dark, felt no fear, except that of dying in some unnamed and remote area of an unknown city. By this time there was no sense as to where I was, nor could I have found my way back to the apartment where Chris and I were staying. As my walk continued, a beautiful but powerful angelic voice spoke "There is a surprise in store for you at the end of this journey."

Assured by the words that I was not alone, I continued to follow the pillar of light, which eventually led into the very heart of the skid row section of San Pedro. What a strange sight I must have been, walking as though entranced through the most dangerous streets I had ever encountered. Still, there was no fear, and time had little meaning, although it was now well after midnight. It seemed that every time there was a possible danger, the force of the Spirit lifted me almost off my feet, creating a sense of weightlessness. Then I was hurried along until whatever danger might have been lurking in the dark doorways of nearby buildings had passed. Coming abreast of a fence, I stood there looking at it and realized that it was not necessary to return to the former ways of human life. Life would proceed without extra clothing, money, or possessions and survive. Apparently that was what this journey was all about; a journey to discover this truth, to understand that life with God is mankind's only true need.

Immediately, on reaching this realization, a car stopped and a man asked, "Would you like a ride?"

Strangely, I did not question whether it was safe to accept the proffered hand. I simply replied, "Yes." Somehow, this mysterious stranger who picked me up seemed to sense where I belonged. Within a short time he deposited me in front of the entrance of the apartment complex. At no time did he give me his name, nor did I ask. Neither is there any memory of having told him where I lived.

Subsequent to my journey through the streets of San Pedro, another mystical experience beyond human mortality further isolated me from the life I had once known. It is said to be one of the two greatest experiences any human being can encounter, the first being the soul's merger with the consciousness of God, or Cosmic Consciousness. This new encounter with the mysterious nature of God would herald my entry into the dark night of the soul, also known as the Battle of Armageddon, a battle of human versus divine will. I would not only encounter the higher plateaus of mystical illumination, but also experience sorrows deeper than any I had ever known or imagined.

As always, it started unexpectedly and descended down through the silent ether mist of an unseen kingdom to encapsulate my soul and draw it into the heart of creation. Once again night had just begun its rule over day. As the darkness deepened, it created haunting shadows under the splendor of an almost-full moon. Although I had gone to bed, I do not know if I was sleeping. Suddenly, however, I was awakened, and felt myself being drawn upward until I became light itself, expanding like a massive balloon. Then, almost as suddenly, all awareness of being human ceased.

There was an indescribable sense of peace as the panorama of creation moved through my expanded consciousness. The silver-lined clouds seemed to float on some unseen breeze, while a full moon shone radiantly within me. My soul had become as vast as the sun, moon, and stars; and I, as Elizabeth, was no more. There was no awareness of individual existence or thought. God had absorbed me completely into His consciousness in order to understand what He really was and how He functioned. Through cosmic consciousness, He had allowed me to experience His mind, and now I was allowed to experience His body.

During this oneness in Him, I experienced the reality of His unconditional love, for it embraced the whole of creation. The love one expresses as a human being is but a mere shadow of that, which flows through the universe. God's Divine love is the cohesive force that binds every star in the sky, for we are more than just a nation, or even a world. We are a part of a brotherhood, a part of that one Spirit which flows through every sun and every planet. Creation has brought forth life through a transcendental love beyond the scope of human understanding and yet one that encompasses total and unconditional giving. His is the true and perfect counterpart of every living form of existence and the ultimate expression of the love, which every soul seeks.

As it had begun, it also ended. When my soul again made its first contact with the physical form, it was like a deep-sea diver who had come up from the depths of the ocean too rapidly. There was a sense of great swelling, and every part of me seemed to extend around the body like an inflated bubble. Neither did this expanded state of consciousness leave immediately on return to the corporeal world, but remained for some time. Getting out of bed I sought to stand up, surprised to discover that movement was still possible in spite of the feeling of massiveness and disorientation.

Eventually I returned to bed and fell into a deep slumber. It was good that I slept, for dawn brought with it a fathomless darkness that I would be unable to pierce for many days.

CHAPTER IV

Dark Night of the Soul

*T*here is no remembrance if it was sunny the next morning following my absorption into the consciousness of God and His universe, for I remember little about the period that followed. At first I could do little except sit and cry, although there did not seem to be anything to cry about. Reading or watching television was impossible. Neither was I able to drive an automobile or go up in elevators. It was as though all light had been closed away, and my soul was now relegated to the dark consciousness of Earth's beginning, living in a dark cave without exit. Therefore, all emotions, such as fear and grief seemed greatly magnified, and everything buried in the hidden regions of the subconscious was now exposed.

The mind may remember fleeting moments occurring throughout childhood, but little does it understand that many of its motivations, belief tendencies and habits have been acquired throughout the formation of the universe and its world. How are we to know, when encapsulated within that part of consciousness relegated to human life that our journey did not begin with our birth through corporeal blood ties, but it began long ago with the birth of creation? Now these portals of the deep subconscious had opened to me and it was necessary to view both the good and bad that had accumulated through myriad of centuries. I would be shown that each person must one day come face-to-face with the inroads of their nature. Otherwise there can be no transcendence over human weaknesses — nor can war, hatred, death, anger and violence be laid asunder. As I had now been called forth to fight this righteous war, so will every living soul when the ties of corpo-reality loses its hold and they reach for their true greatness. It is good to know, however, that no one will fight this battle alone, for God is the co-pilot and He has never lost one single person, as evidenced by the trail left behind by the Great Ones.

Without the assistance of my Angelic Teacher during the days of darkness that followed oneness with the universe, I do not know how long my exile from life might have lasted. Okaji encouraged me to go to the pool and swim for physical exercise. He would often entertain me by diving off the diving board into the water and because of his sacrifice he drew an occasional feeble smile from me. This, I now know, was hard for him, for he had to lower his vibration to create an image sufficiently dense to become vis-ible to my human eyes. Other times the two of us took walks, although these proved less successful than swimming. All too of-ten I found myself crying without provocation, yet unable to tell anyone the reason for this sorrow. Upon reviewing the events of this mystical interlude, I realized later that the abyss had been caused by my extensive soul expansion. Descending from the high-est vibration of heaven into the coarse vibration of Earth was similar to someone jumping into a swimming pool without water and hitting concrete.

During these difficult months there was little comprehension as to the fullness of what had happened to me, for I had never heard of oneness with God. In the churches of my youth, such things had been relegated to fantasies of the mind, or permitted only to saints. Certainly, it is unlikely that any church or minister would have accepted the concept that a mortal such as me could reach the heights accredited only to saints and holy people. How glad I am now that I was but a mere human, for if such a doorway had opened its portals to me I knew it would open to all people.

When thinking back on that period, I am also grateful that I had already reached some awareness that there was no Satan, at least as conceived by the church. Otherwise, I might have been terrified. Through my oneness with God, however, I had discovered that there is but one power governing the universe and that all things within the universe occur through a systematic process of cause and effect.

Even though I spent a number of days in intense darkness, life constantly changes and all things eventually come to an end. In time I managed to read a book from cover to cover. From that moment, my ability to cope with matters of human life began its slow process of recovery. Still, I remained much like a child learning to walk again. It would be years before I could go up in elevators or drive a car in the outside lane while crossing a bridge without deep anxiety. As a measure of stability returned, I bid my past a final goodbye and returned to the land of my two births, Portland, Oregon.

On arriving in Portland I obtained an apartment and found a simple office job, for my mental state made it impossible to handle the more complex corporate positions of the past. Although I was allowed enough sensibility to hold down my job, the nights were long and dark. One could often find me sitting in a chair and staring at the blinds or reclining on the divan, possessed by some deep and intangible anguish. The first explanation concerning this transformational process now occupying my soul came from the Angelic Kingdom. Late one afternoon, while resting in a huddled heap on the divan, an angelic being wrote across the dark inroads of my mind, "You are going through a change of consciousness."

Admittedly I did not know exactly what that meant, but I found comfort in knowing that there was a reason for this darkness.

The book, St. John of the Cross's — *Dark Night of the Soul*, translated by E. Allison Peers explains this metamorphosis in the following manner:

> Into this dark night souls begin to enter when God draws them forth from the state of beginners, which is the state of those that meditate on the spiritual road, and begins to set them in the state of progressives, which is that of those who are already contemplatives – to the end that, after passing through the dark night the soul may arrive at a state of perfection, or that of Divine union with God.

Although I continued to flounder from the recent state of expanded consciousness, and tried to understand the darkness that had descended upon me, there was little warning that more was yet to come. By now, one would think that these experiences, which sought to plant their seeds into the fertile garden of my soul, would have become commonplace. Perhaps it is fortunate that we do not always know what tomorrow might bring, for I was to face yet another mystical pinnacle. This one would plunge me into deep purification of the soul for much of the remainder of my life

The afternoon was warm and as bright as it sometimes is on those rare rainless fall days in the Northwest. Deciding to do my laundry, I went down to the basement facility to put a load of dirty clothes into the washing machine. On returning to the apartment, I sat down in a chair, preoccupied, as usual, with the meaning of this remarkable transformation taking over my soul. Instantly, two angelic beings came. They placed what felt like a band or a crown on my head, which immediately made my darkness even darker. And because it created so much discomfort, I somehow managed to knock it off, but this was but a brief victory. The next time they lowered it, it could not be removed. This band, or *nimbus* as many mystics refer to it, has remained on me throughout the years I have walked the path, although I have never become fully acclimated to it. It is known in the Christian mysteries as the crown of thorns and is the chaplet used for discipline and guidance by the higher Angelic forces.

When I next returned to the basement to complete my laundry, the band seemed to pulse with a life of its own and I would have torn it from my head if it had been possible. At the same time, there seemed to be a radiant Light at the apex of my skull. As I folded my clothes, the Light began to pulsate, but as it did, the darkness within me became darker. Exasperated, I soon realized that everything would have to be refolded more perfectly than before. Thus, each piece was scrutinized, and each piece redone until it met the criteria of the phenomenon that now possessed me.

After the descent of the crown, or band, I found myself entering even further into the depths of the dark night of the soul, for the band became my albatross. Its heaviness brought even more difficulty and an unfathomable darkness. Although the world could not see the chaplet, it could be felt as distinctly as though it were wrought of heavy metal. It felt like some foreign object, but one that human hands could not remove. This alone made it an infringement upon the privacy of individualized existence.

Not only had the Spirit descended to dwell with me, now the power of His possession was greatly intensified because of the band of light that overshadowed my consciousness. Unfortunately, like most humans, my soul was bound to self-will and surrender to Divine Will was not easy to accomplish. In time, however, I would come to bless the Light as I once wanted to escape from it, for it instilled the urge do all things better than I previously ever thought myself capable of. It also built a foundation of determination, and sufficient strength to endure the long and arduous path of transformation ahead.

Driven by this powerful spiritual force, my work began to

extend into long hours and I was able to accomplish more than I could have imagined. My sleep was reduced, but the workload increased. Even my diet underwent a change in order to refine the vibratory frequencies of not only the human body, but also the feelings, emotions and mind. Such changes are not easily made, and sometimes it was impossible to continue without conflict, or on occasion, even anger. More than once I took the picture, *Eyes of Christ* and threw it across the room, breaking the glass into fragmented pieces. After feeling badly for a few hours, I would retrieve it, mend it, and return it to its customary place on the wall.

Because of the ceaseless purifying nature of the crown, it was necessary to cleanse all thoughts and actions. Unlike most people, my thoughts were no longer allowed to flow freely on the wind. The mind now had to learn to transmute the powerful forces and desires which all too often govern human life. Where there was hatred, it was necessary to love; and where there was anger, it was necessary to sow peace. The primary consolation as I walked this path through the Dark Night of the Soul, referred to as the *Via Dolorosa* in the ancient Christian mysteries, was the fount of knowledge that continued to flow like a never-ending spring amid the ever-pervading presence of God.

In the weeks and months that followed, there were lessons pertaining to the utilization of all basic spiritual powers, such as discernment, prophecy and healing. Although every person possesses these powers, I was taught to use them wisely, for they, like everything in the universe, are bound by cause and effect. To use such powers without proper discretion can bring retribution on oneself, not because God orders it, but because the universe is designed that way. The one perfect law that governs the universe assures that every life form not only progresses upon its own merit but also learns its unlearned lessons.

As I struggled to understand the reasons and purpose of life, it became easier than it had been during my youth to see into the future, as well as to penetrate deeply into the subconscious regions of the human soul. Along with these new worlds of prophecy and discernment, there was also an introduction into the world of healing. Soon, I was able to heal by the laying of the hands. Nonetheless, because the Spirit now dwelled within me, the crown of thorns insured that no one suffered. The Law of noninterference was woven into the constitution of planetary progression and bound by cause and effect. This discipline alone kept me from falling too deeply into a quagmire of self-importance.

In order to buy food and pay rent it remained necessary to work in the outside world. Nevertheless, it was difficult to do so because the Light produced a purifying darkness both day and night without cessation. Like a steel vice, the crown could be lowered or raised according to the Will of the Greater Power. When it was raised, it became a radiant light, bringing a sense of wholeness and approval. Normally, however, there was isolation and a pressure to continuously purify the more imperfect aspects of body, mind and soul. Often this brought a deep sense of separation between my humanness and the Divine.

Toward the end of 1971, as the Holiday season fell upon the country I returned to Washington. Still, this did little to alleviate the intense battle raging in my soul. My mind was still wrapped up in the remarkable phenomena occurring within and my effort to cope with the loss of the personal life I had once known. This does not mean that that there were any regrets over the path that had captured my heart, but everything had been shaken loose and everything was rapidly changing. It is not easy to change from the traditional ways of human life into the requirements of this new life. Thus, the battle continued between the habits of the past and the destiny that had now been assigned. In desperation, I decided to choose death over life.

Carefully I planned my assault against life, first making a decision pertaining on the *method*.

One of my pastimes as a lonely young girl was to read incessantly and among the books were a number of the great murder mysteries. Every armchair detective, or at least well-known ones, had become a part of my *family*. Now there was no lack of ideas for my demise. Although it is not my intent to sound flippant about such a serious matter, when looking back upon this decision to die it is extraordinarily humorous.

Under the circumstances, it was a natural inclination to select a painless method for my *Operation Rigor Mortis*. It seems that in such moments of desperation, humans fear that suffering might occur during separation from life. Thus, given a choice, one elects to fly without pain upon the wings of death. After studying the various methods of obliteration, I decided on carbon monoxide, primarily because it was not supposed to hurt. Having made this monumental choice, I proceeded to one of the nearby service stations to get a piece of hose.

It was late in the evening.

On arriving at the station I asked for what seemed to be an appropriate length of hose. At that moment, my Angelic Teacher interjected. He explained to me that the length requested was insufficient to reach from the exhaust to the car window. Failing to see the humor in this at the time, I requested the service station attendant increase the length. It was well that I did. My teacher was right, and had I not listened to him, the hose would not have reached the required distance.

The next step was to find a place to accomplish *Operation Rigor Mortis*. Because of my perusal of detective books, I did not wish to frighten any unknown person or persons who might discover my remains. Had I thought beyond the point of this insubordinate war with God, it would have been obvious that suicide was impossible. Apparently, there is some rule in heaven that requires stubborn people, such as me, to be protected from their own rashness. I am reminded of the last line in Rev: 6:6, "Thou shalt not hurt the oil and the wine."

Finally, having made the necessary purchase for my journey, I drove my car to an old road by a deserted field. It was a cold night, and the stars were glistening brightly, as they do only on a clear winter's eve. The nearby snow-covered fields seemed to touch the horizon, reflecting the light of stars in glistening droplets, while everything around was silent and peaceful. Intent on my project, I took little notice of this surrounding beauty and set about the task of *ending it all.* Turning off the engine, I got out and went around to the back of the car to connect the hose to the exhaust. When finished, I returned to the driver's seat, rolled the windows up tightly, and turned on the motor. As I waited, some kind of a web appeared to weave itself around me and the Spirit gently kept pulling on the hand holding the ignition keys.

After a time, it became apparent that the air within the car was still as pure as it was outside. I increased the RPM. This was to no avail; still the cocoon remained and I, alas, also remained very much alive. Dripping with abject humiliation, I removed myself from the car and angrily tore the hose away. At the same time, peering up to the stars, I spoke loudly to God and whoever else was listening, "I'm going to keep this for next time."

When things had calmed down a bit, it was quite apparent that God had manifested a great miracle on my behalf. Then, and forever after, there would never be any doubt about Him existing as a real and living presence, more real than the sun, the moon, and the stars, and so much closer.

Six months had now passed since my union with the consciousness of God, and yet I continued to reel under a barrage of mystical experiences that left me alternating between highs and lows. I was still having considerable difficulty driving across bridges, riding elevators, and dealing with heights. Nonetheless my fears were not allowed to rule my life. Whatever needed to be done was accomplished. Still the crown continued its restraint on me, much as a caterpillar is restrained within its web-like cocoon. As a caterpillar must become a butterfly, so must a human become divine.

Unlike the days before entry into Cosmic Consciousness, I was now relegated to the task of transmuting my lesser nature. It is only by facing the worst in us that one can see clearly enough to overcome the vagrancies that bind our souls to the painful ways of human life. At that time, I had not yet read St. John of the Cross's book pertaining to the dark night of the soul. Therefore I still possessed little understanding of this Divine metamorphosis. If I had perhaps known more about the process there would have been fewer struggles, and surrender would have come more easily. However, this transformation of the soul is not taught in schools or churches, nor is it elucidated in scientific or religious discourses.

It might be hard for some to believe that the early schools, such as those established by the great philosophers Plato and Pythagoras were based on spiritual principles rather than academia. Pythagoras decreed that the universe could be explained through number and sound (musical notes), and insisted that his students become knowledgeable in such arts. These were not considered academic, but designed to help the student to understand the immutable laws of nature and God. As time passed, however, more focus was placed upon the *effect* rather than the *causation*, and in time the world ceased to remember that the great universities originated from those who had no degree. In today's world the mysteries of transformation are all but forgotten, and would completely be so if those rare individuals who reached for the heavens had not left their work for humanity to follow. It is almost sad to think that the world is entering its greatest epoch without any knowledge of its majestic future.

Through the years I would find numerous references to this great battle of the soul, but these would often be so subtle that most people would have paid little attention to them. One exception to this is St. John the Divine and his "Revelation." Although these scriptures are very explicit, they are presented in an allegory that has stumped some of the greatest biblical experts for 2,000 years. Certainly, they did not benefit me at the time I entered into the *Dark Night of the Soul.* My own lack of comprehension, as well as the difficulty experienced, would later cause me to carefully teach this process to my students. Some, of course, left because they found the path too difficult. Others remained, but when they too entered this arduous transformation they were better prepared and absorbed the spiritual changes more easily. As difficult as it may be for some to accept, in years to come the mysteries of this remarkable *resurrection* will be known by all and accepted as a natural process of soul progression.

Shortly after my attempt to cease living in the human world, I put away any further efforts to hasten my transformation from earth to heaven. Now that both my inner sight and inner hearing had increased, it became possible to hear the voices of the Angelic Kingdom almost as easily as one hears voices in the human world. Also, I became quite comfortable with the numerous angelic presences that came from time to time, and often it seemed almost as though I was living in both worlds simultaneously.

CHAPTER V

Highway of Miracles

hile working full time for the City of Tacoma, Washington by day, I began teaching in four different locations around the city at night. I had moved into a modest studio apartment off of Puget Sound, and it became my custom to go out early each morning to walk along the water. To pay a measure of homage to God, Jesus and my Angelic Teacher, it also was my habit to draw three hearts in the sand with a stick. Inside of each heart I would carefully etch a word, or number of words, to express my affection. Then the search on the beach would begin for something to serve as a gift to place with the words, such as a shell or unusual piece of driftwood.

One morning, rising late and afraid that I would not arrive at work on time, I made the decision to not follow through with my daily beach ritual. Also, there was a need to prepare for my lecture that night on, "Jesus and the East Winds," a comparison between the Eastern religions and Christianity. This was being presented at the Tacoma Public Library which had an auditorium that held 200 people. It happened that I often spoke there, not only because the auditorium was free, but also it had a wonderful stage.

This day, in spite of my tardiness, I was not allowed to put aside my beach ritual. Immediately, after having made the decision to forego the walk, the crown on my head began to tighten. This was not good news and one my usual arguments ensued. I tried to emphatically explain that there simply wasn't sufficient time for a walk.

Having lost the argument, I grudgingly departed for the beach. As soon as I arrived I tried to hasten the process by drawing the hearts. I got the first one done and left a message for God, and then went on to the second one. This was always for Jesus. After the heart had been drawn, I was inspired to write the words, "Jesus is here." Immediately, at the tip end of the word "here" there appeared a fragment of glass. "Perhaps," I thought to myself, still in a hurry, "this piece of china will make a suitable gift to put inside the heart and I will not have to delay going to work any longer."

Digging up the fragment of china, I turned it over and wiped it off. I was stunned. It was heart shaped and had apparently come from a hand-painted plate of the *Last Supper*. The piece in my hands was of Jesus and one disciple. "How could such a thing be possible," I wondered, particularly on the very day I am going to speak on "Jesus and the East Winds?"

For many years I carried the "Last Supper" fragment in my purse, but one night, while on lecture tour, the piece was taken. Perhaps, it too had become an attachment, although I still wish that it were in my possession.

Working, lecturing, teaching, and appearances on the local talk shows, kept me exceedingly busy. Nevertheless, another project was soon added to my already-heavy workload. I took over the ministry of one of the local churches. The church had been having financial struggles and really could not meet the expenses of a full-time minister. Therefore, I proffered my services without expectation of pay and quite happily began to fill the wonderful role of a minister.

A distinct and holy feeling enveloped me each Sunday morning as I donned my ministerial robes and walked out on the platform to talk about God to the church's modest congregation. It was my expectation to be there only until they could find a regular minister, although I deeply appreciated the opportunity that the ministry afforded me. But one day I looked up toward the heavens and said, "God, you have proven to me that you can be all things, but I want you to know that I am still paying the rent."

Such a statement obviously could not be ignored. Within a week, the church offered me a full-time ministry position and, along with it, a large parsonage on the adjacent lot. As I moved into my new quarters, I looked up, shrugged and shook my head at heaven.

Even now, I still smile over my sojourn in the ministry and never cease finding it remarkable that God is aware of our smallest desires and hears every thought and every word we say. Over the years, it has been my delight to watch Him move both people and things to create specific events or answer some prayer. My fascination with this phenomenon has never diminished. Every aspect of life is a part of His consciousness, and He has an entire universe to move at His will. Yet, He works for the good of the whole and does not grant one person a favor at the cost of hurting another. It is little wonder that Jesus found a relationship with Him to be alone sufficient.

The immensity of God's power and protection truly became evident one night as I traveled to teach a class in Lacey, Washington, which was a small city outside of Olympia. It was a very dark, early spring night, and the rain was falling in torrents. Turning off the freeway I was in deep thought concerning the forthcoming class. With my mind thus preoccupied, I completely forgot about an old, four-lane highway that had previously been used as a main route between Seattle and Olympia. Suddenly, it appeared in front of me like a ghostly ribbon of dark concrete, almost opaque because of the heavy torrent of falling rain. Something warned me that driving through the intersection would result in a terrible accident. Immediately, my mind became startlingly clear. Turning off the ignition, I put my foot on the brake as the car rapidly began to slide toward steel supports, some holding signs and one serving as a brace for the streetlight illuminating the intersection.

It is interesting how objects can appear to move so rapidly and yet in slow motion at the same time. The steel supports stood there like silent specters waiting to embrace the impact. They were ominous and frightening. My mind, however, remained remarkably clear, waiting to hear the sickening thud of metal against metal and the sound of breaking glass. The car abruptly came to a halt. For a short time, I sat quietly, saying to myself, "I heard no breaking glass and have apparently sustained no injuries. However, the car must have hit the supports. Perhaps I am suffering from shock."

After remaining still for perhaps several minutes, somewhat perplexed over what action should be taken; I decided to see if the car was still operational. I got out and walked around the vehicle fully prepared to see considerable damage. There was none, and I was stunned. Lack of damage seemed impossible given the speed with which the car had skidded toward the steel supports. Although I circled the automobile once more, there still appeared to be no visible evidence of damage. When I arrived at the home of the students who were sponsoring the classes, I got out and went around the car one last time, still unable to believe what had just occurred.

When class was over and I headed homeward, I drove past the spot where the car had gone into a skid. Getting out, I went over to look at the pavement and followed the skid marks toward the metal signposts. They ended about an inch or so short of impact. Obviously, some power or force had abruptly stopped the car before it collided. The miracle of that moment has since overshadowed my life and the magnitude of God's power and love then, and throughout the remainder of my life, has never left me. If only the world realized how immediate this great power that controls the universe is. Villain or Saint, rich or poor, no one is without the guiding hand of the vast Angelic realms and the consciousness that rules it. The events of that night were neither the first nor the last demonstration of God's power to control time and space. Just as He had tended to my need the night I attempted to turn away from life, so was He always there throughout the good, the bad, and the difficult. I drove thousands of miles without automobile damage or bodily harm.

Another such auto rescue also remains etched in my mind, almost as powerful as the one that occurred on that rain-swept night. Late one morning, while traveling on the inside lanes of a freeway section just outside of Olympia, Washington, a car in the right lane abruptly lost control. Veering across the road in front of me it crashed into a concrete divider running down the middle of the highway. There seemed no possible way to avoid crashing into the other vehicle. Yet, even as the moment of impact seemed inevitable, I saw something that resembled hands begin to stretch out time like a rubber band.

Although the accident had happened right in front of me, by the time I reached it, the driver had left his car and was running down the highway bleeding from cuts on his face, in an obvious state of shock. I easily turned the wheel, veered around the wrecked car, and continued on my way, hoping to find help. Within a very short distance, I happened upon a state patrolman and was able to report the accident and the injured man.

Several months passed following the two incidents just described. My work as pastor of the church continued to be very fulfilling, and before long I began holding classes one night a week in the parsonage. On subsequent nights, I traveled to Olympia, Seattle, and Bremerton. By now, I had managed to dispose of my first automobile, which collected water in its trunk every time it rained, and replaced it with a rebuilt taxi purchased from my former landlord. Because the taxi had a new engine and had been repainted, it felt like a Mercedes, and I was happy to be driving it.

Teaching differed somewhat from preaching, for it opened
doorways of exploration into worlds beyond the scriptures, such
as psychology, philosophy, and science. These new explorations
proved that earth was not built in seven weekdays as some conceive, but rather in seven epochs spanning millions of years. This
also disproved the theory that there was, or is, an opposing force
in the universe. Instead I came to more fully comprehend the
perfect Law of Cause and Effect flowing through all life. These
revelations shifted the burden of life's responsibility from an outer
demon to each individual.

There was a hunger during those days to see the greater truths
become the topic of all pulpits preaching, because I wanted, and
still want, the people of the world to seek their commonalities
instead of their differences. However, the world has never changed
swiftly, nor have the beliefs of mankind. When doubts and dis-
couragement assailed me, the memory of that morning in June
surfaced, when the consciousness of God prevailed over my finite
mind, and revealed the magnificence of mankind's future.

The dark night of the soul did not release its grip during
those busy days, and I knew little difference between the hours
of day or night. My attention was not allowed to turn toward
the outside world of objects, although there were momentary
glimpses of the warmth of the summer sun and the beauty of
the winter snows. However, these were but momentary
glimpses, fleeting and elusive. As soon as my thoughts turned
outward, He who now guided my soul brought my mind
abruptly back into the inner world. How many times I wanted
to escape, not because my heart did not wish to follow the
Will of God, but because my body and humanness had long
been bound to worldly affairs. Therefore, the days were long
and exhausting, sometimes passing with little attention as to
whether it was dawn or sunset.

This new routine eventually became my standard way of
day-to-day living. Quite naturally, it could not remain this way

forever, for the Spirit continued with His unveiling process in order to reveal the inner and greater depths of potentiality. As the months passed, I gradually became accustomed to my busy life and settled within the parameters of a new comfort zone, despite the constant pressure of the dark night of the soul. Although much of my time was relegated to purification, my spiritual powers continued to develop, as did my comprehension of the nature of the universe.

There were moments of great clarity and sometimes wonder during my time with the church. One morning, at three a.m., one of my parishioners called to inform me that her husband had just suffered a massive coronary. She asked me to go to the hospital where he had been taken and to pray for him. Hastily I dressed and drove to the hospital. On my arrival I found he was on life support, with little or no hope of recovery. On entering his room and going to his bedside, I was faced with a dilemma. Would God's plan for this man be interfered by praying for him to have a peaceful transition? However, might it not also interfere in God's plan if I prayed for him to live? Finally, I simply prayed for his peace and departed from the hospital.

On arriving home around five in the morning, I was unable to sleep. Sitting in a chair by the window, there was deep concern over the suffering this man's family was going through. He had a wife who loved him and two pre-teenage children who needed him. How could this be evaluated against my own life? Bowing my head I prayed, "Please God, spare this man. He has a wife who loves him and children who need him. Take my life instead, for I will not be missed."

Upon finishing the prayer, I was instructed to begin preparation for the funeral service. As I wrote the service, I questioned God, "Why are you having me write this, for he is not yet dead?"

As the day wore on, no answer was forthcoming. At four o'clock that afternoon I completed writing the service. The phone rang.

It was the man's wife calling to tell me that the hospital had said her husband would live, but that he would remain a vegetable for the rest of his life.

"No," I told her, "God does not do half a job. Wait and see."

A few weeks later, as I sat on the platform near the pulpit, the miracle man walked in with his entire family. He would die exactly ten years later, but after his children were grown. Looking back on that day, I realize God had me write the funeral service in order to keep my mind focused upon the dying man, so that His power could work this miracle through me. During this period the man had been healed. I knew that my prayer had been answered because I had offered my life for his.

Not long thereafter, my comfort zone was disrupted again. The Angelic Kingdom informed me that I must go on a United States lecture tour. I, who had never been in a city larger than Seattle, was suddenly looking at the prospect of facing an entire nation. I felt much like Moses, as he stood on Mt Sinai before the burning bush and questioned God, why he, a man of quietude, had been selected to lead the Children of Israel out of Egypt. At first, the idea of a United States tour did not frighten me a great deal, perhaps because a quest of such magnitude seemed unreal. Not having traveled a great deal, it was, however, difficult to think about appearing in cities such as San Francisco, Los Angeles, Houston, and New York City. Large metropolises such as these were beyond the scope of my imagination. For this reason, I thought about traveling only to the small suburban areas existing on the outskirts of major cities.

As spring approached, the call to leave the sanctuary of the church became stronger. Soon, I gave the Church Board notice that I must embark on a United States lecture tour. The church had fared well under my ministry, and the board was sorry to see me depart, but they understood that I had been called to fulfill a different mission.

Finally the morning of my departure arrived. My rebuilt taxi was packed and waiting in front of the parsonage. The day was beautiful, and the sky was clear and blue. I rose early, intending to make my first stop in Portland, Oregon. If I had thought about it, it would have been obvious that the finger of God had woven this decision into the fabric of my destiny, for what would seem more appropriate than to start the first phase of my United States tour in the city where I had been twice born?

Perhaps most people would have considered my sendoff a lonely one. There was no one to say goodbye except one of the former ministers of the church, and she was not living in the physical world. Nonetheless, her comforting words bridged our two worlds and drifted softly over me as I proceeded down the walkway toward the car. I heard her say, "May His angels walk with you."

After starting the car, the enormity of what I was doing began to set in. Here I was, leaving Tacoma, Washington and the sanctuary of the church in a rebuilt taxi. My possessions consisted of only my clothes and three hundred dollars. In the eyes of most people, such a departure would have appeared suicidal rather than adventuresome. Nonetheless, the power of the Spirit held me in His vise-like grip and I could no more stop this journey into the unknown than I had been able to resist the call to follow the pillar of Light through the skid row of San Pedro.

CHAPTER VI

Despair to Triumph

$\mathcal{A}$s I drove toward Portland, Oregon on that April morning, the idea of a successful tour across the United States was beyond the scope of my comprehension. By this time, human frailties had produced enumerable reasons why the tour might never work. While driving, I looked up at the sky and decided that it was time to have a rather serious conversation with God. "God," I said, "the United States is just too big. I have never even been in city larger that Seattle, Washington. The best I can do is to go from state-to-state."

It was nice to think that he patted me on the head in order to comfort me, but if He did I was too deeply concerned to feel it. My first United States tour would, however, progress one state at a time, and I would not realize what a monumental undertaking it had been until it was over. And when it ended, I would muse over the limitations that we often impose upon ourselves. Johann Wolfgang Von Goethe, a renowned German poet born in the latter part of the seventeen hundreds said:

"Until one is committed, there is hesitancy, the chance to draw back, always ineffectiveness, concern all acts of initiative. There is

one elementary truth the ignorance of which kills countless ideas
and splendid plans: that the moment one definitely commits oneself then providence moves too. Whatever you can do or dream
you can, begin it. Boldness has genius, power & magic in it. Begin it now. "

Here I was, alone and an unknown, driving across the bridge
on the outskirts of Portland, Oregon, and attempting what many
would consider impossible. Surprisingly, I felt no fear, for almost
two years had passed since that morning of June 6th and unusual
things had become the wine that nourished me. In spite of this, I
still had difficulty conceiving a complete United States lecture
tour.

The City of Portland welcomed me like a prodigal son. Some
of my acquaintances that lived there had rolled up their sleeves
and worked on publicity. They had posted and handed out flyers,
and, to my surprise, they had even arranged for an interview with
the *Oregonian*, Oregon's number one newspaper. This story is still
one of my favorites, and the article made a nice addition to my
rather sparse press kit and served to enhance my profile. As it was
a rather large feature story, it drew a good attendance.

Walking into the meeting room the night of my talk, I was
surprised to find every seat was filled, although there was never
any doubt that this had been accomplished in order to show me
the tour's potentiality. While preparing for this appearance, I had
tried not to think about the possibility of speaking throughout
the entire United States. I could still not imagine ever doing so.
Yet, I did not know how or when my current assignment might
end. In committing my life to God, it was with the understanding that I would serve him forever and go where I was assigned.
Alas! Sometimes the magnitude of the heart is not always in harmony with practicality of the mind.

While appearing in Portland, there were a number of impres-
sions that, for financial reasons, it might become necessary to live
outdoors. Therefore, as I departed from the city I decided to have

another serious conversation with God. Certainly, it was neither the first, nor would it be the last. There would be many other times, as I was sadly still far more human than Divine. "God, I said, "we really have a problem down here. You see I can't sleep outside because I am afraid of snakes."

In my mind's eye appeared a terrifying picture. Waking up some morning, I would find that one of the slithering monsters had taken up his abode in my sleeping bag. I could almost hear the rattle of its tail and see its beady eyes angrily staring at me because its comfort zone had been disturbed. Of course, it would probably sink his fangs into me and I would die alone in the wilderness. The only positive aspect of the situation, as I saw it, was that it would end my new career. There seemed to be but one solution. It would be necessary to buy a tent.

Entering the first sporting goods store I saw, I went in and purchased a two-man tent for the great sum of twenty-seven dollars. At this same time, prayers were fervently flowing from my lips that I would never have to live in it. If there was any consolation at all, it was the fact that I would at least outsmart the rattlesnakes. Putting the tent into my rebuilt taxi, I headed south toward some of the smaller towns located near the California border.

The places I appeared during those next few weeks reminded me of the towns I had grown up near. The primary difference was the scenic beauty that adorned the land everywhere. In place of dusty fields and sagebrush, great mountains rose toward the sky. Behind me lay the majesty of Mt. Rainer and ahead of me the pristine beauty of Mt. Shasta. To say that I fully enjoyed the marvel of God's creations would be wrong. His Will was moving me into a heretofore-untried arena and compelling me to step from the known into the unknown.

Bound by many narrow limitations of the past, I tried to make my money last as long as possible and was quite frugal. Meeting rooms cost about ten dollars a night, and I stayed in the least expensive motels. In spite of this, my funds were disappearing more rapidly than the financial resources coming in. An unknown, even in a small town, does not draw much of a crowd and only four or five people would show up.

A doomsday prediction had also cast its black shadow over the inroads of my mind, further intensifying my concern. This was given to me prior to leaving Tacoma by a person claiming to be a prophet. He said that my tour would not go well and that within six weeks, I would be sick and out of money. Facing lack of success, I felt that I might also be staring into the face of this prophetic disaster. It wasn't the small number of people who came to hear me speak that was of concern, for I fully realized that I was an *unknown*. Rather it was the idea that I might disappoint God and fail to complete the tour.

By the time I reached Mount Shasta, California, my vocal chords were infected, and my money had dwindled drastically. In spite of the dire circumstances facing me, I stayed in a motel at the base of the beautiful mountain.

Not only was Mt. Shasta reputed to be a place of great spiritual activity, but also it had another reputation. A number of people claimed to have seen unidentified flying spacecraft. While such rumors were of little importance to me, for a moment I could not help wishing that something from outer space might possibly fly my way. Certainly, I knew that the universe was vast and it was inconceivable to believe that we, the human race, were the only third dimensional life forms among billions of galaxies.

The mountain was magnificent. Mt. Shasta is located at the northern extremity of the Sierra Nevada range and the cone of its now extinct volcano rises to a height of 14,162 feet above sea level. As I observed the mountain through my motel window that night, it looked strangely aloof and remote, a snow-white crystal dome etched in grandeur against a now darkening horizon. As I went to sleep that night at the base of the great mountain, I am sure that my thoughts must have been filled with intangible questions about the potentiality of other life forms existing in the universe of the stars.

On the following morning upon leaving Mount Shasta I was still quite ill. Yet, I was awed by the beauty of a snow-crested mountain summit reaching to the sky in chivalric surrender. Even now, this wondrous mountain remains in my mind as one of the great scenic beauties of California. Looking back to take one last look at its very feminine and graceful snow-covered peak, I was once more aware of the panoramic beauty of God's creation. The mountain was imperial as it hovered like a sentinel over the small town. At that hour of the morning the sun bathed her dome with golden hues, while her deep ridges came almost to the edge of town like the folds of a bridal dress. In spite of the beauty at the moment, however, I still could not resist asking, "God, why haven't you ever allowed me to see a space craft?"

While I did not expect an answer to my rather ridiculous question, one was forthcoming anyway. Immediately, I heard, "You are already on one."

As this bit of information got dissected mid the ever-constant mental indigestion that all too often occupied my mind, I knew that He was right. We do live on a rather small planet, at least when compared to our larger relatives in the solar system, and we are indeed floating in space. Content, I turned on to the main freeway and headed south. Although I would see Mount Shasta many times during the ensuing years, she would always appear as graceful and elegant as she appeared then.

The next morning, I reached the outskirts of San Francisco. It was my intention to go directly to Sacramento, but the power of the Spirit did not permit me to be such a coward. Suddenly, I found myself heading right into the heart of the big city itself. It occurred spontaneously. One moment I was driving down the I-5 freeway, which runs between the Canadian and Mexican borders, and the next moment found me on another thoroughfare headed directly into San Francisco. The city seemed huge, for I had never been in a city so large. How I could possibly appear in a place of such magnitude?

My home city, Seattle, had often been referred too as "Little San Francisco" and now I knew why. Never had I seen such steep inclines. Everywhere I looked everything seemed to be uphill. Fortunately, due to God's powerful influence over my soul I thought little of the outcome of this adventure at the time. Had I done so, I probably would have had to balance rattlesnakes in one hand and this huge city in the other in order to determine which terrified me the most.

After registering at one of the local hotels, I occupied myself with the task of putting up flyers along the nearby cable car run. Also, I tried to contact a few groups that I thought might have some interest in my work. These were selected from the Yellow Pages of the telephone directory. After that, there seemed little more could be done but to wait. Sadly, I was not yet experienced in arranging my appearances. If I felt like a small and unknown fish in small ponds earlier, now I was a *very small* fish in a very large pond. Disaster seemed imminent.

The night of my appearance finally arrived. True to my premonition, disaster struck. Only five or six people came and I was devastated — not so much because of the attendance, but it seemed that my United States lecture tour was finished. Even worse, I did not know what to do. Returning to my room, a deep sense of failure engulfed me. It was not the same sense of failure that once prevailed in human life, but a deep abject sorrow, further intensified by my current journey through the dark night of the soul. It was obvious that there was nothing to do but go to bed and try to sleep. However, no sooner had I retired than I was instructed to take my tent and go to Sacramento the next day.

There was less than $150.00 remaining, but I had not yet been relegated to living in a tent and was very dubious about doing so now. As usual, the humanness in me balked, and I refused to surrender to Divine Will. The struggle through the night was long and hard. I sobbed and told God that I did not want to live in a tent. Each time I would drift off to sleep, He awakened me and told to go live in my tent. Again, I would sob and occasionally wad up my pillow so that people in adjoining rooms could not hear me. To continue with the tour appeared ludicrous. Obviously, it was destined to failure. "How could I possibly continue?" I asked, "And if I did not continue, where would I go? What would I do?"

Even as these doubts assailed me, I was still being told to depart for Sacramento the following morning and put my tent up there. To me, the idea of living in a tent, for what I believed then would be the rest of my life, seemed a fate worse than death. Thus, the war with God raged on throughout the night. The next morning, completely exhausted, and after some pretty loud words to God, the Angelic Kingdom, and anyone else who might have been listening, I climbed into my car and headed for Sacramento.

While traveling in Oregon, I had learned about Kampgrounds of America (KOA). Fortunately, Sacramento had one and I decided to start there. As I drove, I was still greatly agitated and still complaining loudly. However, it became rather obvious that a rescue out of my current dilemma was not to be. Every mile brought me closer to what seemed a horrible fate. The only redeeming feature I could conjure up during this struggle between human and Divine Will was the concept that a KOA might be somewhat better than being in the wilds. It would possess a measure of physical protection against rattlesnakes and scorpions.

On my arrival at the KOA, I paid for a full week's lodging. In those days a tent site cost $1.50, and even less if one paid by the week. Going to the counter to register, I was pleasantly surprised to learn that anyone staying in the camp had access to laundry facilities, indoor restrooms and showers, and a swimming pool. Later, as I put up my tent, my disposition improved and a little

bit of happiness crept in. By now, I was also suffering less indigna-
tion and was somewhat reconciled to the possibility that I would
probably have to live this way the rest of my life.

It was now June, and while the weather was warm by day, it was
cold at night. Very soon darkness descended over the campground,
and as it did, I found that I had nothing to occupy me. There was no
television to help pass the time, and this was long before the computer age...or at least my computer age. Also, as soon as the sun went
down, a chill began to permeate the nylon walls of my new home.
Wrapping myself in an army surplus sleeping bag in an effort to get
warm, I soon found that night produced its own particular type of
abject misery. It was cold and dark. Finally, to pass time away, I started
to carry on a conversation with myself.

"What do you need, Elizabeth?"

"I need to be famous," I replied.

"But you are not famous," I answered

Then I thought, "What I need is a good public relations secretary."

Of course, the practical part of me replied, "Well, you can't
afford one, so now what are you going to do?"

At that moment I developed a plan. During my earlier years
in the corporate world, I had worked for the telephone company,
first in the Commercial Department and later in Personnel. I held
these positions until becoming the Oregon Plant Clerical Training Supervisor in charge of two states. During my service in
the telephone company's Commercial Department, I served
on the Public Relations Committee. It was wonderful to participate in this activity, perhaps because everyone is a humani-
tarian at heart, and doing something for the townspeople and
our customers brought a great sense of satisfaction. In time,
our public relations work led to some interesting alliances between the company and its customers.

Now I decided to use this public relations talent, as well as the
experience gained during my tenure in the telephone company. I

would become my *own* public relations spokesperson. It was a daring plan, but there was nothing to lose. I little knew on that first cold dark night that this decision would deeply affect the success of my future work. About the time this decision was reached, the sun rose and warmed the inside of the tent. No longer cold, I fell into a deep slumber.

Later that day, full of resolve and courage, I gathered up some dimes and began to make calls to radio and television stations, as well as to the primary Sacramento newspaper. These contacts were subsequently followed up with little packets of promotional material. After waiting a couple of days to make certain my material had been received, I again called each contact. If the media seemed a bit obstinate, I became more persuasive. Fortunately, my background in the corporate world made it possible to remain relatively detached from the entire process, particularly since there seemed to be no other choice. Here I was, traveling alone on a United States lecture tour. I knew no one, and no one knew me, yet I had a job to do.

While I waited for the media in Sacramento to respond, I went about the process of procuring a lecture hall. By this time I had only a small amount of money remaining. Boldly, I made the decision to gamble my last dollar, feeling that it was a sink or swim situation. In the past, I had spent only small amounts on places to speak, and my attendances were equally small. Now I decided to look for a popular place. My selection was the Capitol Hotel, directly across from the California State Capitol. The room held about a hundred people, and it cost an equal amount. It also depleted the last of my funds.

Never will I forget the night preceding my appearance in Sacramento. I was down to my last two and a half dollars and a half-tank of gas, although I still had sufficient food. As I prepared for another evening of cold and darkness, a voice told me to go to a movie. "A movie," I cried, "Do you realize that we only have two dollars and fifty cents left?" Again, I heard, "Go to a movie."

With great reluctance, I climbed into my car and headed for the nearest group of theatres. After paying for the ticket, He told me to buy some popcorn. Looking at my last fifty cents I decided, "Why not? Nothing can be accomplished with so little money."

Returning to the campsite, my mind was in a state of mental indigestion, still perplexed over the events that had just taken place. Although I knew that there must be a reason for what had happened, the reason escaped me. Only later did I realize that this had been done to keep me from worrying, and that the angelic forces which guided me apparently knew how things were going to work out.

The next night at precisely eight o'clock, I entered the lecture hall. To my surprise, it was not only filled to capacity, but there was standing room only. I, who stood at the brink of despair, had suddenly been rescued from the jaws of defeat. When the talk was finished and people left, they began to fill the donation basket with money. Before long it was overflowing. It was as if some silent voice inside of them knew of my financial dilemma and responded accordingly. Certainly, it was not I who drew such favor, but His Power was working this wonder through them.

The miracles continued. My subsequent seminar was also well attended. This increased my financial resources and made it possible to continue with the tour. In spite of this encouragement, however, the concept of success still seemed more of a dream than a reality.

After the Sacramento seminar, I turned toward the I-5 freeway once again, intending to travel south to San Diego. However, I had barely left the KOA when I found myself saying, "Elizabeth Burrows are you going to let San Francisco defeat you?"

Turning in the direction of the city, something compelled me to try San Francisco again. I could not believe that I was doing this, but it was useless to argue. It was obvious that I was given the courage to return, and before long I found myself once more entering this beautiful *City by the Bay*. At least circumstances were such that it would not be feasible to live in a tent, so I sought a modest place to stay.

Once settled, the work of contacting the San Francisco media began. Again, boldness bred success. While I did not win over the local television stations, I fared better with radio stations and obtained an interview with the *San Francisco Examiner*. Ultimately, the rather large feature story which appeared in the *Examiner* helped me not only in San Francisco, but also opened many doorways during my subsequent travels. Apparently, when a major newspaper from a large city chooses to cover someone, other newspapers follow suit. In turn, if newspapers run feature stories, the media does not wish to be left behind and accepts that person also.

On entering the hotel lecture hall on the night of my second appearance in the *Jewel of the Pacific*" following thirteen radio shows and a feature story in the newspaper, it was quite a different story than my appearance some weeks before. The lecture hall was filled almost to capacity, and the past agony of defeat became buried in the throes of triumph.

On Monday morning following my seminar, I departed from San Francisco. Little did I know as I drove away, that the future success of my tour was written in stardust. At that particular moment, I was still bound within the perimeters of state-to-state and city-to-city travel, and many months would pass before the United States would become small enough for me to feel confident and comfortable.

CHAPTER VII

Voyager of
the Unknown

*A*fter leaving the Bay area, I continued southward toward San Diego. While driving along on the southern California section of I-5, I spied a branch of the freeway heading directly toward Los Angeles. Once more, as in San Francisco, I found myself moving toward the center of a very large city. Although my senses claimed that this was a disaster in the making, heavy traffic kept me so occupied that there was no time to present the subject to God. To further compound this surprising turn of events, I boldly decided that I would like to appear in Hollywood.

Having made, what would seem to some, a most ludicrous decision, the search began for a place to stay. By this time, I had learned a good lesson about practical living from previous experiences and decided it would be best to find some place where it would not only be possible to prepare most of my meals, but also there would be easy access to a telephone. As I moved closer to the city my mental turbulence increased, for here I was in a place that I had never intended to be.

Los Angeles, named on August 2, 1769, the day of *Our Lady Queen of the Angels,* was formally recognized by the Mexican Congress in 1835 .On August 13, 1846 General S.W. Kearny and Commodore Stockton entered the city as its defenders fled and the United States flag was raised. It was better known during its years before and after statehood for its natural resources, such as petroleum and water rather than for its sub-division, Hollywood; home of the stars – and, of course, Zorro. Having spent most of my time in the cooler regions of the Northern United States, the unchanging warm weather, smog and dessert-like terrain of Los Angeles held little appeal for me. On the other hand, its beaches, which form a part of the California coastline and touches the Pacific Ocean, were both breathtaking and beguiling.

The ocean seemed far away as I faced the terror of the massive Los Angeles traffic. Even more frightening was the fact I did not know where I going and there was a gnawing fear that any exit off of the freeway would cause me to lose my way. Having once driven over a four-lane freeway while searching for it did not enhance my courage. That God and his angelic emissaries were about to produce a rather big surprise might have been of great comfort, but if He tried to tell me I fear that my severe case of mental indigestion was too active to receive the information.

This particular miracle originated in Tacoma prior to leaving the church. One of my parishioners had told me about a hotel that one of his friends owned in Los Angeles. I happened to write the name on a piece of paper. The information did not mean a great deal, because I had no intention of approaching large cities. He did say, however, that it was a very nice hotel, modestly priced, and that it would be a good place for me to stay.

Here I was, on one of the major arterials and headed in the direction of Los Angeles, my future in the hands of God and His angels. Although mankind's intuition is a reflection of the Spirit which dwells within, it must be freed from the boundaries of self-control before it can function perfectly. At the moment my intuition was free to fly with the wind. I had no map, and if I had possessed one it would have been of little value because I had no idea where I was. As I drove, there was a definite awareness that a great power was in control and sizing up the different areas along the way. A distinct feeling that this section of Los Angeles was not a particularly good area hung over me for a time. Abruptly, after passing through the next traffic light, however, a sense of peace descended. On my left was a rather modest, but nice hotel, and seemed to be exactly the right type of situation. Happily I went in to register, glad to be out of the traffic. I was even happier to have arrived at some destination, although there was no definite understanding as to exactly where that was.

A few hours later, after settling in, I happened across my note bearing the name of a hotel. To my amazement I found myself to be in the very hotel my parishioner had recommended. In spite of self-will and human errantries, the power of the universe moves through every human being, often motivating one to do the right thing whether they are aware of it or not. While some may believe that such things actually happen by chance, a coincidence is never really a coincidence. Rather miracles are brought about by the extensive work of unseen hands from an unseen world existing beyond mortality.

The very first thing, after unpacking, was to obtain a map of the city of Los Angeles. The next day, I boldly headed for Hollywood to seek a lecture facility. Hollywood, however, turned out to be a disappointment, for it appeared unkempt and far-removed from the glory days of its youth. Realizing that an appearance there would not be fruitful, my field of endeavor turned to the old and historical Biltmore Hotel.

Once the matter of finding a place to speak was settled, I began the titan task of publicity. My contact with the newspaper met with no success, but the radio and television stations were considerably more receptive. Eventually I secured a guest appearance on most of the major shows in the area.

To some people, having to appear on television and radio might be an alarming experience. However, I was, and still am, a bit of a ham at heart. The elocution lessons my great-grandmother had imposed upon me in my youth instilled in me a sense of enjoyment for the entertainment field. Therefore, I considered, and still consider, every appearance a form of art. I love enchanting audiences and students, whether in person, or as a guest of the media. In fact, after one appearance, someone said, "If you ever get tired of doing this, you would make a great actress."

Because the media welcomed me, my appearances usually drew capacity crowds now. I did not charge, for it was my wish to make my talks available to rich and poor, without religious or racial difference. Although I did charge a nominal fee for my seminars, it was my rule that no one would ever be turned away because they could not pay. Yet, in spite of this outer success, I drew little satisfaction from it, as the dark night cast its darkness over my soul without letup. There was always an inner conflict, although I now had a better understanding of this struggle involving purification of the senses and subduing the ego. My Angelic Teacher, Okaji, also made certain that I continued to work on other unlearned lessons, for Heaven is good and everything in it must be good. The ego has no place in the angelic regions.

St. John of the Cross presents a reason for this trouble in his book, *Dark Night of the Soul.* "For, as the soul finds not the pleasure and sweetness which it was wont to find, but rather finds affliction and lack of sweetness. As a rule God gives to those whom He leads into this night humility and readiness, albeit with lack of sweetness, so that what is commanded them they may do for God's sake alone; and thus they no longer see profit in many things because they find no pleasure in them."

One afternoon, while driving on one of the numerous Los Angeles freeways I found myself going in the wrong direction. This produced a deep concern, and again there was fear of taking a wrong exit. There is little recourse in times like this, but to pray.

Although I have argued with God, complained to Him on occasion, and suggested better ideas for His use of me from time-to-time, I still resorted to prayer when all other things failed. This was one of those times. "God," I said, "I am going in the wrong direction and I don't know how to turn around. Help me."

At that moment, a wonderful voice spoke, saying, *Paramahansa Yogananda.* Unfortunately, there was little time to relish contact with this great spiritual master who had departed from his earthly body in the nineteen fifties, because I was far too concerned over my dilemma. Within minutes, although I had no immediate memory of what, or how it happened, I had not only exited and turned around, but had returned to the freeway. Now the automobile was going in the right direction. Giving thanks for my timely rescue later, I wondered if the famous teacher had even driven a car while he lived on earth. In all that had been said about him, there was no indication that he had.

This was not the first time Paramahansa would appear to me, for he would make his presence known again several times in the years ahead.

The first lecture tour through the United States lasted fifteen and one-half months. During the first seven or eight months, living in a tent became a way of life. I would be a bit remiss, however, if I failed mention that a space blanket, costing twelve dollars, and an air float, costing three dollars, had been added to my camping accessories. These new additions made the nights a bit warmer and the rocks a little less formidable. By now I was better able to surrender to the possibility that this was probably the way I would have to live much of the rest of my life.

Following my appearances in Los Angeles, I headed for the beautiful San Diego, with its cooling sea breezes and blue skies. If there is a heaven on the west coast it must be San Diego, a Pacific coast city situated 16 miles N. of the Mexican border. It has one of the greatest zoos in the world, Balboa Park, with over 1,400 acres of exotic animals, and, yes, snakes. There is also racing, aquatic shows, speed boating, yachting, deep-sea fishing, swimming, and even a marine and recreational park.

By this time the unknown territories that drew me into their midst were not as frightening as they had been at first. And, soon after taking up residency in San Diego, I rented a small meeting room in one of the most prestigious hotels in the city for my talks. The public relations work went well, and I had the opportunity to appear on every talk radio show and television show in the area. Also, the newspaper did superb feature story. Yet, nothing could have prepared me for what happened.

At 7:20 on the evening of my appearance I sensed something was wrong, although my speech was actually not scheduled until eight. Immediately, I went downstairs to see what the difficulty was. On arriving outside the meeting room, I found it not only filled to capacity, but a long line of people waiting to get in. The line stretched around the hotel and continued for about half a block down the street. It was almost surreal to think that such a great number of people had come to hear me. As I stood there, wondering what to do next, the manager of the hotel came to my rescue and opened the large Crystal Ballroom. People rushed in, some carrying their own chairs. In the end, even this room was not large enough to contain everyone.

No one could ever forget the feelings which enveloped me that night as I entered the Crystal Room. Walking down the aisle I made my way through the audience, feeling like a lone swimmer in a great ocean, small and humble. The mass of faces spread before me like a vast sea. Making my way toward the front of, what had now become an auditorium, I heard someone whisper loudly "There she is," and for a brief moment, I knew what a movie star must feel.

In the years that followed there would be many capacity crowds, and sometimes standing room only. However, only one other appearance would affect me as deeply as the tremendous response in San Diego, my first standing ovation.

During my stay in beautiful San Diego, two additional events took place. Both of these subsequently brought about major changes in my life. I was sitting quietly in my hotel room the morning after my appearance, when a member of the higher Angelic Kingdom appeared and told me that I should establish a counseling practice. This was not the first time this had been suggested, but until now I had resisted. It was not an unwillingness to follow the Will of Heaven, but more because I was afraid that counseling would detract from my primary work, teaching. It seemed more important to help mankind understand the nature of the universe, than to tell them about their future. Ultimately, however, counseling became a wonderful teaching instrument and educated me in ways not fully covered by many of books written on the human mind.

Having experienced the usual number of financial ups and downs as a spiritual teacher, it was easy to see that a counseling practice would create additional income. I could also see that it would help sustain my primary work. Thus, with great misgiving, I acquiesced to the angelic request. Fortunately, a well-developed intuitive sense had existed since my birth, and I had often been able to perceive the events of the future. This power was displayed many times to entertain and amuse others during my youth. Because my Great Grandmother who had raised me had a fascination regarding prophetic knowledge, I had not been prohibited from dabbling in the world of prophecy. Raised without suppression of the natural intuitive ability all people possess, there was little surprise at the angelic suggestion.

The next step was to make a decision on exactly what kind of counseling would best benefit humanity. After considerable thought on the matter, I decided to develop a holistic practice. It seemed important for every human to know their destiny, or God's plan for them. In that His plan for every life form had been established in the origin of creation, and long before the birth of the universe, I knew that people could not find ultimate fulfillment until they became what they were designed to be. As a noted wise man once said, "When you have found your work, what need have you for anything else?"

To add a more complete work to that of destiny alone, I felt that it was also important to look at longevity, health and any emotional problems that might prove an obstacle to the well being of the client. Although many people have shied away from knowing their approximate life span, it is much more important than they think. By looking twenty-five years into the future, it becomes possible to determine future illnesses in people's lives. Such insight can reveal any serious diseases, and forewarned is prepared. It then becomes possible to help an individual to negate any potential illness by suggesting that they change their current lifestyle today. As Leonardo daVinci once said, "Vitality and beauty are gifts of nature for those who live according to its laws."

Counseling allowed me to probe into the depths of the soul and its corresponding subconscious. As a result I came to understand that people are the way they are because of their thoughts and actions through human existence. As the Divine Plan is constantly unfolding, the difficulties that plague humanity are due to the lack of expertise in working in harmony with this Plan. The degree of healing at any level, however, depends greatly on a person's individual capacity to make the necessary changes. Changes in a person's life can result in greater harmony within the body, the emotions, and the mind, and can produce amazing results, even miracles.

The subconscious mind is not just a storehouse of knowledge existing from childhood, but a storehouse of knowledge existing from the beginning of the universe. Since all creation, including humans, dwells within the consciousness of the Creator, He sees all things. In time these are revealed to those who walk with Him, but only if the revelations are in the best interest of a person, or persons. Such power, of course, also bears the responsibility of non-interference and non-judgment. While no secrets were kept from me that would help my clients to have a better life, I was bound by His Will to use this knowledge with discretion.

Eventually, psychiatrists and psychologists, who were universally oriented, would occasionally enlist my aid with difficult patients. Under normal psychological care, it might take several weeks of scream therapy, ink blots and dream interpretation, for an analyst to reach the deeper recesses of the subconscious. With my now heightened intuition, it was possible to pierce the core of the mental and emotional makeup of the individual within a half-hour or so. This does not mean that the patient was immediately cured, but rather that the healing process could begin much sooner because the source of the trouble had been defined.

Today, in looking back, upon what has been a long and successful counseling career, I no longer wonder why our world is so full of anger, sorrow, and fear. The human race is still in its infancy, but the basic nature of every individual is good. This good is visible every day in the men and women who risk their lives in earthquake rubble, floods, and fires to rescue the wounded and the lost. As I developed a deeper understanding of human nature I also developed a deeper love for humanity. With this deeper sense of love, my ability to help people also grew.

Before leaving San Diego another event occurred, which subsequently brought additional changes in my life. This came in the form of a small booklet. Someone gave me a soft cover copy of the translation of a Vatican manuscript, referred to as "The Secret Jesus Scroll." Since having started my research on the life of Christ sometime earlier, I found this new material fascinating. It was difficult to contain my excitement as I perused the contents of the writing, little knowing that I would present the complete "Secret Jesus Scroll" to the world a quarter of century later.

At first there were questions regarding the authenticity of the book, although its translator had remarkable, as well as brilliant background. Professor Edmond S. Bordeaux held degrees in Biochemistry from the Sorbonne, with degrees from Paris and Leipzig in Archeology, Psychology, and Philosophy. He had been an Associate Professor at the University of Cluj in Experimental Psychology and was fluent in fifteen languages. These facts alone created sufficient cause to review the writing with great interest. During my work with the material in the *Scroll* I could not find one flaw in its content.

The complete work consisted of three sections, the first: Jesus' teachings on health and nutrition. The second: Jesus' teachings on communions with the angels. The third: Jesus' teachings on merger with the holy streams of Life, Sound, and Light. Each application described in the *Secret Jesus Scroll* was a workable reality and capable of enhancing the good of the body, soul and spirit, if practiced. Another thing also became apparent. The material presented strong evidence that Jesus had been directly affiliated with the ancient Essenes in his early years. Later, of course, I would explore this possibility more deeply, but for the moment I was satisfied that the manuscript segments were authentic.

When the public appearances and consultations in San Diego finally come to an end it was time to leave California, or so I thought. During my preparations for departure, however, the Angelic Kingdom informed me that I must remain longer. This did not make a great deal of sense at the time, because I had appeared in every major metropolis in the state, from Redding to San Diego, from San Francisco to Los Angeles. Usually things like this brought on a determined argument with God which I always lost, but this time I did not fight against my new instructions. Rather I sought for some area to bide my time until permission to leave granted. All of the major areas had been covered so I drove to the coast and set up an appearance in Santa Barbara.

There has always been a love in my heart for the sea because its beauty reminds me of the magnificence of creation. Whenever I sit by the ocean and watch the waves break softly upon a sandy beach and then slowly recede, it is as though one is watching God breathe. How many times I have sailed in the eye of my mind to far distant shores and merged with the horizon, as it embraced the sea with its coral and pewter sunset. Like John Masefield wrote, "I must go down to the seas again, to the lonely sea and the sky, and all I ask is a tall ship and a star to steer her by."

For a time I was content to meander along the California coast, reveling in the sea's beauty.

CHAPTER VIII

Encounters with Destiny

T he area of Santa Barbara is not very large when compared to San Francisco and Los Angeles, so my appearance in this lovely coastal town was not highly attended. This did not seem important at the time, for the angelic forces had me in a holding pattern. They had given no explanation for this, but I knew from experience that there was a reason and that the answer would be revealed. Six weeks elapsed while thus occupied. When this period passed, departure for Arizona was granted. Even as I drove, it was difficult to understand the reason for the delay, for I had met no special person, nor undergone any unusual experiences.

On my arrival in Phoenix, Arizona, I faced a disaster. My hostess, who had attended both my appearance and later my seminar in Portland, had moved to Phoenix, Arizona. Aware of her forthcoming move, she had invited me to be her guest during my stay. She had also promised to set up several appearances. Unfortunately, I found that the latter commitment had not been kept because of her busy schedule. In spite of this, it turned out to be one of those rare cases where the lack of commitment on my hostess's part was an advantage. Her oversight forced me to step into a world that would broaden the scope of not only my spiritual understanding, but would unite me forever with a far away land. Had I not been detained in California, I would have missed a doorway that led to the feet of a great living teacher.

At loose ends following my arrival in Phoenix, I faced the necessity of seeing what could be done to salvage the situation. As we sat at the kitchen table discussing the matter, my hostess happened to glance down at a newspaper in front of her. Apparently she spied a small article about the forthcoming appearance of some swami at a small college on the outskirts of the city. Looking at me, she asked, "Would you like to go and hear a swami tonight?"

For all I knew a swami was someone who wore a big turban and told fortunes. However, the evening was open, and who could pass up such a delectable opportunity. After dinner, we made our way to the college and took our seats among a somewhat large gathering of people. Before long a tall, thin man dressed in bright orange and a most remarkable beard, took his seat on the stage. Then he tucked a pair of long legs under himself like a twisted pretzel and began to speak.

Very little time passed before it became obvious that this Eastern teacher, Swami Chinmayananda, really understood the nature of God. He was explaining this unlike anyone I had ever heard and I was mesmerized; for this was the first real, living spiritual teacher I had met in person. "Somehow," I thought, "this must be what the disciples felt as they gathered around Jesus on the shores of Galilee." Of course, it was not possible to travel back in time and sit amongst those who came to hear the Master when he dwelled in Israel. Now, however, I was experiencing the same form of direct teaching. Apparently my tour in California had been extended for just this reason, as there was no doubt in my mind that this remarkable spiritual teacher and I were destined to meet.

The story of Swami Chinmayananda's journey to this small college suburb of Phoenix was as unusual as my own. While I was being detained in California, so was he. Apparently, one of the professors at the college where Swami was now appearing had been touring in India when he met the famed man. Enthused by what he heard, the professor invited the renowned man to speak at the college when he came to the States. At the time Swami Chinmayananda's schedule was very full and he felt it necessary to decline the invitation. Upon the Swami's arrival in the States, however, a complication pertaining to his passport surfaced. Suddenly, he found himself with nothing to do for five days and decided to have his staff call the professor at Phoenix and inform him that he could come for five days. So here this famous Swami sat before me, teaching according to the customs of the east. For a brief moment the curtain opened and allowed me a glimpse into a spiritual world that seemed far removed from the religious culture of the west.

In time, a deep friendship evolved with this great teacher. It would last until his death in the later part of the nineteen nineties, and the beneficent touch of this great Eastern Scholar and Master would bless me many times. Later, some people would accuse me of not following the path of Christianity, and insist that I combined the Christian teachings with those of the East. However, this is not true. I am reminded of something Swami said at the end of one of his discourses during the question and answer period. He made the statement that all of the great masters came from the East. Someone in the audience took offense at this and immediately asked about Jesus. Swami, looked at the woman with a bit of amusement, and replied, "Jesus was of the East."

As with others from the East, Swami Chinmayananda was a practiced ego carver, meaning one who is efficient at chipping away the self-centered part of one's humanness. While he never completely annihilated my own ego, he managed to stick a sword into the wily, old dragon many times. In the years that followed, I could not refrain from thinking of Benjamin Franklin's well known quote: "I have accomplished almost everything I have wanted to, except the annihilation of my ego. However, I suppose if I had succeeded at this, I would have been proud of having done so."

My studies with Swami were more inner plane than outer, for an attempt to subdue the ego cannot be done simply through reading text or researching scholarly material. In fact, the intellect can sometimes become the soul's worst nightmare in its search for God. The intellect thinks and reasons but often does not see clearly, for it usually follows its line of reasoning from the outer world to the inner, rather than from the inner world to the outer. While it is possible to dissect a nut because it can be seen with the human eye, the cause, or source of the nut, still remains invisible.

After Swami Chinmayananda's discourse, I decided to see if I could get an appointment with him. At this time, some tangible answers to my questions would be welcomed. It is not that my Angelic Teacher did not try to answer my multitudinous requests, but some things were tests and lessons. He did not clarify these lest they influence the process of my development. Still deeply involved with the purification of the senses, the dark night hung around me like an albatross and I thought that this great scholar could perhaps alleviate some of my suffering. Besides I had a burning question on my mind. Can dedicated spiritual people watch television? While this may seem trivial to most people, it has become an obsession to me because of an incident that had taken place a number of weeks before.

During my travels I began dreading the long dark nights in my tent. Since most of Kampgrounds of America had electrical outlets at the campsites, I decided to purchase a small inexpensive television to help pass away the long hours. Traveling over twenty miles into the night I eventually reached an old familiar K-Mart store. Going in, I made my way to the electronic section where I found a small television for purchase. As I drove back toward the camp grounds, one of those customary battles with God began to rage. He wanted me to return the television. As usual, I wanted to argue, although I preferred to think of it as reasoning. It was to no avail. As I continued to drive, the bands tightened around my head and depression descended upon me like swarm of locusts. Before long, I wanted to throw the television set out of the car window and allow it to break into a thousand pieces by the side of the road.

Soon the conflict between human and divine will developed into a full-scale war. As it was very dark and becoming quite late, I was loathed to turn the car around and return to the store. Neither did I wish to face the humiliation I felt I would have to undergo. Suddenly, out of the dark, my headlights picked up a sign indicating a nearby hospital. Immediately I made the decision to take the television in and donate it to the children's wing. On completing this task I left the hospital and returned to my car. As I walked His voice spoke to me, saying, "This is in token of the television that was once given to you by a boyfriend which you never returned."

Due to this incident, the question of whether a spiritual aspirant could watch television had become paramount in my mind. What had once been an issue of pleasure had now become a full-blown obsession, and the memory of my television war was clearly etched in my mind as my hostess drove me to my appointment with Swami Chinmayananda.

On arrival at Swami's temporary residence the next day, I realized that my visit had to be timed to the minute. Because of my Angelic Teacher's guidance, I knew that if I arrived early I would have to wait. If I were late, Swami Chinmayananda would probably not agree to see me, as tardiness shows a lack of respect. On this occasion, it seemed wise to be on the safe side and, arriving early I sat outside the door until it was time to meet with him.

When I entered the room I was amazed to find Swami Chinmayananda watching television. It was an old western movie, and he seemed to be enjoying it very much. He did not speak, and for a time I did not know exactly what to do because it is considered impolite to speak to a spiritual teacher from the east until spoken to. Therefore, as we sat side-by-side my mind resembled a tornado whipping over the Idaho deserts.

Time passed as we watched the movie, but the holy man still did not acknowledge my presence. It soon became apparent that he was going to continue to watch television. Therefore, I decided that I might as well settle down and watch with him. Once my body and mind relaxed their concern, answers to my many questions began to pour through my mind in rapid succession. This was fascinating to me, for it was my first experience in meeting someone in physical embodiment who was capable of teaching in the unspoken word. Prior to this, all such communication had come strictly from the angelic world.

Only when the film was over did Swami Chinmayananda finally speak. Getting up, he said, "That was a very nice picture. Now I will give you a mantra."

Just before we left, Swami Chinmayananda presented my hostess with a little book that he had written called *I Love You*. It was a book he had created for children in order to help them understand the true meaning of love. As Swami gave it to her, I thought how much I would like to have one also. However, I sensed that it was not right to ask. Some weeks later, much to my surprise, a copy arrived in the mail addressed to me. Obviously, Swami had known my thoughts.

Unfortunately, my visit with Swami Chinmayananda did little to alleviate my suffering. The dark night of the senses remained very intense and I was a seething cauldron of mental and emotional turbulence. Not one little error, even those of childhood, had escaped God's scrutiny. Every crook in the path of life had to be made straight and atoned for. Thus, the war between human and divine raged unceasingly. While I was allowed to negotiate with God on occasion, He always remained the Will that overshadowed my human weaknesses. Sadly, during this early part of transformation, I fear that I wasn't too adept at resisting temptation and spent a great deal of time in trouble. It had been much easier when I was twelve years old and believed that I had been saved from the terror of the *Last Judgment* because Jesus had died on the cross for my sins.

One day, completely beside myself, I turned my eyes upward and roared up to the Heavens, "God, I am really aggravated at you, so I have decided to get me a flesh and blood husband."

Pausing for a few moments, I then added, "And while I am at it, I am going to get a rich one."

Again I paused for a few moments and then added my final ultimatum: "I'll find one when I get to New York City."

Of course, I really had no desire for a husband and felt quite safe with my threat — primarily because I never expected to reach New York. Nevertheless, I felt it necessary to emphatically let God know that this *dark night of the soul* left much to be desired. Threatening Him with a human husband seemed about the most catastrophic thing I could think of. Ah! Ignorance is such bliss, for the veil of the future carefully guarded God's perfect revenge.

The next destination was Oklahoma. Soon after my arrival, I walked into one of the major television stations in Oklahoma City to do an early morning show. Since God encourages punctuality, I arrived early to insure that I would not be late. While sitting in the reception area and waiting to be taken into the studio, a conversation incurred between a nice looking gentleman and myself. It seemed that he and his company owned the television station where I was appearing, along with several others. As the conversation proceeded, he said, "I want you to be my guest when you come to New York." Then he gave me his business card.

It was a wonderful invitation, although I still did not expect to ever reach New York. The thought of visiting such a huge city was beyond the imagination of the girl who had grown up on an Idaho farm. Nonetheless, I tucked his card in my purse, where it was promptly forgotten; and went on to do the show.

Television and radio were not the only media that seemed to welcome my appearances. As I traveled throughout the country, newspapers also opened many doorways, and numerous religious editors seemed particularly interested in my spiritual journey. The stories they wrote were not small articles, but often filled a half to full newspaper page. On occasion there would even be two pages in the special Sunday supplement section. I enjoyed these interviews and always tried my best to be honest, forthright, and unique.

After the Oklahoma television show, I departed for my appointment with the primary newspaper in Oklahoma City, little knowing that I was about to meet another person who would further prove that God is aware of even the smallest details of our lives. Apparently the newspaper reporter, who had scheduled the interview with me, thought that James Morris, author of *The Preachers*, might wish to sit in on the interview. At the time, Mr. Morris was under contract to do a sequel to *The Preachers*, entitled *The Prophets*.

The reporter was a very nice young man and the interview was proceeding well, when James Morris looked at me and asked, "Young lady, has anyone ever done a book about you?"

I shook my head.

"Someone should," he commented.

Following the interview, James Morris arranged to come out to the campground and interview me for his next book. By the time he arrived, the mosquitoes were so bad that we had to relegate ourselves to the recreation room. He sat in the barber chair, designed for things other than interviews, while I stood nearby. We talked for a very long time, or rather, he asked me questions and I answered. As he was leaving, he handed me his tape recorder and left instructions to record anything that might be interesting to readers. He arranged to pick the recorder up the following morning. This meant that it would be necessary for me to work far into the night.

On Mr. Morris' arrival the next morning, I crawled out of my two-man tent on hands and knees. Apparently my tent home seemed to bother him a great deal, because the author looked down at me and said, "Elizabeth, I can't leave you like this."

Camping had become a way of life since my appearances in Sacramento and I thought little of how this might appear to someone more affluent. "Please," I said, looking up at him from all fours, "I am really quite content and doing well. It may be difficult for you to understand, but I am used to this and you must not worry about me."

Eventually I convinced my would-be benefactor that things were not really as unbearable as they appeared, and he departed.

Later the two of us corresponded for quite some time, but ultimately we both became too preoccupied with other matters to continue. After my first book was published, I heard from him only once or twice. Nevertheless, our meeting in Oklahoma was fortuitous and brought about a partial fulfillment of a teenage fantasy; one of becoming a famous writer and having dinner in New York with a publisher like authors did in the movies. At the time of our meeting, I little knew that James Morris would be the instrument for partially fulfilling this dream. Unfortunately, it would not be my book, but his book, which would bring this dream into fruition.

After a very successful tour through Oklahoma and later New Mexico, I turned my trusty rebuilt taxi toward Texas. Oblivious to my future, I drove innocently into the jaws of God's remarkable and premeditated fate.

CHAPTER IX

Southern Exposure

hile I was in route to Texas, the Angelic Kingdom informed me that I should have a camper for my travels. This was one of the more astounding instructions I had recently encountered. Thus far, the tour had been, for the most part, a state-to-state obstacle course. Although my needs had always been met, and I had never known hunger or lack of shelter, the bulk of available funds always had to be reserved for the next destination. By the time my public appearances in an area actually started, my financial reserve was always very low.

Somewhat amused at the idea that I could afford a van, I looked upward and said, "God, I have never seen a thousand dollars at one time in my whole life, let alone the money for a van camper. If there is to be one, you will have to buy it."

Perhaps I would do well to explain that these conversations with God never lacked respect on my part. God is different to different people and becomes to each whatever they might conceptualize. Because He is everything that mankind can conceive He can sit on a throne, as some believe, or He can be the water of a powerful river, or the stars in the sky. Since the descent of the

Spirit He was to me the Intimate Consciousness and Master that now abided with me. Therefore, He was personal, as well omnipotent. By this time, I had been on the road for the better part of a year and had undergone heat, cold, isolation, and the continued hardships of inner transformation. Sometimes the dark night of the senses bore down with unrelenting steadiness and I would pray to God to remove the crown, which seemed to intensify the darkness. My salvation during this great struggle of Armageddon was work, although I admittedly complained many times.

In order to subdue the senses, my Angelic Teacher had me rise early in the morning and my days were filled with things that had to be done. This included public relations work, traveling, teaching, and counseling. By nightfall, I usually flung myself into bed in absolute exhaustion. Day after day, there was little to do but to put one foot in front of the other and take one step at a time. Sometimes I never knew the outcome of my next destination. Had the poverty and desolation of my youth not prepared me for such a life, it is unlikely that I would have been able to accomplish, what has so often seemed to others, such a Herculean task.

In spite of the long, hard days on the road and my not too infrequent feel sorry for Elizabeth bouts, I would learn that humor is also a part of God. While God and His great Angelic Masters do not participate in riotous laughter, they are not without subtle amusement. The humor of Heaven, however, is superior to that of Earth. God, or one of His emissaries, may do something that is extraordinarily funny, but it is done with great elegance. Although they may chastise and reprimand, they never debase. Therefore, their humor never belittles anyone, nor in any way shows disrespect to any living creature.

While traveling, Okaji sought to lighten my load by doing unusual things, such as singing with me. This was done through the art of superimposing his consciousness over my vocal cords.

When this occurred, a magnificent and miraculous voice flowed out of me. Sadly, when he stopped singing my singing career also came to an abrupt halt.

Along with both the discipline and the humor, there were those wondrous times when miracles were the dessert of the day. Many times I had to face putting my tent up in heavy rains, and when this occurred, I would lift my eyes to Heaven and say, "God, I have to put this tent up and it is pouring down rain. While I do not wish to interfere with your weather, it would be wonderful if you would stop raining until my tent is up."

The rain always stopped.

When the task was completed, I would again look upward and say, "God, the tent is up and you can rain again."

The rain always began.

On the other hand, when I occasionally tried to demonstrate the power I felt I possessed, it would backfire. One such incident occurred when a group of us decided to embark for lunch midst a deluge. As we prepared to step out of the car and go toward the restaurant, we found ourselves inundated with heavy rain. Never dreaming that God would deny the opportunity to show what His power could do, I said, with a measure of self-importance, "Never mind, I will stop the rain."

Lifting my eyes toward the Heavens I asked God to stop the downpour. To my consternation, upon my request, it rained even harder. There was no place to hide, and deeply embarrassed I had to turn to others who were with me, and say, "That will teach me." Nevertheless, this well-taught lesson was never forgotten. It clearly illustrated that all powers must be administered with love and humility, and that no human being has the power to calm the seas. That belongs to God and God alone and He works such miracles through those people whom He chooses.

Continuing with the tour, I again faced new adventures and looked forward to what was in store. My next destination was Texas, known as the "Lone Star State." It is a fascinating state, bounded on the southwest by Mexico, on the west by New Mexico, on the north by Oklahoma, on the east by Arkansas and Louisiana and on the southeast by the Gulf of New Mexico. In some ways it was like a gently sloping amphitheatre, rising from the Gulf coast toward the north, and northwest to plains and mountainous plateaus of more than 4,000 ft. elevation. There is a saying that everything is big in Texas, and I could not help believing this as I drove miles and miles across its vast territory.

The history of Texas is as remarkable as its miles of often desolate landscape, and its' heroes are many. It endured the Spanish-French conflict, the revolution against Mexico and the republic, and an occasional skirmish with the Indians. Although it entered U.S. statehood around 1845, it was still subjected to the southern Confederacy for four years. Texas could also boast of its own privateers, which took place along the Gulf coast under such notables as Luis Aury and Jean Lafitte.

It was difficult for me to enjoy this historical state, however, for it was summer and the hot, desolate miles stretched out ahead of me like an endless black ribbon, while intermittent mirages appeared in gloating formation against a backdrop of concrete pavement. The heat was oppressive to one who had lived most of their life on the West Coast. The automobile had no air conditioning, so the idea of a van camper, or any vehicle with an air conditioning, sounded about as close to Heaven as a human could get while living on Earth. Although I had acknowledged God's suggestion that a van camper would be wonderful and concurred with Him that it was a good idea, it was still financially impossible. Therefore the entire matter was eventually disposed of in the hidden realms of my subconscious mind.

After driving, for what seemed an eternity, I arrived in Houston, which had been named after Sam Houston, the commander of Texas army who defeated the Mexican army and captured Santa Ana. Once the long drive was over, the history of Texas went back to history and I busied myself with the customary public relations work that had to precede all of my appearances. During the process of contacting other organizations for the purpose of securing supplementary talks, I met an amazing woman, Dr. Zoe Troupe, who had once been a nightclub entertainer and now held five doctorates.

Jointly, with her husband, Dr. Troupe owned the largest health food store and restaurant in the country. They had purchased a Safeway store, along with other adjacent businesses. This was located on a piece of property on the western side of Houston. After the purchase, they converted the main building into a lecture hall, health food restaurant, bakery, and nutritional center. Called *Ye Seeker's Bazaar*, it drew people, as well as speakers who were interested in broader concepts and spiritual development, from all over the country.

Within a short time, I became a frequent visitor at the store and just as frequent at the restaurant. Also, I developed an addiction for carrot juice milkshakes. These may not sound very appealing, but there is only one way to find out. Pour one glass of carrot juice into a blender and touch it off with three scoops of honey-vanilla ice cream. Blend until smooth.

During my many discussions with Zoe, I learned that she had been a nightclub comedian when she discovered "The Path." Subsequently, she entered a series of illuminating experiences similar to my own and decided to return to school. Eventually, she earned several doctorates in alternative medicine, and became what was and still is one of the greatest woman alchemists to have ever lived. Her work is so complex, even some of the finest scientists have found her concepts astounding and futuristic. As both a homeopathic and naturopathic practitioner, she successfully treated hundreds of people over the years. She even created the compounds she used, admitting openly that her hands and mind were always under the direct tutelage of the higher Angelic Kingdom and God.

The study of Homeopathy fascinated me and, had I not had certain work to accomplish, it would have been easy to become sidetracked. This form of alternative medicine deals with the law of similarities, meaning that the remedy has much the same properties as the disease. While it may seem somewhat strange to give a patient a dose of something that resembles their illness, this is not the case.

A homeopathic remedy has been taken from its base nature, such as a leaf or serum, and through a potenizing process it is then developed into a more powerful reflection of its original state. It can be transformed into the tenth power, the hundredth power, or even the thousandth power, and it is therefore closer to the non-manifested vibratory nature of a disease. When a plant or serum is a thousand times more powerful than an illness and comes in contact with its causation, it transmutes, or refines it until the disease returns to its original state of non-existence.

Unfortunately, while homeopathic remedies are available in many grocery stores and health food stores it is wise to remember, when taken incorrectly, or in the wrong potency, they can be dangerous. One of these dangers is in ante doting, or taking the wrong remedy because of lack of knowledge. It is always best, when trying to overcome an illness, particularly a serious one, to place oneself in the care of a physician, or at least a qualified and trained practitioner.

One important thing evolved from my friendship with Zoe, which would last until her transition in the early part of the 1990s, and that was a deeper understanding of alternative medicine. This information enabled me to greatly improve my own health, although I have never foolishly allowed herbs and homeopathy to replace traditional medical help when it is needed. My assignment with destiny, however, was that of teaching, and thus it became necessary to lay aside my fascination with alternative medicine and focus my attention on the task at hand.

Because of our similar experiences, Dr. Troupe became interested in my cause and offered the use of her guest cottage during my visit in Houston. My stay in the cottage lasted for a number of weeks and I was fortunate enough to be a participant in many interesting conversations with Zoe during the ensuing days. As the holidays approached, however, I decided to take a break from the hard months on the road and return to Tacoma, Washington to perform the Christmas services at my old church.

During the holidays the dark night of the senses abated somewhat, which was a welcome relief. I also enjoyed the enveloping love of the Church Board and my old congregation. In a sense, it felt as though I had come home, or as close to home as one can experience who is on United States lecture tour. Of course, the easement of the dark night lasted only until my return to Texas.

Originally, I had driven from Houston to Dallas to catch a plane to Seattle and consequently stored my car there. It was therefore necessary to land in Dallas in order to recover it from storage. Once this had been accomplished, I departed for Houston and the wonderful cottage Zoe had turned over for my use. Just as I turned onto the freeway, immediately the familiar, impenetrable heaviness that is such a familiar aspect of the *Dark Night of the Soul* descended again. This time, two long years would pass before I would again experience much relief.

It was evident why the Spirit did not allow more respite. Nevertheless, this did not lessen my uncontrollable desire to reach up and tear the source of my discomfort from my head. Had I been allowed to follow this inclination, the purifying work, which had already been accomplished would have been lessened and too much ground work lost in this battle for supremacy over the lower nature. It was not without tears and groaning that I again took up my cross and struggled along the *Via Dolorosa*, a Christian term used to define the inner path of mystical transformation.

The way of the *Via Dolorosa* is not something that has been openly taught in churches, but rather it has been taught in secret and hidden in allegory. Its secrecy began during the first three centuries with the early Bishops, and to quote St. Augustine, Bishop of Hippo, who was born A.D. 347, "Having dismissed the Catechumens, we have retained only you to be our hearers; because, besides those things which belong to all Christians in common, we are not to discourse to you of sublime Mysteries which none are qualified to hear, but those who, by the Master's favor are made partakers of them. To have taught them openly, would have been to betray them."

Most people do not realize that all mankind will eventually pass through this remarkable transformation, also known as the Walk of Fire, Armageddon and the Dark Night of Soul. In time, when the task of transformation is complete, the human race will bring a true peace on earth. Somehow this wondrous knowledge removes the sting from self-introspect and one's awareness of their own iniquities. I have always liked the description Jesus gave his disciples in the "Gospel According to Thomas," when they asked, "Shall we then, being as children, enter the kingdom?"

"Jesus said to them: 'When you make the two one, and when you make the inner as the outer and the outer as the inner and the above as the below, then shall you enter the Kingdom."

Even as my soul struggled through this arduous process of purgation, I knew that there was no other way to remove those things adverse to the way of Heaven, either in myself or in any one else. Alone, we, as human beings are not strong enough to change, but with the power of the Spirit to change us, all things are possible. Yet, as Kabir, an East Indian poet once wrote: "He removes the veil from the eyes, and gives the true Vision of God: He reveals the worlds in Him, and makes me to hear the Unstruck Music: He shows joy and sorrow to be one: He fills all utterance with love. Verily he has no fear who has been lead to such shelter and safety."

Although I intended to immediately schedule my departure for Louisiana, I was now detained in Houston as I had once been detained in California. The angelic forces gave no explanation. It would be another six weeks before permission would be given to me to travel to my next destination. During this period, I felt that any attempt to do more public appearances would not be advantageous, particularly from a financial point of view. Therefore, it seemed wiser to fill my time with counseling engagements. As usual, when it pertained to counseling, people seemed to materialize out of the woodwork and soon, my schedule was heavily booked.

At the end of one of my afternoon consultations, a client told me that she was from New York, and that she was in Houston to attend a conference sponsored by a broadcasting company. I recognized the name of the company and mentioned this to her. She was somewhat surprised when I told her that I had met the Vice President during an appearance at their station in Oklahoma. Rummaging through my purse I finally located the business card he had given me. She smiled when she looked at it and said, "Oh yes, Alex is Vice President of our broadcasting company. He is here in Houston, but very busy. Unfortunately Elizabeth, I doubt that he will have time to see you while he is here."

This did not disappoint me, for my conversation with Alex preceding my show in Oklahoma had lasted only a short time. Actually, I wasn't even certain that I would recognize him if I saw him on the street. Therefore I replied, "I have no wish to see him now, but will see him when I get to New York." I was still certain that I would never see the Big Apple. Although one may think about such things from time-to-time, as one does when musing over possibilities, I do not remember having done so. If I did, the idea probably seemed almost as terrifying my fear of snakes.

"You know," my client added, "his wife died several months ago."

This did not register with me either. I simply shrugged, concluded the counseling and bid my charming client farewell. With other things to occupy my mind, our conversation was placed on a shelf somewhere in the subconscious, where one files most superfluous material and promptly forgets about it.

At the end of six weeks, it became apparent I could now leave Texas and travel to New Orleans. Packing my belongings,

I bid Zoe farewell, and set off into the sunrise for Louisiana, popularly known as the "Pelican State," still in my rebuilt taxi. While driving along, however, a sudden thought struck me. There was now one thousand dollars over and above expenses in my checking account.

No one can travel in Louisiana without becoming enchanted with it, for its history belongs to the romance of American history. From the beautiful bayous, excitement of crawdad fishing to its great cuisine, Louisiana, and particularly New Orleans, is a place of intrigue. Cotton crops and cane sugar, plantations, slave trading and privateering, it was all here, including the famous Mardi Gras Festival.

As I drove, stopping only for a brief time to witness the fascinating science of crawdad fishing, I remembered a long forgotten movie titled *Mardi Gras,* which I seen when I was a young, teenager. As my mind drifted back to this teenage memory, I was suddenly infused with a vision. I would be attending this legendary pageant. Only then did I realize that I had been kept from leaving Houston just long enough to arrive in New Orleans in time for the festival.

The history and symbolism of *Mardi Gras* is seeped in the mysteries of soul transformation. It began long before the Europeans set foot in the New World. In mid-February the ancient Romans celebrated the *Lupercalia,* a circus-like festival, not entirely unlike the *Mardi Gras* of today. When Rome embraced Christianity, the early Church fathers decided it would be better to incorporate certain aspects of the pagan rituals into the new faith, rather than attempt to abolish them altogether. Carnival, therefore, became a period of abandonment and merriment preceding the penance of Lent, thus giving a Christian interpretation to the ancient custom.

Carnival season extends from the twelfth night to Lent, reaching its climax the eve of Ash Wednesday. Beginning on twelfth night, there is a series of brilliant balls; and during the last week, the balls of *Momus, Proteus,* and *Comus* are preceded by gorgeous pageants that bring the *Season of Mirth* to a conclusion. *Mardi Gras,* meaning Shrove, for Fat Tuesday, signifies the day of the *shift,* or confession, which is made in preparation for the great fast.

The number twelve, as in most mythology and ritual, signifies a spiritual rebirth of the soul as it prepares to become one with its divine counterpart, the indwelling God. The twelfth night of *Mardi Gras* illustrates this, as the Revelers present a young woman (soul) with a golden bean (wisdom) in a cake (corporeal sweetness). When the soul is unmasked, meaning its true nature stands revealed, it must return to its beloved, the indwelling God, through penitence and fasting (*Dark Night of the Soul*). Thus, *Fat Tuesday* depicts the last gasp of the soul's decadence before its period of austerity and atonement. How fitting the symbolism of *Mardi Gras* was for one who was as deeply entrenched in the purification of the soul as I was. Nonetheless, my own *Fat Tuesday* seemed to stretch out indefinitely.

When I arrived in New Orleans, I found that motel and hotel prices had escalated due to the forthcoming festival. As usual, my budget was little equipped to handle such expenses, and it became necessary to come up with some other solution. I had received a letter from New Orleans, prior to the Christmas holidays, which contained an address of an apartment house located on the outskirts of the city. It was my hope that the manager would consider renting an apartment to me for sixty days. In that most places required a year's lease, short-term rentals were rare. I was fortunate, however, for there was one furnished vacancy remaining and I had no trouble negotiating a sixty-day lease.

Many people had warned me against appearing in the south, particularly those who frequently traveled around the country to speak on spiritual matters. Nevertheless, I was fulfilling my allocation with destiny and encouraged by a power beyond the will of people. Because of this, I paid little heed to the warnings. It was good that I did not do so, because New Orleans was wonderful and gave me VIP treatment. The major newspapers, as well those in outlying areas, did feature stories, and every radio talk show host and television media in the state held out a hand of welcome. Overall, the responses to my public appearances in Louisiana were massive.

During this time I decided to create a new dimension to my work and add the *Magic World Healing Clinics*. These were designed to educate people in not only how to eat their way to better health, but also how to administer self-healing treatments during illnesses. Since one can do a great deal to improve their health through diet alone, it seemed feasible to teach nutrition first and healing second. Food is a science, and one I had studied well, particularly Biogenics.

The Science of Biogenics is based on a four-food classification, *Biogenics*, or active food between the seventh & twenty-first day of growth, Bioactive, living food that is not cooked, *Bio-static*, cooked food that is not harmful to the body, yet does not replace the body's life force. This *Bio-static* category includes rice, grains and legumes, and supplies much of the needed protein and minerals to sustain the organo-vegetative system. Last, of course, there is *Biocidic* food, otherwise known as committing suicide with food. The latter always brought a few chuckles from my audiences, because we all have our weaknesses and these weaknesses are normally taste centered in food that is not necessarily healthy to the body. These clinics also enabled me to introduce aspects of *The Secret Jesus Scroll,* which I had received in San Diego earlier.

The science underlying the four different food classifications has always been interesting to me, particularly *Biogenic* and *Bioactive.* Biogenic has a similar affect on the body as homeopathic remedies. Food in its first twenty- seven days of growth is drawing nutrients into its body in order to grow, therefore containing a greater life force than food that is preparing to reproduce. Normally this would be considered the sprouting period through baby-green development.

Like homeopathy, the heightened vibration of young food helps to refine the denser vibration of the human body, thereby reducing the aging process, reducing pain and lessening the amount of illness a person may have to undergo. Like homeopathic remedies, excessive use of Biogenics can also destroy, or weaken the immune system. Because the average body is accustomed to cooked foods and meat products, it is relegated to the more dense vibratory nature of earth. Along comes *Mr. Biogenics*, which starts the process of refining or transmuting. Consuming large quantities of Biogenic food can increase the process of transmutation too quickly and refining then becomes like a bulldozer in the system, thereby destroying. How rapidly this can occur depends on weight, age and current diet of the human body. Under no circumstance should the amount of biogenic food consumed be more than 20%. For beginners, 10% is sufficient.

More can be done with food in its bioactive stage, meaning uncooked, but mature. This would include all fresh fruit, as well as raw vegetables. However, even these should not constitute more than another 20% of the human diet. In that the normal organovegetative system has been dependent on meat products for millions of years, and this is an intricate part of the genetic makeup of the human race, the balance of the diet should include a fair amount of protein. For the vegetarian, this is accomplished through grains and legumes, such as rice, beans, soy etc. For others, a modest amount of meat, fish or poultry is necessary. The raw food dinners I often prepared for the clinics were basically intended to be an experience, rather than an immediate way of life.

My new spiritual life was filled with many difficult moments, and the *Magic World Healing Clinics* proved to be no different. These covered a period of two nights, usually Thursday and Friday. My first evening began with an introduction to Jesus' teachings on health and nutrition. Later, after the usual *Science of Biogenics* discourse designed to help the audience understand why Jesus taught in the manner he did, I served a raw food banquet. This was to insure that those attending the clinics would discover how delightful natural food could taste, primarily because this subject was covered quite thoroughly in the first section of *The Secret Jesus Scroll.*

These first adventures into the creation of raw foods dinners were based strictly on intuition. Somehow I managed to develop over a dozen entrees and a dozen or more desserts without the necessity of a stove. Because I was now traveling in the South and a hot sun was the customary situation of the day, I was even able to bake bread in much the same manner Jesus described in the *Scroll.* He had taken wheat, crushed it and made it into small cakes. These were then baked on top of hot rocks. Since hot rocks were not readily available, I made large flat pieces of sprouted grain and baked them on the hood of my car.

As time passed, these Magic World Healing Clinics became one of the most successful aspects of my work.

Two months elapsed before I finished with my public appearances in Louisiana. Finally, bidding farewell, I headed for Alabama. Along with my departure, I took with me the memories of southern hospitality, as well as some of the magnificence of the *Mardi Gras* pageantry. And, as I drove, I assessed my tour, and was surprised to discover that there was now two thousand dollars in the bank over and above expenses.

A rather unexpected incident took place a short time after my arrival in Alabama. Early, during my first discourse, I was abruptly confronted with an unpleasant situation. I found that the *Klu Klux Klan* was not something out of a movie or television show, when one or more of their members infiltrated lecture hall. As soon as I was standing before the audience, a young, rather nice-looking young man rose up and began to quote scripture. Apparently, he thought that I was filled with something other than a

Holy Spirit and that he had the right, in the name of Jesus, to cast the old devils out. In that demons, at least as many traditionalists conceive them, do not really exist, the entire situation was more disruptive than harmful. Unfortunately I had to have the young man bodily removed from lecture hall, which put a damper on the evening.

Perhaps more people would have besieged me over the years, but no one ever knew where I was staying. It was not a matter of hiding out, but a matter of finances. The places I appeared were simply too expensive for anything but short-term occupancy, and for the sake of good health, it was better to prepare my own food. If I was fortunate enough to consider a motel, I usually chose ones that offered weekly residency. These had lower rates, swimming pools, and kitchenettes. Also, I had access to a telephone, remained healthy, and sometimes succumbed to the relaxation of a swim and some sun bathing. Although some of these amenities were also available at various campgrounds, it was nonetheless a joy to stand up to dress and to wash the dishes in a sink.

Toward the end of my initial appearances and seminars in Alabama, I again featured a *Magic World Healing* Clinic. This time, it was necessary to enlist help in preparing my raw food dinner. A hundred people signed up for the clinics and I could only single-handedly prepare food for thirty-five. Fortunately, there was seldom any lack of assistance, for there were always those who attended every function and relished having some personal time with me. I selected some of those who had been present during the two-day seminar, and with their assistance, the feat of preparing a raw food dinner for one hundred people was accomplished.

The first night of the clinic brought an interesting turn of events. Governor George Wallace was speaking in the room adjacent to ours. For some reason his campaign manager seemed to find our group more interesting than listening to the Governor, and so he dropped in for a few minutes here and there. Just as I was about to conclude for the night, he drew me aside to ask me if I would consider doing a healing on Governor Wallace, who was now in a wheelchair as a result of an assassination attempt.

Although the Clinics were new in my agenda, it was, and still is my belief, that only in doing everything one is asked to do, can one adequately carry out God's Will on earth. Thus, I agreed to meet with the Governor, although the meeting never took place. Governor Wallace declined. At the time I felt that it was probably for the best, as the Angelic Kingdom gave no indication that a healing would be granted in this case.

The incident with Governor Wallace left me wondering why some people were healed and some were not. This question became particularly paramount when the Angelic Kingdom told me to focus on teaching self-healing. To some degree I could understand this, as my assignment was teaching. Because I was focused on teaching and moved from place to place, it was impossible for me to be available for long term healing treatments. It had become apparent through the years that healings are not always instantaneous, but that some required several healing sessions. For this reason I knew it was more expedient for one to help others learn to heal themselves, in that every one possesses this power.

In answer to my question, "Why are some people healed and others are not?" I was taught that all requests and prayers are answered according to cause and effect, and often dependant upon the unlearned lessons of the soul as well as the interrelationship with others. Again, as I have said before, God works for the good of the whole. To the soul, which must endure the hardships of human life, God always lends His strength, His courage, and His love, but He does not usually grant miracles when there are lessons to be learned.

Healing is somewhat like the growth of a grain of wheat. The single stalk alone cannot withstand the forces of the elements, such as heavy rain and wind. It succumbs and is laid flat in the aftermath of such disasters. On the other hand, a field of wheat is strong and endures the hardships of the elements, for each stalk strengthens its neighbor. In that nature reflects strength in unity, I felt, and still feel, that a collective healing force can be more intense with a group healing than with the power of a single individual. The exception to this rule, of course, would be a master, such as Jesus.

On the second and last night of the clinics, after training the audience on how to heal, it was customary to select someone who was ill. I felt it absolutely imperative that the collective healing force should be of one mind, and I did not knowingly allow each person to do things their individual way. God is one force, one mind and one will, and the systematic progression of an entire universe is subject to this Will. Thus, I felt that we would be more powerful if we were of one mind, and that this one mind should be completely submerged in the consciousness of God.

As my work with the *Magic World Healing Clinics* gained momentum, I noticed remarkable miracles beginning to occur. Like everyone, I marvel over such supernormal experiences. Although I was fascinated by these miracles that took place during the clinics, I was not usually allowed such wondrous experiences while working on a personal basis with individuals. In part, this was because I was being trained in all the powers and an ego can become massive when it thinks it has special powers which other may not have. Through the years I have observed many enthusiasts who could have played much greater roles in the world and had much greater power, but pride forbade them further study. These always believed that they had reached the apex of development because they discovered in themselves what everyone has always possessed. Therefore I well understood that God was continuing the process of purification and surrender in me, and taking great pains to see that I did not fall into this quagmire. To permit the ego to grow would have been extraordinarily detrimental to spiritual progress.

When the work in Alabama was finished, I turned my trusty rebuilt taxi toward open road, this time Georgia. I now had a total of thirty-seven hundred dollars over and above expenses. My newfound wealth was short-lived. As I drove past an auto dealership on the out-skirts of Atlanta, I was instructed to go in and buy a car, a voice saying, "If you are going to get it, you had better get it now."

A short time later I was driving a brand new white van out of the dealership and, within a few days, had converted the van into a camper. I carpeted the floor and walls and bought a folding bed, a small refrigerator, and other amenities. By this time, I had learned to be careful in my purchases, lest I be instructed to part with some because of overindulgence.

Now that God had made it possible to buy a car, the doors of my extraordinary success closed. For the next few weeks, the large crowds I had come to expect were greatly diminished. The re-sponse in Georgia, and later West Virginia, was sufficient to meet my needs, but not enough to give my ego a boost.

By this time, as I mentioned earlier, a heightened ego in a spiritual seeker can be a detriment, not because the soul seek ag-grandizement, but because it is less willing to do the inner plane work brought about by the dark night of the soul. In my case, the heaviness and darkness again increased, cutting off the magic that had been needed to gather funding for a new car. This bothered me somewhat, for I rather enjoyed the larger crowds. I like to think that it is not because of my ego, but rather an aftermath of my childhood studies in elocution. It brought me great satisfac-tion to disperse a bit of magic here and there and see the joy on people's faces when they learned that life was eternal.

Unfortunately, inner purification shows no immediate results and one often falls into the quagmire of self-doubt. If this happened to me once, it happened on many, many, occasions. Yet, I understood that purification, reduction of the ego, and inner development could create a greater work than that which is accomplished through an ego-centered self. As a result, what little enjoyment I was now al-lowed to have came from beautiful scenery, camping in my camper, and, of course, the *heavenly* air conditioner.

CHAPTER X

Hello! New York

While still in Georgia, I received a note from Swami Chinmayananda telling me that he would see me in Boston during July. Apparently he planned to conduct a Yagna (a series of talk meetings) at the Massachusetts Institute of Technology. His discourses were scheduled to last ten days, beginning on the Fourth of July. "Boston?" I thought, "I do not expect to go to Boston." Nevertheless, after thinking on the matter while driving toward West Virginia, I decided to contact some of the people I had gotten to know quite well during my travels and encourage them to meet me there so that they spend time with Swami.

To my surprise, I found myself in Boston on the Fourth of July. No one was more astounded than I was, although I am still not exactly certain exactly how this came to pass. Like many Americans, I knew little about the historical aspects of the city except for the famous Boston Tea Party. Boston and its harbor are situated at the head of Massachusetts Bay. During the colonial days the city was almost an island and connected with the Massachusetts mainland only by the very narrow Roxbury neck. It was also the birthplace of one of my favorite American statesmen, Benjamin Franklin.

Most people know Benjamin Franklin because he assisted in drafting and later signing the Declaration of Independence. However, he was also a philosopher and a genius. To those who have followed the path of inner awakening and transformation, Mr. Franklin is recognized as one of those illumined people who helped lay the framework of a nation based upon the principles of nature and the rule of one God. For those who may doubt this, they have but to review the statesman's prodigious achievements, for only those whom God has come to embrace can become so omni-lateral. Benjamin Franklin had one of the broadest and most creative minds of his time, as evidenced by his theory of electricity, his ideas on the aurora borealis, and the origin of the northeast storms in America, earthquakes, natural history, and mathematics. He attracted my fancy so much that I later made it a point to do an in-depth study of his life.

Unfortunately, I did not get to enjoy the historical culture of Boston during my stay, for I soon found myself, as usual, in a rather extraordinary situation. A number of the people I had contacted about Swami Chinmayananda's visit decided to join me. In order to help them minimize their expenses, I suggested that they plan on camping. Perhaps the memories of my childhood and sitting around an open fire with a group of friends roasting marshmallows had gotten the best of me. At the time the idea seemed to be one which would be very enjoyable for everyone concerned. I fear that my concept of enjoyment turned out to be a bit of a misnomer. Some of those who joined me had never camped before, and ultimately this was to prove more hazardous than the Boston traffic.

The morning of the Fourth of July dawned with blistering heat. Some of the people, who were new campers, became highly disgruntled. In spite of this, we somehow all piled into the van with our tempers in check and tried to find our way to the college. Eventually we arrived, somewhat disgruntled but intact. The heat and humidity caused our clothes stick to our bodies as we moved and perspiration poured down our faces. This discomfort unfortunately expressed itself through the attitudes of some, but I was adamant about continuing this adventure.

Because I did not wish to be tardy for Swami's appearance, I took no chances. Swami's letter to me had contained only the sparsest instructions concerning his Yagna and even less information on how to locate him. His directions had merely stated that I should go next door and talk to Leah. She would tell me everything.

Upon our arrival at MIT, we found no evidence of Swami's appearance. However, at my insistence, everyone started canvassing the nearby houses and apartment buildings. I had no address and no last name for the mysterious Leah, so there was no alternative but to go door-to-door. This venture proved unsuccessful. By this time my students were even more disgruntled, as well as hot and hungry. Since we had come this far, however, I, decided that no stone should be left unturned and we returned to MIT to take another look in the hallways for any posters or notices indicating that Swami was scheduled to speak. Believing that I had led them on a wild goose chase, some members of the group stated they were convinced that he was not coming. However, the Spirit had taught me a great deal about endurance during the long months on the road, and I had no intention of giving up. I said, "I know he is coming, and I, for one, shall sit here until he does."

At last, one of the members of our group found a small notice confirming Swami's appearance, and that the ten-day Yagna was supposed to begin that very evening. With a measure of contentment, but with decidedly frayed nerves, we made our way back to the campground, intending to return to MIT later that evening.

Standing at the end of the hall that first night, watching Swami approaching with his followers, made all of our difficulties melt away. Having brought a basket of fruit, I waited outside at the end of the hall. When Swami saw me standing there, he stopped and looked me straight in the eyes. I knew from his expression that he was aware of the traumatic course of the day's events, and for some reason it apparently amused him. As the years passed and I came to know Swami Chinmayananda better, I realized that he had also been aware of the loyalty and persistence that had brought all of us to MIT that scorching day to hear him.

Many people turn away from the path of Western religion because they are disenchanted with its dogma. They seek the ways of the East to find new spiritual values. Others seek the East for the purpose of coming to an understanding between the Eastern religions and that of Christianity. However, my objective was to know God. Although I had found Him, or shall I say, He had found me, there was still much to learn.

The East is a path of discipline, little understood in our Western culture and certainly not generally accepted. In the East, the seeker of God accepts the theory of re-entry into embodiment for the sake of soul progression as easily as the West accepts Jesus as its savior. However, because I now bore the Spirit, I had no conflict with the ways of East, for the worship of God unites. The argument over who is right and who is wrong in a corporeal sense leads to separation. Everyone everywhere is searching for something, but all too often people become entangled in a web of multitudinous concepts spawned by the limited capability of individual understanding.

One of the major differences between the East and West is the Master/disciple relationship. Most Westerners simply cannot endure the disciplines of the East, primarily because the egocenteredness of humanity dislikes being told what to do. Westerners do not always understand that the ability to surrender to the guidance of a teacher can better prepare them for surrender to God. In the end, God is Master over all, and all will serve Him.

When a student surrenders to the instruction of a spiritual master teacher, a mental link is formed between the learner and the instructor. To better understand this, perhaps one can imagine a Vulcan mind meld, your mind to my mind. In such a way, the disciple, meaning one who seeks the disciplines of God, begins to learn, not only the ways of the teacher but also the knowledge that the teacher possesses through the unspoken word. This gives a much deeper and more expedient understanding of any study, as opposed to that which is only spoken orally and read.

A spiritual master teacher does not accept everyone on the inner-plane who comes, for there is a price that the teacher must pay. As the student is raised in consciousness, the teacher must work even harder to remain centered in God. Every thought of anger, jealousy, and hatred on the part of the student or disciple makes the weight of his or her consciousness heavier on the teacher.

This process was depicted well in the Old Testament, when Jethro, the priest of Midian and father-in-law of Moses, said to Moses (Exodus 18:17-18): "The thing that thou doest is not good. Thou wilt surely wear away, both thou, and this people that is with thee: for this thing is too heavy for thee; thou art not able to perform it by thyself alone."

Due to the natural self-centeredness of the student, a teacher must first search deeply into the heart of anyone who seeks to study with him or her. If the student is not centered in their search for God and not willing to dedicate themselves to "The Path," a spiritual teacher would be unwise to accept them on the inner-plane. A disgruntled and negative attitude on the part of the student can tear at the consciousness of the teacher like a lion rends a carcass.

The criterion of a master is captured in the following story.

Once upon a time, a young man came to a spiritual teacher and told him that he wanted to be taught. The Master ignored the student.

Again the student came to the Master, and again he was ignored.

Finally, he came a third time and asked the Master, "Why will you not teach me? Please explain your reason, for I have a great wish to study with you."

The teacher then took the enthusiastic student down to the nearby Ganges River, and taking hold of the young man's head, the teacher held him under water until he almost drowned. Finally, pulling the student up by the scruff of the neck in order that he might breathe, the Master asked, "When you were drowning, what did you want more than anything?"

The young man looked into the face of his mentor and said, "I wanted a breath of air."

Then the Master replied, "When you want God as much as you wanted a breath of air, come back and I will teach you."

If anyone assumes that a master from the Angelic Kingdom will be easier in their administration of the necessary disciplines, they are sadly mistaken. Those from the other side are actually more powerful than those still bound to the material world and are much more difficult to dispose of. When people do not like what a human teacher tells them, they simply leave to find someone else. With an Angelic Master, there is no place to run, and one's human displeasure may as well be directed to the wind.

Fortunately, I was able to endure the disciplines of the East just as I endured the disciplines of the Angelic Masters. Not only was the Spirit with me every moment, bringing with Him the purifying forces of the *dark night of the senses,* but my Angelic Teacher was also there to see that I continued to walk in the ways of what I have come to know as *The Path*. The constant discipline, heaviness, and inner conflict brought distemper to my soul and tears to my eyes many times, but just as some are locked outside the gates of redemption, I was locked in. Therefore, I did not struggle as others might have, when Swami Chinmayananda added his own particular style of inner and outer teaching.

On the tenth day of the Yagna, Swami prepared to leave MIT for his next destination. Before he left, several of the women decided to wear saris to honor him and the ways of the East. Happily, we went shopping at one of the Eastern store outlets in Boston. While there, I too purchased a sari, which consisted of several yards of beautiful flowered material. Along with the fabric, I also purchased an Indian-style blouse that allows exposure to the arms and mid-section of the body.

The woman who sold me my Eastern attire was kind enough to show me how to put it on, and it seemed easy enough. All one had to do was to wrap five to six yards of straight fabric into a flowing and graceful dress. This had to be done in such a way that the dress would not fall off at some inopportune time. Blatantly thinking that I had learned the art of wrapping a sari I happily departed from the store with my purchases, looking forward to surprising Swami in my newly acquired Indian attire.

That afternoon, while standing in my van and trying to tuck the five-plus yards of material around me, I found the situation much more difficult. After several false starts, I finally managed to maneuver the material into a semblance of proper dress. By this time the group was ready to leave and we again assembled, got into the van and headed toward MIT for Swami's final lecture.

By now I had learned that it was Swamiji's custom to hold what is called a Sat Sangh, or a sit and talk period, during the late afternoons. These were a smaller and a more intimate session than the evening discourses, which often drew hundreds of people. During Sat Sangh, we were allowed to ask questions of Swami, and other times we simply sat around and listened to him talk about one thing or another.

This particular afternoon, I imagine Swami Chinmayananda must have had some difficulty concealing his mirth over my poor attempt to favor him by wearing my Eastern attire. He took one look at me and said, "Elizabeth, the tail, it is too long," meaning the drape of the dress was over-extended.

Turning desperately to one of the nearby Indian ladies, I asked if she would kindly dress me. Taking me into the small adjacent kitchen, she rearranged the material into a graceful sari. However, she did not tell me that I had the blouse on backwards.

When I made my appearance, Swami looked at me gently and said, "Come here, Elizabeth."

As I approached him, Swami reached up, took the end of the drape and tucked it into the neckline of the blouse: thereby covering up the fact that I had the blouse on backwards. I have never forgotten the subtle dignity with which he performed this sensitive act. Eventually, of course, I did learn to drape a sari halfway decently and get my blouses on correctly. From that time on, I always wore one on the last day of my visits with Swami Chinmayananda as a way of honoring both him and his country.

On the morning following Swami Chinmayananda's last discourse we broke camp and each person prepared to depart to his or her home state. We all breathed a sigh of relief, for this particular adventure had not always been easy.

By now, I had been on the road for almost a year and a half. Travel had become a way of life for me, and the United States no longer seemed as intimidating as it had when I first left Tacoma. At this time I received a letter from Alex, Vice President of the broadcasting company that had hosted me in Oklahoma. In his letter, Alex gave me instructions on how to reach his home in Connecticut. Apparently, I was not only being invited to do a television show at one of their stations, but was to be Alex's personal guest as well. I was very grateful for this, because the words *New York City* were still able to strike terror into my heart. I had also decided that New York would be the place where I would conclude my first United States speaking tour. Thus, bidding Boston farewell, I then said hello to New York.

My sojourn in New York was like a fairy tale. Alex's home in upstate Connecticut was beautiful and spacious, and its grounds literally dipped into the waters of the Atlantic. My stay was well chaperoned by his sister and her husband, as well as his two children. Nonetheless, the light finally dawned and I realized that this was the man God had selected as my rich New York husband.

With this revelation, I looked up at the heavens, and shaking my head at God, I said, "You couldn't even wait for me to pick my own, could you?"

It seems inconceivable that such a vast Omnipotent intelligence would bring about such a remarkable individual experience, just to respond to my challenge so many months before. Alex was very rich, nice-looking, dignified, and intelligent. What more could any woman ask for, unless she really did not want a husband, and I did not.

Each day I drove my new van from Alex's estate to the railroad station, and leaving my car at the small depot I then boarded a train for Grand Central Station in New York City. It was hard to believe that this city, one of the largest in the world, had once been the roaming grounds of prehistoric creatures. One cannot help but wonder how many of New York's finest remember the epochs past, when the Great Ice Age moved steadily over the state and destroyed the majestic beasts that walked where their city now stands. How clearly this illustrated to me, what everyone knows so well, that the world is perpetually changing and that it cannot be tomorrow what it is today. If there was sadness over these remembrances of what once was, there was also a joy over the modernization of our once primitive world.

As I looked up at the massive skyscrapers, I tried to remember that in 1615 only a few huts and a forte built by the New Netherlands dotted the south end of Manhattan Island. In its place now stood a great concrete jungle, formed by architects and builders, raw sinew and stonecutters. At the same time, I found everything extraordinarily exciting, for excitement is really the pulse of New York City. Certainly there was little foreknowledge when I gapped up at the giants before me, that a bond would develop and link us together for the rest of my life. It came first in the form of a subtle thought and grew into a colossal titan. The time had come for me to officially close my first United States tour. Where better, than to lay it at the feet of the Statue of Liberty in New York Harbor.

To me the Statue represented the mother of wisdom who, holding forth her light, signifies the divine birth in all mankind, as well as the birth of a new nation centered in God. Her crown consisting of seven points, suggests that this new birth will one day take humanity into the seventh and final epoch (day) of creation and bring forth the brotherhood of all mankind. Then, the Lion (Spirit) and the Lamb (Soul) will unite, or lay down together, forever; and peace will come to all of Earth.

This magnificent wonder represents the future of humanity, who will one day bring forth the great Light of Cosmic Consciousness and forever free itself and its world from human bondage. Manley Palmer Hall wrote: "This is the destiny for which we were brought into being. The plan, which was devised in secrecy long ago, and in far places, shall be fulfilled openly...as the greatest wonder born out of time."

The Statue of Liberty stands on Bedloe Island in New York Harbor. Soon after the establishment of the French Republic, following the Franco-Prussian War in 1870-71, Frederic Auguste Bartholdi was commissioned to design a gigantic statue as a present from the country of France to the American people. Thousands visit the Statue each year, and most see her as a symbol of freedom and liberty. Yet, she is so much more, for she reveals the destiny of America and its people.

The wondrous moment of our first and only meeting had an even more significant meaning for me. Not only did the statue reveal the destiny of America, but also my grandfather, several generations removed, had been the Marquis de Lafayette, the French General who had battled side-by-side with General George Washington for the liberation of this nation. Both General Washington and my grandfather were Masons, as were Benjamin Franklin, Thomas Jefferson, and others. I still possess a book that shows a picture of the red, white, and blue Masonic apron my grandmother, the Madame de Lafayette, made as a gift for General Washington. At last, I would now behold this great lady of two countries, who raises her light to welcome the world, with my own eyes

I will never forget boarding the ferry and setting off across the harbor to meet the famous lady for the first time. As the boat drew closer to the statute I was careful not to raise my eyes, because I did not want to look at her until we landed.

When the boat docked, I went and stood before the Statue of Liberty, as tears filled my eyes. After my emotions were somewhat contained, I finally looked up into the face of this wonderful woman with the light. The two of us stared steadfastly at each other for a very long time, for we had both accomplished that which was said to be impossible.

> *Give me your tired, your poor,*
> *Your huddled masses yearning to breathe free,*
> *The wretched refuse of your teeming shore,*
> *Send those, the homeless, tempest-tossed to me:*
> *I lift my lamp beside the golden door.*

Shortly before leaving, I folded my hands beneath my chin and bowed toward this woman who symbolizes the freedom for all mankind and who holds the key to America's future destiny.

CHAPTER XI

The First School

The remaining days in New York were few, but I did not leave before James Morris, the author who had been present during my Oklahoma interview, contacted me. He invited me to have dinner with him and his publisher. While sitting in the restaurant with the two of them, I again marveled over the fact that another youthful desire of mine had been brought into fruition. Unfortunately, while I was allowed the experience of having dinner with a publisher, it was not my book we were celebrating. Nonetheless, I had not given up on this matter, for I fully intended to write someday; and, like all writers, I dreamed that I might indeed write a bestseller. As of yet, I had not been oriented into the world of rewrites, proposals, synopses, outlines, agents, and editors.

During my last days in New York, my mail caught up with me. Among the correspondence was a letter from the church in Tacoma where I had been a minister. They wanted me back. Thus, I turned my van westward to return to Washington and to the ministry.

It was still summer when I crossed the Midwest, and the hot weather was, again, almost unbearable. Because of this, I made a decision to approach Washington from the northern part of the United States. I assumed the journey would not only be cooler by traveling northward, but it would also enable me to see the Dakotas, as well as parts of Wyoming and Montana. The drive was leisurely, the scenery beautiful, and I enjoyed it very much, particularly since I was no longer under the pressure of PR work and public appearances.

While traveling through the Dakotas, I found a beautiful campground and decided to stop there for the night. When I checked in, I learned about the renowned Black Hill Passion Play. It was considered one of the most famous in the United States and was being performed nearby. Since it was August and still quite hot, the play was presented during the early evenings in an open outdoor arena. I arrived in sufficient time to find a good seat, under a cloudless Dakota sky. While I waited for the pageant to begin, I watched the early evening's descending dusk with its phantasm of color conjoining with the flow of a cool northern breeze.

The tableau was beautifully executed and I was grateful to have an opportunity to witness it. However, one thing was quite humorous. The actor playing Jesus had performed the role for over twenty years, and during those years he had developed a bit of an expanding mid-section. Also, he was a brunette. The original Jesus had been of medium-brown hair, young, of nice appearance, and slender. I not only knew these things because of Jesus' appearances to me, but because Lentulus, a Roman official in Judea, described him thusly in a letter to the Roman Senate following the crucifixion:

"A man in stature middling tall, and comely, having a reverend countenance, which any that look upon may love and fear; having hair of the hue of an unripe hazel-nut and smooth almost down to his ears, but from the ears in curling locks somewhat darker and more shining, waving over the shoulders; having a parting at the middle of the head according to the fashion of the Nazarenes; a brow smooth and very calm with a face without wrinkle or any blemish, which a moderate color makes beautiful; having a full beard of the color of his hair, not long, but a little forked at the chin, and eyes gray and glancing." (E. von Dobschutz, Christus-bilder 318 – Translation: Montague. R. James, Litt.D., F.B.A., F.S.A. Provost – Eton University)

A bit of mirth therefore invaded my soul when thinking about the play and I felt that the producers should perhaps first talk to me before picking a Jesus. Still, I enjoyed the performance of this rather aging replica, and there was definitely a special magic as night began its descent. The waning rays of magenta and purple spread across the sky, while the lights played amidst the gathering shadows. It was against this beautiful and natural backdrop that the hero walks off into the sunset carrying his cross, to live immortal amid the stars of heaven.

There is a stark beauty to the Black Hills, and it differs from the rising snow-peaks of the Rockies and Cascade Mountains, or even the Appalachian ridges of the east. The hills rise on an average about 2,000 feet above their base, with exception of South Dakota's tallest peak, *the Harney*. In large part, they are enclosed by the North and South forks of the Cheyenne River and surrounded by semiarid alkaline plains. Because of this, the land is enveloped in a mystical and haunting silence, which slowly penetrates the soul during periods of quiet contemplation. It is a magical form of enchantment, bringing with it a sense of deep peace. And sometimes, for a moment, one could almost perceive the silhouettes of great Indian warriors riding through the ever-present shadows and dancing between the ridges of the hills.

The morning after the pageant I veered westward, taking me across Montana and Idaho. While driving, my mind was still on Jesus. The pageant had left that feeling of closeness, which sometimes possesses a person when a magic wand of heavenly influence has touched the soul. Over the years, Jesus had appeared to me in wondrous ways. One time, when the dark night of the soul had engulfed me in its web of purgation and my tour was undergoing great difficulty, I talked to God about Jesus, saying, "I wonder if Jesus knows what I am doing down here."

At the time, I thought little about it. However, a few nights later I was awakened from sleep by a figure standing over me. I opened my eyes, only to look into the face of Jesus. He was bent over me, his hands behind his back, and he said, "I want you to know that I am aware of the woman in white on earth."

In that instant, all the difficulties that I had undergone seemed worthwhile.

Now, as I traveled westward, I reflected on that experience, and the other times the Master had touched my life. My love for him was constant, deep, and at times indescribable. He came as he chose and always when asked, although I never asked unless the situation was extraordinarily important, or the need very great. He had millions of people requesting his help and there was no desire to increase his burden on my part. That was, and still is, my gift to him.

By the time I crossed the border between Montana and Idaho, I possessed the van, three hundred dollars, and a tent. Mumbling to God, I said, "But you told me that I would return with $2,000.00." He responded immediately by saying, "Sell the van."

This was devastating. The *Seagull I*, which I had named the van, apparently had to go. As usual, I belabored God with extensive reasoning, but there was to be no negotiation. Finally, I agreed that it would be sold upon my return. At the moment, however, little could be done but to enjoy it during these final days on the road.

The first sight of the familiar mountains of the west was like touching a part of Heaven. I did not know until that moment how much I had missed the Northwest with its majestic mountains reaching upward toward the ever-moving clouds. Even now some of the higher peaks had patches of snow dotting their rocky ridges, and fragrant forest pines stood tall and serene on their mountainous precipices. The hills of the east seemed but dwarfs to the splendor that now held me entranced, and I realized how often westerners take such great beauty for granted.

One other beauty that touched me deeply was the hills of home. After driving across the Eastern Washington desert I entered the Cascade Mountain Range and crossed Snoqualmie Summit. For the first time in fifteen and one-half months, I felt the welcoming arms of the mountains of home with its valleys, and rivers. Here the air was fresh, the water blue, and the mountains still pristine. And there was something more, for in a sense I was also coming home victorious. My Angelic Teacher confirmed as much when he told me that I had far exceeded the expectations of the Angelic Kingdom.

When I arrived in Tacoma and entered the parsonage, I found that it was just as I had left it. Little things, which normally would have been moved, were in exactly the same places I had put them. Obviously, no one else had occupied the early nineteenth century house since my departure over a year and a half earlier. Because everything was very clean, however, I knew that the women of the church had been in recently to make proper preparations for my return.

For a moment, as I stood in the middle of the living room, it seemed that I had never left. Yet, in a sense, I was no longer the same person. A seasoning had taken place in my soul. In my mind, the previously unknown vastness of the United States had been reduced to beautiful scenery and wonderful people. The cities had become chessboards and I a player. Having left as an unknown, I had now returned a conqueror. This seasoning would soon remove me from my role as a minister in the church and cause me to set sail once more on the uncharted waters of destiny.

Shortly after returning, I had dinner with the same people who had sold me my rebuilt taxi. During my visit, we reached an agreement that they would purchase the *Seagull*, and I would take another one of their cars in trade along with $2,000.00 cash. After the deal was completed, I ended up with exactly what God had told me: $2,000.00, a paid-up car and my tent. Unfortunately, the money caused yet another inner struggle to ensue, for I was then instructed to paint and freshen up the parsonage.

Just as I had not wanted to part with the car, now I did not wish to part with the money. By this time, surrender should have been somewhat commonplace. Yet, I was still an infant when compared to a saint, and the tentacles of my human past still clung to me like barnacles. It seemed to me, that the money should be saved and used for survival. However, God appeared unconcerned about this sensitive point, and indicated that any place where classes such as mine were conducted should adequately represent Him. As always, He won and I lost. With paintbrush and pail in hand, the laborious task of painting the interior of the parsonage began. Neither did it stop until most of the money was spent.

In spite of my good intentions, my sojourn in the ministry was destined to be short-lived, and soon I received instructions to depart on another lecture tour. By now, America was no longer frightening and I set out on my new assignment with confidence. Like its predecessor, however, my current car, which had been named "The White Knight," had no air conditioning. Therefore, it was back to cold oranges on ice to keep cool, and tenting.

After several appearances throughout Oregon, I once again crossed the border into California. By the time I reached Sacramento, I had made the decision to leave the western world behind and to go to India to study with Swami Chinmayananda. It was not that I planned to give up my western disciplines or my loyalty to Jesus, but I wanted to expand my horizons. I had never been out of the country, and now there was an opportunity to study for little or no cost at Swami's ashram, Sandeepany, in Bombay. Besides, my research had revealed overwhelming evidence that Jesus had studied in the East, and I had a motto: if Jesus did it, I would try it.

After completing my work in Sacramento, I drove to Redding, California to do one last seminar before leaving for India. It was my intent to drive from Redding to Seattle, store the car and depart from my home state. However, on the morning following the seminar, as I began to pack my car for the return to Seattle, a voice from the Angelic Kingdom said, "Go home."

"Go home?" I asked. "What am I supposed to do when I get home?"

"Establish a school."

At last I began to understand the seemingly small delays that had bound me to the West Coast. There would be no trip to India for me, at least not in the foreseeable future. Fortunately, this time I was able to acquiesce more easily, but not without a complaint that I felt God needed to hear: "Why didn't you tell me this before I had all of my shots?" I asked.

As with many people, the vaccine shots required to enter India had made me quite ill, particularly the cholera. Now it appeared that my severe illness subsequent to the cholera vaccination had all been in vain. I felt that I could have been told about the school before being subjected such misery. Like the Children of Israel, who followed Moses across the Sinai Desert, I sometimes questioned the practicality of God's reasoning. This was not because I believed that He ever made mistakes, but rather *The Path* was, and is, sometimes very difficult. All too often, one is allowed to make a mistake simply to learn a lesson. Therefore, it seemed to me that it would be much easier on God, if He just stopped me before I made them in the first place. At the moment, this included the cholera shot.

Having been told to go to the northern part of Seattle, I soon settled into one of the motel-kitchen style units that I had become so accustomed during my travels. Picking up one of the two major Seattle papers, the search began for an affordable location for a school. Whatever I selected would have to have a large open area suitable for a classroom.

When I think back on my first school, it is with a measure of amusement. God never made any school of mine easy. Usually, because of financial reasons, these were established in buildings or homes that had been neglected and needed a lot of work. My first school was no different. It would begin in the bottom portion of an old brown house once used for commercial purposes. Not only did it possess dirty walls and unkempt floors, but also the upstairs, which was still occupied by a women's lib movement at the time, was in near total disarray. Although the downstairs had a perfect area for a classroom, it needed a lot of work before it could be used. What would later become the hospitality room where refreshments were served had a concrete floor saturated with grease.

Again, the poverty of my childhood served me well, for over the years my talent for turning nothing into something had become quite well developed. And during the ensuing years, the Angelic Kingdom never declined the use of this talent, nor, as a matter of fact, any other talent I possessed.

Once I had settled on a building and signed the lease I rolled up my sleeves and began the work of transforming the barren surroundings into a suitable school. With the help of my landlord, the task of renovation came out remarkably well. The location was excellent, for it was only about three blocks from one of Seattle's more charming neighborhoods known as Greenlake. It was also an area that was easily accessible.

As soon the location of the school had been resolved, it was necessary to search for a nearby place to live. I found an apartment within walking distance, and by cutting across the back alley I was virtually standing at the back door of what would ultimately become the most successful school I would ever have.

When the school opened, it offered such courses as *The Life and Secret Teachings of Jesus, St. John's Revelation*, and the mystical teachings of Moses' "*Genesis*." To me, it was somewhat like presenting each student with a glass of fine wine. Although I respected the fundamental values of Christianity, I felt that fundamentalism was but a shadow of the wisdom which Jesus taught as he walked along the shores of Galilee. For me, the Christian Mysteries held the key to those things Christians, as well as others, have always wanted to understand about themselves and their universe.

Teaching was not a role that I chose, but rather, a role that had chosen me. In my early state of devotion to God, when I made the decision to serve Him, I wasn't yet certain of the best way to do so. Reviewing my experience in the corporate world, I had decided the obvious solution was to teach, for talking was apparently my greatest talent. The elocution lessons, which my great grand parents had sacrificed so much to give me from the age of three and a half years old, had developed a fondness for the public life. Therefore, I was not only comfortable speaking in front of large audiences, but could also enjoy the more personal relationship with students.

It has always been my belief that good teaching requires a measure of good acting. Certainly, I realized how difficult it was for some who came to study and to remain alert. Many who attended classes worked all day and by the time they arrived at the school, they were tired. While I do not believe that classes should simply be entertaining, they should be sufficiently so as to keep the students awake.

One such incident of putting on a performance for the students occurred when I decided to introduce some Greek culture to the class. Realizing that the *Hymns of Orpheus* could put even the hardiest scholar to sleep I made the decision to lend some enchantment to the writings of the Greek Lyric Poet. Dressing up in a long robe adorned with stars and moon, I seated myself on a high chair against a backdrop of the night sky. Then I proceeded with the enchanting evocations and lyrical poems of the poet. In this case my enthusiasm for teaching created an unforgettable consequence, for during the presentation, I accidentally set myself on fire.

The stage for this debacle had actually been set earlier that day, when I decided that it would be keeping in the tradition of the great magicians to simply disappear in flames at the end of the program. Not possessing any knowledge pertaining to magic, I did the next best thing: I created an illusion. By placing a small candle amid some rocks in a planter, deep enough that the students could not see the flame, I planned to produce controlled bursts of flames by sprinkling lighter fluid onto the fire. Perhaps, I thought, the students will think that the fluid is water, and as smoke and flames billowed out, they would be caught in the momentary magic splendor of Orpheus.

That night, things actually started out well. Several times during my performance, I took the glass and flicked my hand over the candle. To the delight of the students, smoke and flames shot up for a brief interval, particularly when Orpheus said:

> O Ever untam'd Fire, who reigns on high
> In Jove's dominions ruler of the sky;
> The glorious sun with dazzling lustre bright,
> And moon and stars from thee derive their light;
> All taming pow'r, aetherial shining fire,
> Whose vivid blasts of heat of life inspire:

Unfortunately, I decided that the flames and smoke needed to be much higher to create a moving finale. This required a heavier dose of lighter fluid, but while flicking my hand over the flame disaster struck. Suddenly, my arm was engulfed in flames. Not wanting the students to know that this was not part of the act, I tried to put the fire out by rubbing my arm against my back, hoping that my robe would not catch on fire. To my amazement, and perhaps theirs, I succeeded in putting the fire out, and escaped without a single burn. At the completion of this *performance* a guest of one of the students came up, and taking my overly red and warm hand, she looked at it with a measure of concern. When she did not see any burns, she shook her head and walked away. She never returned. Thereafter I decided to become less vigorous in my approach to the finale of Orpheus.

During this early period of the school's development, it was necessary to work very long hours. I rose early in the morning and returned home after late evening classes. Usually, the students seemed loath to depart and often remained until they were told to leave, which was typically around eleven o'clock at night. Sunday was no exception, for I would often go to my sparse office after the classes and try to catch up on paperwork.

As the days passed, I blessed those years I had spent in the corporate world, for it would have had much more difficult to set up the business aspect of the school without such valuable experience. Continually exhausted, I was also tremendously productive during those years. In spite of this hard work, the bands of discipline around my head never failed to keep me well informed of my inadequacies. I learned that true success comes to those who give and risk all. In part I gathered strength from a Benjamin Franklin quote; "He who would give up essential liberty for a little bit of safety deserves neither liberty nor safety."

My years at Northeast 72nd, as I fondly referred to the location of the school, would herald the end of another comfort zone. I was about to exit that part of the dark night of the soul known as the purgation of the senses, and enter into the *Dark Night of the Spirit*. Soon the success of my earlier years would drop away like a worn-out cloak, and a new struggle would ensue. St. John of the Cross, writes; "And the second night, or purification, pertains to those who are already proficient, occurring at the time when God desires to bring them to a state of union with Him. And this later night is a more obscure and dark and terrible purgation."

Sometimes, when the *dark night* lay heavily upon me and seemed too much to bear, I was led to the lake to photograph seagulls. While I sat on the shore taking pictures and watching the gentle ripples of the water break against the backdrop of a late-afternoon western sun, I thought about the music to *Jonathan Livingston Seagull*, as well as Richard Bach's book by the same name. How akin I felt with Jonathan, for he was made an outcast by the flock, and ultimately spent his days flying alone over the far cliffs. I too was an outcast, banned by New Age groups because I was a follower of teachings of Jesus, and banned by the Christians because I taught the Christian mysteries, which many believed to be against the Word of God. At the same time, I was also exiled from the consciousness of the masses because they could not, and would not; believe that I, who was so mortal, had directly experienced God.

During these difficult years my strength was in God. He and His Angelic Forces were my only comfort and solace. Many times they produced some magic phenomena to help me when I thought I could not go on, phenomena that those who denied and exiled me would have perhaps given their lives to have experienced.

The months at the school were not only busy, but also filled with interludes of unforgettable memories. Among these was the meeting with my second living master teacher. During my appearances in the mid-west, I had written to Professor Edmond S. Bordeaux, translator of *The Secret Jesus Scroll*.

Included with my letter to Professor Bordeaux was my promotional flyer on the Magic World Healing Clinics, which were based on the teachings contained in the scroll. Professor was kind enough to respond and stated that I had been invited to his last seminar in San Diego, but had not come. I was surprised and, perhaps a bit flattered, to think that this great man was actually aware of my absence from his presentation. After reading his letter, I felt it was necessary to attend his next seminar. This was obviously one of those situations in which I was the recipient of a message that needed to be listened to.

Following some internal debate about the importance of my school versus the opportunity to study with a man of such obvious genius, I wrote again to Professor Bordeaux, saying, "I am willing to give up everything I own or possess if you will allow me to come and study with you. What I have is not much, but nonetheless, I will be most happy to give it up."

Time passed, and there was no response. Later, the memory faded from my mind. Then, one day, I received an announcement about one of Professor's Essene seminars. This was to be held in San Diego. In order to not to be remiss again, I immediately made plans to take my new would-be assistant, Nikki, along with twenty-six other students, and attend Professor's classes.

Never will I forget my first sight of this remarkable man. He was of short, stocky build with a band of graying hair outlining a rather round, bald dome of a head. His face appeared ageless, and his eyes deep and penetrating. Sitting up on the stage, he seemed as powerful as the mountains and as deep as the sea. Some intangible magnificence exuded from his presence. I was not only taken by him at the moment, but would remain in awe of him for the rest of my life. Because I did not wish Professor to think that I had once again missed his presentation, I arrived early, along with my students. After they had found seats, I climbed up on the stage where he was sitting and introduced myself. "Professor Bordeaux, I am Elizabeth Burrows from Seattle, Washington."

Looking up at me, with a rather long probing gaze, Professor Bordeaux said, with eloquent humor, "My, I am glad to see that you are not a myth."

Feeling the necessity to remind him I had been willing to part with all that I owned in order to study with him, I looked at him quite seriously and said, "You know, Professor, I once wrote to you and offered to give up everything if you would but accept me as a student."

On hearing these words, Professor Bordeaux simply nodded his head and dismissed me, as it was time for him to begin his seminar.

Realizing that he must be quite busy, I thought little about it and hastily went down to take a seat.

The Professor was not only a brilliant man, but also a remarkable teacher. He preferred to participate in what he called Socratic Dialogue, meaning that someone would ask a question and he would answer. It was fascinating to watch him work, not only because of his expertise, but because Professor was an adept in fifteen languages. Actually he claimed to speak only fourteen and a half languages, saying that he had never completely mastered English. Those who attended these discourses came from various countries throughout the world, and Professor made it a point to answer each person's question in his or her native language.

Quite the adventurer, Professor Bordeaux's own entry into Cosmic Consciousness had taken him from a fever epidemic in Equatorial Africa to a leper colony in Polynesia. A renowned scientist as well as a philologist, he performed scientific experiments in alternative health care which not only stopped the fever epidemic in Africa from spreading, but also worked their cure on lepers in Polynesia.

One of the great stories about Professor occurred while he was en route to America and his ship sank. As one of two survivors, he kept himself alive on a small island by licking dew off the plants in the early dawn and eating raw bird eggs. When he was finally rescued and taken to Central America, he had no money, no passport and no clothing, other than what he wore. Everything had been lost at sea, except for his life savings and this was tied up in Swiss banks as the result of World War II.

On reaching Central America the government would not allow Professor to cross the border from Central America into Mexico without proper papers, the focal point of his destination,. Complaining about the complications of bureaucracy, he obtained a horse and set out across the desert on horseback. As he made his way across the hot desolate sand his horse died, but this did not deter him. Eventually, he reached Tecati, Mexico, although not without a series of difficult mishaps. By this time, Professor was without money or passport; hence his impoverished financial state compelled him to take occupancy in a tiny horse stable. In spite of such overwhelming odds he went on to establish his first school, and a prolific writer, he wrote his first books on meat wrapping paper.

The morning following my self-introduction to Professor, he signaled me to come up on the stage. As I stood in front of him he said in the slow, well-thought-out words, so much a part of his style, "I have wish to see that letter you wrote."

"Oh, Professor," I replied sorrowfully, "if you have not received it by now, you never will. I wrote that letter many months ago."

Looking at me thoughtfully for a brief moment, Professor then said, "I have decided to help you."

At the time, it was not apparent what Professor Bordeaux meant by that statement. However, I would soon learn, and also understand the price that these great spiritual teachers pay, not only for our individual advancement, but also for the advancement of the world. From that day on, my mind, which had run rampant since my entry into Cosmic Consciousness, and resembled a team of wild horses, was harnessed. I could not think with the rapidity of the past, nor perform any action as hurriedly. While this may sound like an infringement upon the process of God's dark night of the soul, it is not. Control of the mind is the major key to utilizing all powers.

Through my inner plane connection with the Professor, the process of stilling my mind took a new direction. The mind became quieter and the senses less rampant, making it possible for the Spirit to work more efficiently through my human consciousness. With this development came an ability to also exert more control over my actions in the physical world. Subsequently, all of the powers also became stronger. This does not mean that the powers, such as discernment, prophecy, healing, knowledge, and wisdom had been perfected, for the use of any power is relegated to the level of one's own soul attainment. However, I did become more adept in all areas. Later I would puzzle over why people spent years developing a single power when they could possess them all by seeking God first.

Another profound effect came out of this new link in consciousness with Professor Bordeaux. Although it is always God who makes such a link possible, this remarkable teacher had chosen to allow it. Now Professor's knowledge became my knowledge through unspoken words. Before a year had passed, I had not only absorbed Professor's eighty-plus books, but had also learned basic biochemistry without having studied it. When I next attended another of Professor's seminars, he looked at me kindly and said, "I told you I would help you, and I have been paying for it ever since."

By this time, I had been exposed to the teachings of two great men. Swami Chinmayananda had not only opened a doorway into Eastern understanding, but he had never ceased diligently carving on my ego. Professor Bordeaux instilled me with his scientific wisdom and helped me to harness the rampant nature of the mind and senses. And there was to be one more teacher who walked the Earth with an illumined mind, Manly P. Hall. It would be he, who would open a doorway into the secrets of the great mystery schools and the illumined Masters of the ages. His appearance in my life, however, would not occur until I stepped out of the lower mysteries and the purification of the senses, into the higher mysteries and the Dark Night of the Spirit.

CHAPTER XII

India –
Land of Enchantment

Shortly after the students and I returned from San Diego I heard about the mysterious materialization phenomena of an Eastern Guru named Baba Mayananda. There were many stories pertaining to the remarkable things he did, although I admittedly had some doubt. It has been proven many times that such phenomenon is usually magic or illusion, but Jesus had performed many miracles and I believe that everyone seeks another Jesus. I, like others, was attracted to anything that might expand my search for truth.

The story uppermost in my mind is about one of our Western teachers, Gene, who traveled to India to meet the famous Guru. When he departed from the States, he remarked that if he ever saw Baba Mayananda he would ask him to materialize a ruby ring. His search was successful, and on the last day of his visit with the Guru, Baba Mayananda turned to Gene and asked, "Is there something you would like?"

For a moment, Gene reported that be became completely tongue-tied. Finally, he managed to stammer, "Nothing except your blessing."

Accordingly, Baba Mayananda reached in the air, materialized a ruby ring, and then presented it to Gene.

Although some people may think such a feat is impossible, I
took into consideration the fact that everything existing around
us has been materialized from subtle ether. Because all creation
was only a potentiality once, I did believe that some spiritual teachers might have developed the art of changing ether into solid matter.
If so, then materialization is comprised of actually solidifying ether
substance already containing the potentiality of the object and
this would differ little from the manifestation of earth itself. The
same principle would apply to both. Therefore I maintained an
open mind, but it was quite apparent that the greater spiritual
wisdoms in today's world did not usually participate in such a
practices. Certainly I would later discover that such phenomenon
is not necessarily the mark of a great teacher.

Due to my soul agitation, because of the dark night, I had little
fascination with ruby rings. My primary concern was finding a
reprieve from the Dark Night's constant pressure. Thinking perhaps that Baba Mayananda was somewhat like Jesus, I felt that he
perhaps could remove, or at least ease, the chaplet of restraint that
had so long been my albatross. Looking up at the sky, as I usually
did when talking to God, I said, "God, I know what I would ask
Baba Mayananda for if I ever met him. I would ask him for liberation."

Later that same night, just before I went to sleep, the face of
this Eastern Guru suddenly appeared before me. I thought little
of it at the time, for God sometimes created images on the inner
plane in one form or another. Smiling to myself as Baba
Mayananda's face floated past me, I turned over and went to sleep.

On the following morning the phone rang. It was a woman
named Ann whom I had met in Oregon during my first United
States tour. She said, "Elizabeth, I am going to India to meet Guru
Baba Mayananda and I have a feeling that I am supposed to take
you with me. If I pay for your trip, will you go?"

Although not exactly shocked at the invitation, I was deeply amazed.

By asking for the removal of the chaplet, I hoped that there would be some abatement in the Great battle. The purgation of the senses had been going on for almost five years without much easement. My abject discomfort had become even more defined, when one day while I was exercising and my spiritual teacher removed it for brief moment. This felt like the next best thing to Heaven. Now I wanted this uncomfortable restriction removed forever. I had some vague concept that by going to India, this teacher who was accredited with materializing a ruby ring out of the ethers for John, would be able to lessen my discomfort.

How naïve one is to think that someone, or something, can remove that which God has ordained. Nonetheless, just as He had previously arranged things when I threatened to get myself a human husband, obviously He had now decided to make arrangements for me to see Baba Mayananda and seek my liberation. At some level, I suppose I did know that all any teacher can do is to assist in raising the consciousness of a student or disciple and thus guide him or her through their unlearned lessons. Nonetheless, I departed for India bearing some small fragment of hope that my discomfort might soon be lifted or perhaps ended altogether.

The night before my departure, I was taken to meet Baba Mayananda in much the same manner as I had been taken to meet with Jesus. Such incidents enable me to have a better sense of an individual's personality and a deeper comprehension of their nature. Usually such meetings are relegated to great spiritual people and angelic presences, allowing me to make contacts I would never have been able to make otherwise. In Baba Mayananda's case, I found him to be a rather simple man and not as spiritually evolved as his followers believed him to be. When I was first introduced to the guru in the inner worlds, I remember being somewhat surprised that there were so few people around him. Later I realized most that followed him would not be able to circumnavigate the vibratory differences between the two worlds. My own ability to do so was made possible by the Spirit I now bore and by those who guided my steps from the Angelic kingdom. Nonetheless, I have always been grateful for such opportunities to travel between Earth and Heaven, and certainly enjoyed my pre-meeting with this Indian teacher. At the end of our brief visit, I returned to my physical state and found that my watch had stopped. This caused me to smile, for I felt I was being shown that time did not exist beyond the human senses. Much later, however, I realized the incident was actually pointing out that my desire to be removed from the dark night of the soul was bound to time.

The next morning dawned bright and clear, a good omen for my first trip abroad. After some last-minute packing, it was off to the airport to catch a plane to New York. Anne and I had agreed to connect there for our flight to India.

Although there was a four-hour layover when I arrived in New York, I found that getting from one end of the airport to the other was a Herculean task. After disembarking from the plane that carried me from Seattle, I met Anne. We took no chances on being late, and immediately began to make our way to the opposite end of the field where Air India was based. This required tipping various and sundry porters, boarding an airport bus, and subsequently a very long and tedious excursion through customs. In the end, we did not even have time for a cup of tea, let alone dinner.

As soon as the door of the plane closed it felt as though I was in India already, for the flight attendants wore Indian saris and looked like beautiful flowers. The music was also Indian as was the food. Having had no dinner, I was delighted when they began to feed us almost as soon as the plane departed from New York. No airline I have ever traveled on since has ever treated their economy passengers with such graciousness, nor provided such wonderful food. By the time we landed in Bombay many hours later, I was completely addicted to both the food and hospitality of the East.

To stay for any length of time in India is ultimately to love India. While its lack of sanitation, overall uncleanness, and poverty can understandably discourage some Western tourists, the spirituality of India is a beacon light that never seems to dim for those seeking spiritual asylum. Since my return, I have often said to people, "You cannot go to India without India becoming a part of you forever."

India is a great subcontinent of Asia, with a population that matches the whole of Europe, excluding the Soviet Republic. Inhabited by many different races that embrace about 200 distinct languages, India is beautiful to the eye and oftentimes magical to both body and mind. Its beauty extends from the Indian Ocean to the mighty Himalayan mountain range. There is also another side to India, however, the side with its poverty, tenements, and tent cities. It is the latter that sometimes engulfs a tourist and leaves an unforgettable mark. The tent cities have no sanitation and spring up on any open block of land, even in the middle of a city. The stench that rises from them is overpowering, and one has the tendency to turn away from these ugly sights and smells.

As much as I wanted to visit the Himalayas, particularly Nepal, where Jesus had supposedly once lived for a very brief time – it was not to be. Instead, my destiny, as well as that of my traveling companion, rested in southern India and the small village of Bangalore. Before leaving Bombay for Bangalore I took a side trip to visit Swami Chinmayananda's ashram, Sandeepany, and to visit some of my former students who had gone there.

During Swami's visit to the States, he had accepted nine of my single students into his study program and now they were here in India. This two-year opportunity to study in the East was sustained by those who supported Swami's work. The only out-of-pocket expense had been the students' airfare from Seattle to Bombay. It seemed like a wonderful opportunity for them to merge the Eastern and Western cultures. It was my hope that they would later return to the United States and become teachers, thereby hastening the universality of mankind.

Almost everyone in India speaks English, so I was able to hire a taxi and travel without mishap to the ashram, located in a secluded five-acre area outside of Bombay. As we traveled, I got my first good view of the tenements and tent cities, and to smell the vagrancies of human life.

As I rode along in the taxi, my thoughts focused on my former students and how they might be faring in India. I also looked forward to meeting their teacher, Swami Dayananda, who was Swami Chinmayananda's primary disciple. Swami would not be present, for he was again on international tour. Neither would I be able to see Pilauni, a beautiful Hawaiian girl, and one of the best students I have ever had. Apparently, Swami had also recognized Pilauni's special qualities and had taken her with him on tour as his private secretary.

Visiting with the students turned out to be a joyous occasion and fortunately, I arrived at the ashram in time for lunch. Having heard stories about the Eastern ashrams, including the horrible disciplines and primitive living conditions, I feared the worst. None of these things were true at Sandeepany, although the students rose faithfully at four o'clock every morning and went to the temple for prayers and meditation. Later they returned for breakfast, which was followed by more classes; including Sanskrit. After that, lunch was prepared. From lunch until four o'clock in the afternoon the students worked at various tasks, such as maintaining the grounds, washing clothes by hand, and studying privately. After this, it was back to school for more classes, followed by dinner. Their day ended with an evening discourse and a chanting session. Bedtime was about ten o'clock at night.

The day I arrived at Sandeepany was one of those perfect days, which usually occur during the early part of spring in our Western world. It was a beautiful sight to see both men and women students dressed in white, walking with their teacher, Dayananda, to the temple for studies. The young men were dressed in two-piece tunics, which hung loosely over trousers that tied at the waist, while the women wore saris. I tried to imagine what it would be like to have to hand-wash five yards of white fabric every day and decided that washing machines were better. Nonetheless, it was both enchanting and peaceful, and as we all walked together I realized how much we missed in our mad Western pace.

After my all-day visit at Sandeepany, I returned to Bombay, where Ann and I again met and caught our flight to southern India. At my first sight of the charming area of Bangalore, my concerns about the impoverished condition of India were greatly reduced. Bangalore was one of the larger villages in the south and some of its surrounding land was used for farming. The village did not have the squalor of Bombay, although it certainly had its beggars, misshapen, and poor. Yet, Bangalore's delights and hospitality far exceeded any deficiencies.

During my stay in Bangalore, I found that I could explore the city streets in a manual or auto rickshaw for a dime, have the laundry done daily for sixty cents, and attain modest hotel accommodations for three dollars a day. The weather could not have been more perfect, and my anticipation of adventure crowded out any fatigue from the long trip.

The adventure began almost immediately, although many people probably would not have considered it exciting. To most, perhaps it would have been more of an annoyance.

The young man carrying my luggage had barely left the room when I went to the bathroom and saw some kind of lizard by the washbasin. It looked at me, and I looked back at it. Not exactly caring much for the idea that this lizard was so nonchalant about my presence, I decided to ring for help. Immediately, two members of a cleaning crew responded, but they were unable to speak English. With multitudinous hand gestures, I tried to tell them about the lizard. They apparently thought I was telling them that the bathroom was dirty, so they went in and started some very serious scrubbing. Then they left, smiling and bowing. I think they were trying to tell me they had taken care of the matter, that the bathroom was now clean.

As soon as the cleaning crew had gone, out came Mr. Lizard. Again I called for help. In they came again and began scrubbing the bathroom. "No! No! No!" I cried. "The bathroom isn't dirty! I want you to catch the lizard." Another round of hand gestures began. Finally, in desperation, I got a piece of paper and drew the creature. They laughed loudly, and then went in and caught it. Had they not, I would probably have spent the night trying to sleep with my eyes wide open. Besides snakes, scorpions, and spiders, I especially disliked unfamiliar creatures that stare back. Later, I learned that this particular lizard was actually very shy, as well as harmless.

The following morning I went with my hostess to see Baba Mayananda. There were other Americans staying in our hotel for the same reason and so we combined our resources. Six of us caught a taxi and headed toward the Guru's school.

Usually people began to gather at the school at five o'clock in the morning. The devotees, those who worshiped the guru, would spend hours plucking leaves from flowering blossoms and arranging the delicate petals in artistic designs on the walkway. Later in the day, at approximately four o'clock, Baba Mayananda would come out of his private quarters and walk the flowered-strewn path. Sadly, this long awaited daily event lasted only for a brief period of about five minutes, after which he would raise his hand in blessing and promptly disappear. For some reason the devotees seemed satisfied with this very brief encounter. Early the following morning they come again to go through the same process.

During my own fusion with the pure consciousness of God, I came to a deep understanding of exactly what God is. Therefore, I found it objectionable when anyone, East or West, considered himself, or herself, to be God. Although the Spirit of God may be incarnate in them, or has descended to dwell in them, to say that they are God is a misstatement. God is the consciousness that contains and pervades the universe, and we are each an intricate part of Him whether we are aware of it or not. Therefore, all living things in the universe of the stars can say nothing other than they are a manifestation of Him. Only those with an illumined mind, who have become one with God, can truly consider themselves an actual manifestation of Him on Earth, and few are those who have achieved this state.

It was from my own understanding pertaining to the differences between the truly illumined and those who claimed that they were that I derived the terms, Masters of Darkness and Masters of Light. To me Masters of Darkness means not illumed. Although they may be quite enlightened, their personal understanding of God has been passed down from teacher to disciple. On the other hand, Masters of Light signify those rare individuals who have walked on earth with the illumined mind, whose knowledge of God is by direct revelation through the descent of His Spirit. Thus, I have always differentiated between the terms enlightened and illumined.

In that both my inner-sight and hearing had become quite developed by this time, I had little difficulty distinguishing between enlightened and illumined. I did not accept the literal analogy of many Eastern Gurus, or even to that of Western theology. Many times I would shake my head and remember what Professor Bordeaux had said from time to time as he answered student's various and sundry questions, "It does not correlate with the reality," meaning that many of the teachings in both East and West when taken literally do not necessarily correspond to the ancient writing of the great ones, natural law, science, or reasoning.

Certainly, Baba Mayananda did not impress me. He seemed to have one of the most inflated egos I had ever come in contact with, and his materialization of baubles did not seem as important to me as taking care of the sick. While sitting outside with some of the guru's devotees, I saw people carry a very sick man in on a stretcher. Those who brought him put the stretcher down in one of the open sections under the blazing sun. Not one of Baba Mayananda's followers offered to leave their protected shaded gazebo-like structure to make room for him.

Two days passed before the guru saw fit to attend the man's needs. Whether he was ever healed, I will never know, but the incident left me with a decided distaste for this man whom so many worshiped because he frequently materialized baubles. A statement made by another visitor, perhaps summed up my feelings best, "When Baba Mayananda materializes food to feed the hungry, I will then be impressed."

Like a number of the Eastern Gurus, Baba Mayananda considered himself God. However, I had studied under some great teachers, including my beloved Angelic Master. I could see a profound difference between the truly illumined workers on Earth and those whose mastership is passed down to them by their own Gurus through discipleship, or in Baba Mayananda's case, instilled in him by his mother from birth. Baba Mayananda was not illumined and I would meet many other spiritual teachers in both India and America who were not. In so many ways, however, the East is not much different from the West, for wearing saffron-colored robes merely means that one teaches the holy word. This differs little from someone wearing western ministerial robes. As America is divided by denomination, India is divided by guru worship and castes.

While Ann continued her adoration of Baba Mayananda, I left to catch up with Swami Chinmayananda and surprise him. Once away from my hostess, I found that the Indian people seemed determined to honor me as a Holy Woman. This not only surprised me, but also gave me a measure of discomfort, for I was not used to such treatment. In the West, my students merely came in the door and said "Hi, Elizabeth." They did not bow at my feet.

In spite of my discomfort, Okaji helped me to understand the importance of allowing these gentle people of the East to do just that, for it was their custom. Even more astounding, they did not care that I was a Christian, nor did they ever try to convert me to one of their Eastern religions.

One incident in particular remains steadfast in my mind. While traveling in Bangalore, I was invited into one of the Indian homes

for a cup of masala, a richly spiced, sweet tea. There was only one
chair in the humble dwelling, and I was directed to sit on it, while
the others gathered around on the floor. Although this wonderful
family did not know it, I would have felt much less awkward sitting on the floor with them. While sitting there and drinking my
tea, I noticed that the family passed another cup of tea from family member to family member. It was obvious that they were unable to afford individual servings for each person. Through their
simple and gracious gift, I saw the way all people should live.

A few days later, I also had an opportunity to be hosted by the
Sri Krishna Weaving Mills, a fabric mill on the outskirts of Ban-
galore. The senior owner of the mill, whom I have always called
Papa, was a member of the Chinmaya Trust, Swami
Chinmayananda's organization. I had been corresponding with
Dwarkanath, Papa's son, for many months prior to my arrival and
knew that he was looking forward to taking me to the mills.

Picking me up at the hotel, early one morning, Dwarkanath
whisked me away to meet the family. As a matter of protocol, I
was introduced first to Papa, an elderly gentlemen sitting at a large
wooden table. Papa probably knew no strangers, and my meeting
with him quickly turned into an adventure in Indian culinary
magic and hospitality. It was during my visit to the Sri Krishna
Weaving Mill that I ate the longest and largest meal I would ever
eat.

Because Indian people continued to perceive me as a Holy
Woman, food seemed to appear everywhere I went. To decline
their gifts would have been to insult the hospitable hands they
held out to me, although I would have preferred a touch of hunger at times. As soon as Papa had given me a warm welcome, he
clapped his hands and pointed to the table in front of me. Immediately, a little dish bearing a wonderful Indian delicacy was placed
on the table in front of me. As soon as I finished consuming this,
he clapped his hands again. Another delicacy found its way to me.
Three hours later, Papa was still clapping his hands, and I was still

eating. In order to endure, I prayed to God to somehow make it possible for my stomach to acquiesce to this culinary onslaught of hospitality.

Around three o'clock that afternoon, Papa asked if I would like to see the vineyards. I eagerly nodded, thinking that it would be possible to stop eating. At the vineyards, Papa stopped the car and called one of the workmen over to him. It was fortunate that I could not understand their language, or I would have found myself once again in the throes my latest terror, eating. Since my vocabulary did not include any Indian languages it was impossible to understand what was being said. Thus, unaware of my fate, I blissfully sat as one of the workers brought over a large bunch of grapes and handed them to my host. Papa took one of the grapes off of the vine and ate it. Nodding with what seemed a great sense of satisfaction, he muttered something else in his native language.

Off went the worker, while we continued to wait. Before long, the newly washed grapes were back and quite naturally found their way into my lap. I had been eating now for over five hours with little reprieve. My compensation came when I escaped Papa's overwhelming hospitality, and Dwarkanath took me on a tour of the weaving mills. It was a fascinating experience, and before we left, Papa's son presented me with yards of beautiful, white cotton material to make clothing.

The next day, Dwarkanath again picked me up at my hotel. Apparently, Swami Chinmayananda was expected to arrive by plane, for he was scheduled to discourse that evening in Bangalore. Papa had promised me the day before that he would take me to the airport to meet Swami. When Dwarkanath and I arrived once again at the weaving mills, we found Papa eating. He wanted me to join him, but this time I tried to graciously decline, for I had just eaten breakfast. Nonetheless, Papa's meal went on and on, and it became obvious that we would arrive at the airport too late to meet Swami and his entourage.

Even eating must end sometime, and eventually Papa finished. At last, we headed for the airport, with Papa driving. It was the first time I had ever seen four lanes of traffic occupy two. Papa's driving only further compounded this treacherous state of affairs, for he created a fifth lane and expected the other four to move out of the way. It was easier for me to simply close my eyes and prepare to meet death with a measure of serenity and dignity.

Somehow, we managed to arrive at the airport. By this time, of course, Swami Chinmayananda had already gone. Nonetheless, my host was not to be thwarted and began to drive around in what seemed like a big circle. Ever so often, he would stop and ask someone a question pertaining to Museum Road, the only two words that I could understand. Eventually, with both of us still intact, we arrived in front of a house. Papa stopped the automobile, saying with a great measure of pride, "He's here."

"You mean Swami Chinmayananda is here?" I asked with a certain amount of excitement and a large measure of skepticism.

"He is here" Papa affirmed with a seeming sense of satisfaction.

When we entered the house, I noticed a relatively large group of Swami's devotees waiting to welcome him. Remembering my recent brush with Swami's attempt to do some purifying of my ego, I tried to be a bit humble and hung back, sequestering myself behind a wall separating the two rooms. The devotees thought I might be afraid and encouraged me to come forward, but I just kept shaking my head. Eventually, Swami made his appearance. After his devotees had extended their greetings and gathered around him, I stepped through the door. To the amazement of his followers, he opened his arms, and; taking me in them, gave me a big, old-fashioned Western hug, asking, "Elizabeth, how did you get here?"

Hugging is not a customary practice with the great teachers of India, and as I mentioned earlier, one does not speak unless the Guru speaks first, nor does one start eating until the Guru takes the first bite. Neither does one touch the Guru, who is considered

holy. However, Swami had traveled extensively in the United States
and had obviously picked up some of our Western habits. Hugging seemed to be one of them. By this time, Papa, who had observed this Western exchange, was quite impressed because Swami
not only knew me, but he had also given me such a massive bear hug.
In Papa's eyes, this indicated that I was someone important, and he,
Papa, had been responsible for bringing the two of us together.

That night I went to hear Swami's discourse. Although I did
not sit in the back row, as I had threatened to do following some
of Swami's work on my ego, neither did I sit in the very front.
Instead, I elected to sit near the front, primarily because it was
difficult to understand Swami Chinmayananda's Eastern accent,
although he always gave his discourses in English. When Swami
entered the doorway of the auditorium, an entourage of disciples
and devotees accompanied him. It was a magnificent sight to see
the Guru, dressed in silk saffron robes, make his way through
hundreds of adoring people.

As Swami moved down the isle toward the podium, the people
stood up to honor him. When he came to where I was standing,
he stopped and looked at me. Taking a beautiful, white-flowered
mala (a mala is equivalent to a Catholic rosary) from his neck, he
placed the fragrant blossoms around mine, and, standing back to
admire his handiwork for a moment, he said, "That is nice." Next,
he motioned me to be seated in view of all of the people who had
come to hear him, even before he seated himself. It was one of the
greatest tributes I have ever received, although this honor lasted
only until I met Swami Chinmayananda in the States again and
he resumed his dedicated work on my ego.

Before leaving Bangalore, some of my new Indian friends set
up an appearance for me in the public library. I had little hope of
attracting a large audience but felt a need to do something about
my work. It is uncanny how news travels in India. For some mysterious reason, even though there was no direct advertising or formal announcements, everyone seems to know the moment a spiri-

tual teacher is scheduled to discourse. Suddenly, an entire audience appears to materialize out of thin air.

When I walked into the library auditorium, every seat was taken. To make matters more stressful, men occupied most of them.

A great deal went through my mind while waiting to be introduced, primarily whether the spiritual words of an American woman would be accepted. One thing was certain, I did not wish to do what Christian evangelists often do, and use such an opportunity to try and convert the people. Rather, I chose to speak on the process of transformation from human to divine.

Although Indian people have accepted the master/disciple relationship all of their lives, they are seldom taught about the mysteries behind the transformation. The Guru may often allude to these, but the deeper secrets themselves are passed on only from master to disciple through the spoken and unspoken word. Much like Western people who take the words of their minister on faith, the Indian people also accept the teachings of their Guru on faith.

Admittedly, my teachings were considered very bold, particularly for the modern Western world. Nonetheless, I felt, and still feel, that the only way the world can change is to reveal the doorway to the future honestly and openly. Therefore, while speaking in India, I tried to present the realities underlying the mysterious transformation of human to divine in a concise and plausible manner. This attempt was apparently successful, because at the end of my discourse, many of the men gathered around to ask questions.

Immediately following my discourse in Bangalore, an old Sadhu came up and asked where I was speaking next. To me, this was the highlight of my appearance. A Sadhu, meaning an ascetic or one who meditates or contemplates, always has an uncanny ability to suddenly show up where a Guru is speaking regardless of distance. Unfortunately, it was necessary in this case to tell my Sadhu that I had no plans to appear elsewhere in India. When leaving the library, however, I said to God, "I am going to return to India someday and get an old Sadhu for a disciple."

Although destiny has never returned me to India, I have not forgotten the wonder of those days and nights beneath the splendor of the saffron dawns and sunsets. Sometimes when the brashness of the Western world overwhelms me, I threaten to leave America and return to the nation that honored me as a Holy Woman.

On the day following my appearance, I left Bangalore and flew to Madras, the capital of Madras State, to tour the Temples of Kanchipuram. At first sight, this part of India presented a stark contrast from the charming village I had just left. It spread out over a vast area, and parts of the city were almost rural in character.

The history of Madras (called Chemai) seems to extend back into some kind of timelessness, as though it had always been. It is filled with holy places, among them the headquarters of the more Western-oriented Theosophical Society. Therefore, I had not only come to visit the Temples of Kanchipuram, but also to visit the Theosophical Society Headquarters. And, not far away from the headquarters stood the sacred Banyan tree, where it is said that Gautama Buddha had entered enlightenment. A visit to this famous tree was one of the focal point in my travel plans, for many wonderful things had been written about Buddha.

On my arrival, I found a suitable hotel and made arrangements to take one of the tour buses to the holy shrines the following day.

Shortly after boarding the bus the following morning I became involved in a conversation with some gentlemen wearing turbans. They were Sikhs, and one of the few major religions with which I was not yet familiar. After talking with them for some time, I again realized, as always, truth runs through all beliefs. Even though they followed the teachings of Mohammed instead of Jesus, it seemed that we believed in the same God. Therefore, I found my conversation with them remarkably interesting, and because of their openness, I learned much about their religion.

Because they were military men and protectors of India, they assigned themselves the task of watching over me to assure my safety. Every place I went they remained with me, even though I must have embarrassed them terribly when I wandered into a men's restroom by mistake.

One cannot help but marvel over the hospitality of this wonderful land of saints and holy people, and the care it gave me. During my tour of the Temples, my hosts certainly did not lack in Indian courtesy. When the day was over, one of the men handed me a slip of paper and said, "When you get to Bombay (also called Mumbai), I want you to call my wife. We have a large apartment overlooking the Indian Ocean, and Saroj, my wife, is alone a great deal. I would like you to be our guest."

Taking the piece of paper and tucking it into my pocket, I thanked my three hosts fervently for watching over me. Unfortunately, however, it seemed that my self-appointed protectors departed a bit too soon. Just as I stepped off the bus, an Indian man grabbed me, hustled me into a nearby bicycle rickshaw, and began pedaling. Much to my consternation, it seemed that I had been somewhat kidnapped. Knowing, of course, that a bicycle rickshaw was a common means of transportation, there was little doubt that my kidnapping placed me in no immediate danger. Nonetheless I tried to tell the driver the name of my hotel in Madras and asked to be taken there.

My kidnapper continued pedaling, saying nothing, and I began to wonder if he understood even a little bit of English. Unfortunately there was little recourse at the time, but to go along for the ride. The thought of jumping out did not cross my mind, primarily because there appeared little to gain by doing so. The distance from the bus to the hotel was quite far, and if my driver were indeed heading in that direction, it would be some time before we got there.

As he pedaled along, I settled down to enjoy the trip as much as possible. Bicycle rickshaws are fascinating and during my stay

in Bangalore I had used them quite extensively. Therefore I felt a
measure of comfort, as well as curiosity, as we proceeded to where
ever we were going. Once my mind had become quiet I sensed
that my driver did not have any money for food. An evening meal
to him meant getting a paying customer. As a foreigner, I had
been a prime target. My intuition was apparently correct and eventually we arrived at my hotel. Watching him pedal off into the
approaching evening, I was content in the knowing that he would
have a meal that night.

On the last day of my visit to Madras I went to visit the great
Banyan tree where Buddha is said to have entered illumination. It
had been prophesied that Siddartha, a prince, would renounce
his kingdom and become the Buddha when he saw a sick man, an
old man and a dead man. The parents of the young Siddartha did
everything they could to ensure that this prophecy did not come
to pass. In spite of their efforts, however, one day while the youth
was out riding in a carriage, he saw an old man, a sick man, and a
dead man. He asked himself, "Is this all that human life is, to
become old, sick and then die?"

Upon seeing these terrible things, Siddartha renounced the
wealth of his princely surroundings and departed to live among
the dead (those not awakened). The austerities the young prince
practiced were greater than those of other ascetics who wandered
from place to place seeking enlightenment. And because of this
the future Buddha drew a number of disciples.

Five years passed. The skin on Siddartha's head often cracked
open and bled, and his emaciated body was almost skeletal. One
day he came to the realization that he had still not achieved enlightenment. None of his austerities had recompensed him by
showering him with divine light. Thus, having found that starva-
tion and extreme renunciation did not appear to be the way to
nirvana (peace), the former prince decided to partake of a bowl of
rice. And it came to pass; when his disciples saw him eating thus
they departed from him.

As Siddartha sat beneath the Banyan tree eating his bowl of rice, he entered Divine illumination. A powerful voice then told him "to teach," and from that day on he became Guatama Buddha. Shortly thereafter Buddha dedicated his life to help alleviate people's suffering.

Whether the Banyan tree under which I now stood was really the same tree where Guatama once sat made little difference to me. Due to the collective consciousness of those who came to pay homage, the tree emanated a sacred holiness. I bathed in its silence and magnificence, as I pondered on the life of one who sought to take away the sorrows of the human world.

The next day I returned to Bombay. This would be my last stop before leaving for Seattle. Immediately upon landing, I called Saroj, the wife of the Sikh who had been one of my protectors while touring the Temples of Kanchipurum. The decision to call had been a difficult one, for I was in a foreign country and contacting someone I had never met. Although there was some concern that my visit might be an inconvenience, I felt an obligation to my Bangalore protectors to do so. On calling, I was pleasantly surprised to learn that my acquaintance had indeed contacted his wife, and she was prepared to receive me, not just for a visit, but also for the duration of my stay in Bombay.

Catching a taxi to Saroj's home, there was again an opportunity to observe the filth, stench and disease of Bombay. At this time, I had not yet heard of Mother Theresa and her work in Calcutta. If I had, it is probable that I would have traveled there to work with her. Nonetheless, the decay I now witnessed while traveling through Bombay later helped me to have a better understanding of the difficulties Mother Theresa faced, and her remarkable dedication to work among the poor and dying.

In the States, we look at these Eastern countries and their uncleanness with very critical eyes, and it is hard not to. When one walks along the street and sees every empty space in a city filled with makeshift tents, and contemplates this squalor-filled with hungry and diseased people, it is difficult not to be judgmental. However, the sight and smells did not bother me quite as much as they had when I first arrived in India, perhaps because I better understood the ways of this country.

Without proper sewage treatment, the tent communities had to make do in whatever way they could, although it was incomprehensible to think that the poverty of human beings forced them to live in places equal to pig sties in order to survive. Still, I had seen the same thing beginning to take place in America, even in the city where I lived. In Seattle we also had tenements, the homeless, the hungry, and our streets were strewn with trash. It was impossible not to consider a time in the future, as the population of our nation continued to grow, when we too might have to live with the terrifying sight that now met my eyes as I traveled through the streets of Bombay.

If there were a bit of heaven in India, I would experience it during the next three days. My newly found Sikh friends lived in a large apartment overlooking the Indian Ocean. Each morning at sunrise, the sea turned into a cauldron of magnificent, pure saffron. The air was soft; bearing with it just a hint of a breeze; and for a time it was almost as though I was suspended at a gateway that opened to the endless universe. Then the scene would slowly fade away, like a beautiful watercolor fading in the rain. Each night, this painting was repeated as the day was swept away in a swirl of color, giving in to the black cloak of night. Now I understood why the Swamis wore orange robes. They wore the bright-hued garments to honor the days and nights of Brahma, or the days and nights of God.

My hostess was an elegant woman, lovely in form, gracious, and even more gentle and beautiful in her inner world. She made every effort to make my visit memorable. Once again, however, I was relegated to the pastime of dining, so I accomplished little during the days I spent on the Indian Ocean except eating and sleeping. Following the usual custom of Indian hospitality, Saroj and her friends insisted on constantly serving me a variety of Indian delicacies. I was confident that when I returned home the scale would indicate a "titanic" disaster had taken place and a volcanic eruption in the form of fat had consumed my body. Additionally, because of the amount of food I ate, as well as the heat, my eyes would simply not stay open between meals. I fear I was a poor guest. As soon as the sun dipped into the sea, and the temperatures lowered, my hostess took me on enchanting trips along the sea. Fortunately, these events occurred before the late evening meal.

On my last evening in India, Saroj took me by car to her favorite beach. Just as the sea began to turn into deep saffron and various hues of indigo, I found myself mounting the back of a camel. It would be my first camel ride, although not my last; for the next time, I would be riding toward the majestic domes of the great pyramids in Egypt.

The camel was kneeling on all four legs as I mounted, but immediately rose up. The two front legs abruptly stood up first, sliding me downward along the camel's back. Then it gave a jerk and raised both of its back legs simultaneously, giving me the sensation that I would soon be flying over its head without angel wings. Then it began loping down the beach at almost a full gallop. Because camels run swiftly, but differently from other animals, my experience was somewhat like standing on the railing of a ship during a storm. The camels synchronize their two left legs, then the two right legs, trotting in such a fashion as to toss a person from side-to-side. I remember shrieking loudly, although I do not know if it was from the fear of being thrown off or if it was some new form of laughter, the nervous kind one emits when feeling completely out of control. For a short time the dark night of the soul lost ground. Even now, as I remember this episode, that aspect brings me a certain sense of diabolical pleasure.

Later, after dismounting from the camel, Saroj and I walked together on the beach and ate Indian corn on the cob that had just been roasted on low embers in the sand. It was quite spicy, but I enjoyed it immensely, for my taste buds had now grown more accustomed to the seasonings of the East. Never will I forget the image of my lovely hostess standing against the backdrop of the Indian Ocean, a dark silhouette in the fading orange-colored eve.

After leaving India, Saroj and I corresponded for a while, but as with so many people we meet, time and distance become like the fading sunset at eventide. Friendships fade away, buried in the semi-forgotten pages of the soul's scrapbook.

On the following morning, concluding my visit with Saroj, I took a taxi to the airport and boarded a plane for the States. There was a great deal of time to think during the return flight, and as the scenes and sights of my stay passed before my eyes, I wondered which of my experiences had been the most memorable. Then it came to me. It was not the saffron-colored sunrises and sunsets, the wonderful food, or even the fantastic hospitality, but a simple incident that had occurred while I was in Bangalore.

One day, I was walking beside a young Indian boy of about nine or ten, and we struck up a conversation. He asked me, "Who is your Master?"

"Jesus," I replied.

"I've heard of Jesus," he said thoughtfully. Then he added, "My Master is Baba Mayanandaji."

"Oh yes, I am familiar with your Master," I responded. "In fact, I spent several days at gatherings in front of his school."

The boy's eyes got very wide. "You have met my Master?" he asked.

"Yes, indeed," I said.

Then we walked along quietly side-by-side under the azure Indian sky, both of us content in our mutual respect for one another's ideals. For me, it was a view of how the world should really be.

CHAPTER XIII

Toward the Unknown

On returning to Seattle, I found that my students had prepared a true Eastern welcome. The school had been scrubbed spotless; flowers had been purchased; and I was greeted as though every single word about my adventure was more precious than gold. Such devotional fervor can be described as Guruitis, a disease that dissipates quickly when the teacher administers a few disciplines. In this case, the sudden surge of adoration from my students ended before the week was out. Nonetheless, I relished its momentary encounter, not because I needed to be adored, but because it was good for them to show respect to a spiritual teacher.

Back at the school, I was again engulfed with work, particularly since the classes were still large. In spite of the heavy workload, there was still time to intensify my research into the life of Jesus. I was simply not satisfied with the fundamental concepts of traditional churches. Something was not right. The churches were satisfied with the Master as they knew him, so why wasn't I? Perhaps it was because the church could not answer many of my questions, and neither could my investigative nature rest in faith alone. What did Jesus eat? Where was he during those years that were not covered by the scriptures, known as the lost years? What did he really look like? Most of all, however, I wanted to know Jesus the Master, a term so little understood in the Western world.

As my research continued I suddenly found myself faced with a dozen different Jesus', each existing around the same time. The situation was made even more difficult by Professor Bordeaux's translation of "*The Secret Jesus Scroll*" and his book *Exergis of Christianity*. Both gave evidence of Jesus' affiliation with the Essenes, but the latter work hinted that the Essene Jesus and Jesus the Christ were two different people. Professor presented some pretty strong evidence to back up his theory, so much so that it later would cause yet another division among those who were followers of Jesus. This new group considered themselves the "New Essenes" and they believed in the Essene Jesus as vehemently as the traditional church believed in Jesus the Christ.

One morning, while deeply entrenched in research, a rather startling thing occurred. My brain knotted up within my skull much like a muscular cramp in one's leg. Although most people, when they have over exerted or have put undue stress on a muscle, have had such muscle knots in their body, I had never heard of one in the brain. At the time, it deeply concerned me and I remember thinking that it might be necessary to lessen the intensity of my research.

This was not a very easy decision, for here I was sitting in the middle of a boiling pot comprised of several different men all named Jesus. There was Jesus, the son of Phabet deprived of the high-priesthood; Jesus, son of Ananus; Jesus, the son of Sapphais, Governor of Tiberias; Jesus, brother of Onias, deprived of the high priesthood by Antiochus Epiphanes; Jesus, son of Gamala; Jesus, the son of Saphat, ringleader of the robbers; Jesus, son of Thebuthus, a priest; and Jesus, son of Josedek. (Josephus – "Complete Works.")

By this time the situation had become so bad, that I put my head in my hands and cried out, "Will the real Jesus please stand up?"

There was but one solution; to meticulously follow the same line of research that Professor Bordeaux had followed in his *Exergis of Christianity*. It would be necessary to go over each Jesus again one-by-one. Eventually, I found the passage that had caused Professor to divide one man into two. Carefully I went over it again and again, but I knew I was right. The Essene Jesus and Jesus the Christ were one and the same, and now it was possible to prove it. After that it became relatively easy to cast out the other superfluous figures bearing that same name.

One thing I have been extremely careful about is never to allow preconceived ideas take control of my research. Truth is paramount, for it alone can withstand the constant tides of change. When the time came to write Jesus' life story, I wanted it to be based on what he really was, not on what others thought he was.

This tenacious drive to seek the truth in all matters surprised me a great deal, for my dislike for history classes had been rather intense during my youth. Now I was driven to determine the real story behind the man from Galilee. My search for the real Jesus' would span over a quarter of century. Along the way I would become submerged in the lives and histories of two other great biblical figures: Moses, Lord of the Sinai and John the Beloved.

Five years had passed since my entry into the dark night of the soul. Although I was no longer the same person I had once been, the inner war still continued with little let-up. Despite the power of miracles, I frequently experienced the agony of defeat. The things that normal humans take for granted were no longer allowed to me, such as eight hours of sleep, makeup, and long showers. These were considered stimulation to the senses, things that draw the soul continually toward enticements of the corporeal world. It was apparent that my Angelic Teacher deemed my soul needed to continue the development of its inner world instead, and I should devote my efforts toward learning greater understanding, love, and tolerance.

Even as the dark night continued to engulf me, there were greater battles to deal with than diet. No thought or action went unnoticed by the Spirit, or my Angelic Teacher. Things that had happened to me when I was a child and things long forgotten, surfaced in my consciousness like ghostly phantoms. The deep recesses of the subconscious mind, which contain the inherent tendencies accumulated through the centuries, is indeed bottomless. When anger had been worked on for a while, another doorway would open. Out galloped hatred, jealousy, gluttony, and deceit—like rider-less horses bearing guile and treachery.

Allowed to hurt no individual by deed, thought, or word, the dark night of the soul is not just the purification of the body, the mind, and the soul; it is also a period of atonement. Every warped attitude and crooked way must be made straight, and every unresolved issue must be resolved, for God insists upon peace between all people.

During this period, as a bearer of His Spirit, God continued to reveal the nature of His ways. The Angelic Kingdom saw that I no longer read fiction, unless it was something that included spiritual values, such as *The Prophet* by Kahlil Gibran, or *Very Unusual, The Wonderful World of Mr. K. Nakamura* by Manley P. Hall. Attending movies had been reduced to once or twice a year, and those I attended had to exclude extreme violence and sexually explicit situations. This eliminated practically every movie produced. Even newspapers became an almost-forgotten thing.

There is a reason for such disciplines, for where one's mind is, so are we. Therefore, an intricate part of the transformation of the soul is the purification of the mind, for only a controlled mind is capable of utilizing the powers of healing, discernment, and prophecy to their fullest potential. Without purification of the mind, a sense attraction for the dense world of matter is retained, and the union between the consciousness of God and the consciousness of the soul is lessened. The weaker this link, the lesser the individual's power. One has to make a decision: do they want to continue the path of old age, sickness, and death, or do they want to grow angel wings? I chose the latter and accepted the disciplines that came with it. In "The Secret Jesus Scroll," Jesus spoke, saying, "In the world of men and the world of angels, there is a price."

To compensate for this sacrifice of mortality, the Angelic Kingdom continued to teach me in all matters. This new, but extensive education, not only included studies pertaining to the psychological makeup of the human mind, but practical health and alternative medicine. People came for consultations from far and wide, and His Spirit made it possible to discern every ailment, its cause, the destiny of every soul, and the root of every emotional problem. In addition, there were still the mysteries of heaven and earth that had been taught in the great schools of antiquity. These included science, the major religions of the world, and the wonder of the great philosophers.

This was a world that I never dreamed existed, and had I known, I would have believed that for me to reach it was an impossible dream. Sometimes I wanted, and still want, to cry out to a hungry world that seeks for peace, the lonely who seek for love, the illiterate who cannot read or write, and to the masses who walk unknowing when the wisdom of the ages surrounds them. I want to say to them, "Your day is here if you will but reach out for it. It is not in some distant kingdom, but as close as your breath. It is not confined to only saints, for God built this world for all humans."

As Swami Chinmayananda once said, "All Saints have a past and all sinners have a future."

Although I had never learned astrology past its most rudimentary principles, I could plainly see that astronomy and astrology were intricately intertwined. Even today, I am still fascinated as I watch the documentary on the creation of the universe, which was created by Public Broadcasting. This film takes mankind back to 10 to the minus 43 seconds, or a fraction of a second after the universe began. However, astronomers say that they still have not pierced the mystery of that fraction of a second when the universe actually began. Yet, I know that they will, for the answer is found in that illumined moment of the Cosmic Consciousness connection and, not only scientists, but all people shall one day experience it.

When science does pierce the secret of that fraction of a second, which will prove the existence of God, scientific minds shall then become a part of the enlightenment of our future world. Albert Einstein, one of the great-illumined minds of the Twentieth Century, spent a part of his life unsuccessfully trying to prove the Grand Unified Field Theory. However, it does exist; and although he knew this, he apparently was unable to prove it during his life.

As my research, meditation and curiosity continued, I found that there had been a time long ago when science and religion were not separated. The origin of creation was, and had been, well understood by every illumined mind and intertwined with the process of evolution. During these studies of creation vs. evolution it was impossible to find any separation between the two, for both were intricately inter-related. Creationism was, and is, the study of the growing inner consciousness as it created its outer environment. On the other hand, Evolutionism was, and is, none other than the outer expression of matter in its development. It was therefore impossible not to reflect on the great astronomers who opened doorways into an unexplored universe, such as Newton, Coepernicus, Galileo and Kepler. Just how enlightened were they?

While this was a period of great darkness, it was also a period of great learning. To be taught directly by God and His Angelic Emissaries in all matters of education was a miraculous thing for one who had been raised in poverty. To hear and communicate with the great beings of the past was a never-ending source of guidance and revelation. Because the Spirit had now penetrated my body, there was never loneliness or lack of challenge; neither was my soul bound to the humdrum of corporeal day-to-day living. Still, I often tell my students, "If you think a couple have difficulty living in the same house from time-to-time, just wait until you and His Spirit share the same body."

On the first of May each year, I left the school and went back on lecture tour, returning in September to begin classes. Still popular with the media, these summer appearances accomplished a great deal.

One early spring morning, a short time before I was to leave on another tour, a very disturbing sight awakened me. God sat at a table, in what looked like a courtroom, and He was wearing the black robes of a judge. When I opened my eyes, I knew that the school would have to go. This was devastating, particularly in view of the long hours and hard work that had gone into it. In spite of the ominous warning, I struggled desperately to keep the school going, using every means of credit at my disposal to continue the work. In the end, it was to no avail. The doors closed. Putting everything in storage, I purchased another one of my former landlord's cars. This one was named Diogenes, after the little brown-skinned stoic who held the armies of Alexander the Great at bay while he took a sunbath.

One morning, just as I had five years earlier, I bid goodbye to an empty building and headed into the sunrise. This time, however, no one said to me, "May His angels watch over you." Now it was my Angelic Master who sought to give me solace and tried to help me see that this was not the end, but rather a new beginning. Nonetheless, it was many months before I could look back without pain and pay homage to that moment when I had again been uprooted from my comfort zone.

As on the previous United States tours, I began to work my way along the West Coast, although not with the same thoroughness. One reason was because I wanted to relegate more attention toward the Midwest and Eastern Seaboard. This decision was based on research, for I had discovered a rather amazing pattern in the conversion of Asia Minor to Christianity.

While John the Beloved had established the seven churches of Ephesus, other disciples continued the work in Jerusalem. Later, following his illumination on the road to Damascus, Paul went to Rome and began to establish Christianity there. In studying the ancient maps, it appeared that everything had been laid out somewhat like a giant chess game. As the new Christian Religion spread out from Jerusalem, the same thing was beginning to occur in the Roman Empire. Just as a chess player attempts to divide his opponent's forces, John had formed his seven churches as a spearhead aimed directly at the heart of Asia Minor. The teachings seemed to spread in both directions from this spearhead, and ultimately connected with the teaching efforts of Jesus' disciples in both Rome and Israel. Finally, during the third century A.D., Constantine, Emperor of Rome, declared the Roman Empire to be a Christian nation.

After seeing this distinctive pattern envelop the Roman Empire and its subsequent surrender to the new Christian Religion, I decided to use the same principle. Having already completed a rather thorough canvass of the West Coast, as well as the south during my earlier tours, I felt that I needed to focus on the East Coast. It was then my intention to spearhead through the Midwest. Such thinking at least occupied my mind and established a goal, which helped alleviate some of the pain over my loss of the school. Although I knew that God must have a reason for my change of circumstance, He did not reveal it to me. Mentally, I began to prepare myself for the possibility that I would have to remain on the road for the rest of my life.

To say that I was popular with fundamental churches and ministers would be a brash assertion. As the people had persecuted Jesus 2,000 years before because he taught differently, I was now the target of a number of inclement faces along the way. On the other hand, because I was a Christian Mystic, my popularity with the media continued. The media delighted in finding opponents for me from the fields of religion, psychology, and philosophy. I, in turn, was pleased to accept these challenges and learned quickly not to enter my opponent's battlefield. The aim was to draw them into mine. That our views might be quite different did not seem important, for those who watched the programs could decide what was right for them.

Holding onto mythology and legends without trying to determine their origin seemed to be a way of life for many fundamentalists. By this I am not referring to Fundamental Christianity alone, for there are fundamentalists in all religions, all philosophies, and even in science. Nevertheless, in view of modern technology, it would seem that even the young should be able to understand that Earth was not created in six weekdays, nor is it the center of the universe. Every great-enlightened philosopher, religionist, scientist, composer, and poet understood this. Yet, all too many people fight new concepts and fear to step into the unknown to travel a path of new adventure and growth.

During my mystic voyage, the works of the great wisdoms lent their strength, and made it possible to continue in spite of the endless driving, hardships, and inner wars. I was cared for, watched over by, and taught by powerful Angelic Forces, and the presence of God traveled with me. For most, this is a world yet to come and a world that many cannot yet accept. I remember thinking at the time how sad, that such a wondrous doorway is there for all mankind, from the homeless to the rich and from the criminal to the saint, and yet they not only walk in darkness and unknowing, they seemed to prefer it.

Perhaps these feelings would still envelop me today, but they have been replaced by a deeper and greater compassion. The human race is still in its infancy. The great age of man lies yet ahead and will not come into existence until the transformation of human to divine is complete and all humans bear the illumined mind. Then the good shall break forth as the morning sun bursts across the night. This is not an errant prophecy, an imaginative dream, or even a hope; it is a reality.

The human race wants to stop its suffering and it wants more out of life. However, the greatest pain remains, for most, loneliness. Loneliness prevails, in part, because so many humans are not beautiful or handsome by the standards of the advertising media. Too much attention is focused on the body and too little on the beauty of the soul. To God, all of his children are beautiful, and one must learn to see this beauty in each person. Learning to love people and taking pleasure in helping each to find his or her own seed of greatness is life's greatest reward. Einstein certainly did not win an award for having a great physique. He was admired for his genius; and to humanity, he was more than handsome; he possessed some unfathomable beauty.

While traveling, memories of those who had shared my life, as well as contemplation on the nature of God, occupied my mind. This helped to pass the long hours on the road. By the time I arrived in Arizona, it was June, and I prepared to make the pilgrimage to San Diego for Professor Bordeaux's annual seminar. First I made arrangements to appear in Scottsdale, Arizona.

During my speech in Scottsdale, I noticed a relatively young, cute blond woman sitting in the front row. It was difficult not to pick her out of the crowd because her eyes seemed to get larger and larger as the talk proceeded. Although she was an adult, she seemed to have a child-like aliveness that set her apart from the other people. At the end of the meeting, as the more dedicated seekers gathered around me, she was among them, and there was an opportunity to learn more about her. Neither Cheryl, for that was her name, nor I, realized at the time, that this fortuitous meeting would deeply affect both of our lives.

Following the customary routine of past tours, I set up my seminars, as well the Magic World Healing Clinics. To fill in the days prior to attending the Professor's San Diego school, I also saw clients. Cheryl was completing her year's work with the school and preparing to take the summer off. She attended all of my classes, lectures & seminars, coming early to help set up and staying late to assist in whatever way she could. It seemed natural to invite her to go to San Diego with me. I was certain that I would enjoy having company during the drive, and at the same time, she would have an opportunity to meet one of my great teachers.

Sometimes a teacher is blessed by having a student who approaches the spiritual path with their entire heart and soul. Cheryl was one of these. It seemed that she could not learn fast enough. Once we had reached San Diego and settled into the motel, she kept me up late every night with a barrage of questions pertaining to God and the Universe. We would have both marveled that as Cheryl asked her perpetual questions, her own rendezvous with destiny would eventually take her to all parts of the world.

At the conclusion of Professor's seminar, Cheryl and I returned to Phoenix. As the winter approached, it became obvious that Cheryl would be going with me when I left in the late spring. This meant that there would finally be someone to handle public relations. Because motels would be much too expensive for two of us, it appeared that the time had arrived for me to dispose of "Diogenes" and obtain another camping vehicle. Once more, I found myself inside a new car dealership. Cheryl and I both fell in love with a blue van-camper whose exterior reminded us of the sea. Combining our resources, we purchased it. This time it was not necessary to do the renovation myself, for the van came fully equipped with icebox, sink, dining table, and other amenities, including air conditioning. However, in trying to cut costs, such road conveniences as power brakes and automatic transmission were omitted, not realizing that when the vehicle was fully loaded, it would be heavier than anything I had ever driven. Nonetheless, our new vehicle, which we named the "Seagull Too," would carry us on many unforgettable adventures and later serve as my primary home.

By this time, the promotional work that I had been sending abroad was also beginning to open a few doorways. One of these resulted in a contact with a young croupier at a gambling casino in Ghana, West Africa, who wrote asking to become a part of our work. In answer to his request to know more, I sent additional material, tapes and books. Shortly thereafter, he wrote again, telling us that he had now been joined with three other young men who also wanted to learn the way of "The Path."

As a pebble is dropped into a pond and its waves inundate across the water, so too would the work in Ghana. Before long this small study unit inspired an entire organization, also located in Ghana. This group wrote, saying that they wanted to become a part of our work in the States. In time the ripples upon this pond would become 3,000 strong.

Not only had a doorway opened in Africa, but also one in England. The latter had originated through contact with organizations involved in work similar to my own. Due to England's apparent interest, I made the decision to set up a lecture tour in the United Kingdom. This time my journey would not take me from city to city, but from organization to organization.

There was no fear as I prepared for my first tour abroad. Seven years had passed since that wondrous day I found myself walking on God's path. The seasoning of my soul had taken me through the same wonders, hardships and glory that belong to all who seek to journey beyond mortality. Although the road may appear difficult, it is tempered with mercy, and at every turn there is an Angel to light the way. Each soul has a magnificence that will one-day rule over mediocrity. Who then can really turn away from the hand of God, for it is He who helps the soul to soar further than it has ever dreamed? Helen Keller once said, Life is either a daring adventure or nothing.

CHAPTER XIV

Dilemma
in England

As the classes in Phoenix began to wind down, I left the Seagull Too in the care of two of my new students, Benjamin and Judy, and prepared to leave for my first lecture tour in England.

Benjamin and Judy had heard of my work while they were living in California, and immediately hitched up their travel trailer for a move to the Southwest. Despite the fact that they were late in starting classes, they quickly became regulars, not only at the classes but also at our Scottsdale retreats. Benjamin was an excellent electrician who could find work anywhere, and Judy was a housewife, as well as a woman of few words. With Cheryl busy teaching, I soon found Judy on my doorstep ready to assist me every day. I was extremely grateful for the help of this wonderful woman. She and her husband were to remain in my life for many years and share numerous adventures with me. Because Judy and Benjamin made their home in a relatively large travel trailer, they were able to follow me wherever I taught.

As I boarded the plane for England and my first teaching appearances abroad, there was no particularly sense of nervousness.

Ah! Ignorance is such sublime bliss. While flying in the high blue yonder, I felt the confidence of one who has successfully maneuvered many a rocky mountain. Perhaps it was good, however, to be bathed in ignorance and noble sacrifice, for only a few short days would pass before I would be reduced to a blithering idiot. Had I known what lay ahead, I might have sought to open the emergency door and jump without a parachute. Of course, the angelic forces could have warned me, but there were simply too many lessons to be learned. (I believe that the angels secretly relish such times.) In spite of the forthcoming disaster, however, my initial contact with the people of England would affect my relationship with people in all countries forever.

Immediately upon landing, I went to a hotel to recuperate from the jetlag that inevitably results from overseas travel. Prior to leaving the States, I had purchased a Brit-rail Pass, which now enabled me to travel throughout the United Kingdom, as needed, without additional cost. This proved quite practical, particularly since my scheduled appearances would take me all over the country.

The next morning I awoke feeling refreshed and departed for one of many stations to catch a train to the location of my first lecture. Leaning against the seat, the clack of the wheels against the rails created a rhythmic sound and lulled me into a momentary sense of satisfaction. Outside my window, the beautiful English countryside passed in panoramic splendor before my eyes. I quickly decided that this was the only way for one to travel when going cross-country, for there is something unique and exciting about trains. From the dining car to the sleeping compartments, traveling by rail offers a level of comfort that simply does not exist on crowded airlines with their closely stacked seats. Trains also have their effect on the imagination, and many movies have been created around them, from murder mysteries to romance. Caught in the adventure of the moment, I found myself arriving at my destination all too soon.

My first appearance before the English people turned out to be far less successful than my train ride. While speaking that evening I looked into the faces of my audience expecting to see some of same excitement I was accustomed to seeing on the faces of my American audiences. Instead my words were rewarded with cold granite faces and borderline hostility. Unfortunately there was no place to hide. Meeting with some of the people after the talk did not help, for those who approached me were rigid in their polite courtesy. My only consolation was a fleeting reminder that I could leave the following morning for my next destination, and sorry that I had to wait.

The next day I boarded a train for Cornwall and my next appearance, but with far less optimism than on my arrival. While en route, I was scheduled to meet a man by the name of Sir George Trevalyn at one of the train stations. We had made previous arrangements to travel the rest of the way together. Sir George intended to help break the ice by introducing me to my next hostess. Apparently he knew her quite well, for he had conducted a number of classes in the Cornwall area prior to my visit. Formerly knighted by the Queen, Sir George was also the recipient of an Honorary Nobel Peace Prize for his work as an educator. Now retired, he went from place to place, speaking and teaching in order to open spiritual doors for those who sought a greater truth.

It is always interesting to meet someone whom one has never met before, particularly under such mysterious circumstances. I knew what Sir George looked like, but he did not know what I looked like. Once the train came into the station, I disembarked and immediately began to look around for him. In a distance I saw a tall, rather wiry but elegant, white-haired man. He was also looking around, so I moved toward him in order to introduce myself.

He later described our meeting, saying, "I was caught in the throes of excitement over the prospect of meeting some mysterious stranger. I would look at a person and tell myself that it could not be her. Then I would look at another and say the same thing."

Whether I was a disappointment to Sir George in the end, I will never know, for he was too much of a gentleman to ever express his opinion on such a matter.

Unfortunately, my second appearance before an English audience fared no better than my first. I had not been speaking very long before there was a knowing that things were not going well. Once again, I was facing cold, impenetrable eyes, which showed little warmth and no acceptance. Finishing my lecture, I was faced with a very difficult decision. Should I hide until my departure for the States and vow never to return to England, or make some effort to discover what the problem was? Since I still had a number of other speaking engagements scheduled throughout the country, the latter seemed to be the better of the two solutions, although at the moment, the more difficult choice as well.

After my talk was finished and people were taking a bit of time to enjoy their refreshments, I found enough courage to approach Sir George and asked to talk to him. He nodded in agreement. We managed to extricate ourselves from the main group and went someplace where we could have some privacy. As we stood together outside of the lecture hall I said quietly, "Sir George, I have to ask you something. I am failing miserably in my appearances before the English people, and I need to know what the problem is."

Looking at me kindly as though to soften the blow of his words, Sir George replied, "Elizabeth, you cannot come here to England and act as if we do not know anything."

Horrified, I looked up at him. Perhaps I could have gotten irate and insisted that he did not understand, as American speakers have sometimes done to me, but I chose to accept what he had to say. The Light that I bore had endowed me with the fortitude to ask, and now it gave me the strength to graciously thank him for his honesty.

Boarding the train the following day for my next destination, I had much to think about. Although I had never traveled abroad before, it had become rather obvious that American people were not generally well liked. It isn't because we are Americans, but more because we often appear brash and rude without realizing it. We all too often venture into other countries and rush from here to there in traditional American style. Just as often, we are careless in the niceties of good international courtesy. Now, as the wheels of the train clattered along beneath me, I had to face the truth: I too had been guilty of American haste.

As I rode, I reviewed my situation. It was painfully clear that my approach would have to be revised if I was to have any success with the English audiences. I decided to start changing immediately, and began by smiling kindly at the conductor. Next, I engaged in conversation with the person next to me and asked him to tell me something about the history of England. "How remarkable," I thought later. "We can go any place, anywhere in the world, and have a complete geography and history lesson if we are willing to listen rather than talk about ourselves."

Not only were the balance of my appearances in the United Kingdom much more successful, but they became so popular that I spent one month every year for the next eight years lecturing and conducting retreats in the beautiful English countryside.

Sometimes Sir George and I would meet and conduct a joint retreat. One such event occurred on a beautiful old estate, which had been purchased for use as a private college. On my arrival at Hawkwood I was met by the dean, who welcomed me much in the manner one would welcome arsenic or some other poison. This was not totally uncommon, for a female spiritual teacher is simply not as acceptable as most male teachers are. That attitude did not necessarily prevail in my public appearances and seminars, for I had become somewhat of a celebrity over the years. Nonetheless, that mindset regarding female spiritual teachers has been strongly evident from time-to-time throughout my whole teaching career.

Although Sir George was a friend of the dean, his presence did little to warm my welcome. I would like to say that the Dean's rejection did not bother me, but that would not be entirely true. There is always a deep pain when one is rejected, regardless of the reason. However, in a situation such as this, there is little one can do but continue with the work.

By the end of the one-week school, the situation had improved a great deal. The Dean took time from his busy schedule to sit in on some of the classes that Sir George and I taught, and as a result, he seemed to have developed a genuine respect for my work. This later became even more evident, for toward the end of my stay, the Dean invited me into his office to join him and Sir George in a fruit juice cocktail. When we finally parted company, he said, "Elizabeth, you and your people will always be welcome here."

Three years after Sir George and I met at Hawkwood College, an event occurred that summed up my entire relationship with the English people. I was giving my opening lecture one morning and said, "I know that you English people think that we Americans are barbarians, and that we haven't spoken proper English in years. However, I am here, and you are here; so perhaps we are now bridging that gap."

A woman sitting toward the back of the room quickly raised her hand. When I motioned that she could speak, she responded, "But you do not belong to just America anymore."

Apparently England had adopted me.

CHAPTER XV

No Room
at the Inn

*U*pon completion of my first tour in the United Kingdom, I returned to Phoenix and found that Judy and Benjamin had equipped the new van with cruise control. This took some time to get used to, but the feature served me well and eased the stress of driving such a heavy vehicle devoid of the customary driving amenities.

By this time, it was late spring. Cheryl had just completed her classes and sold her home. Thus, as the weather prepared for its Southern summer warm-up, we boarded the van and set sail together for our next series of adventures in the Seagull Too.

The first leg of our journey took us to Maine in response to an invitation I had received to teach there. I have always made it a practice to accept such offers, for it has been my personal belief that God opens many doors for us. If we do not walk through whatever door He opens, neither our work, nor lives, can be as successful as they would otherwise be. Only when we keep our commitments and follow the directions given by God and His

Angelic Kingdom, can He bring the forces into play that assure one of ultimate success. Unfortunately, we are all too often bound by self-will to be conscientious in our efforts to follow Divine Will.

Upon our arrival in Maine, Cheryl and I found that our hosts lived quite some distance from any town. Their home, as well as their adjacent art studio, was located almost on top of the beautiful rugged coastline, but isolated. It was obvious that people would not travel such a great distance to classes, and in the wintertime the roads would have been almost impassable. Therefore, I felt that we could accomplish very little by remaining there, and after taking a few days to enjoy the beauty of the seacoast we bid goodbye.

A rather curious event, with a somewhat humorous aftermath, occurred prior to Cheryl's and my departure from Maine. I received a letter telling me that the Professor Bordeaux had departed from his physical body. On reading the news, I was actually quite excited, for the Professor had been a great man and he deserved to continue his work without the hindrance of embodiment. I had known that his time on Earth was coming to an end for a couple of years now and I rejoiced that his present work was finished. I wondered, however, why he had not come to tell me of his departure himself.

There was barely time for me to ponder this question before there was a sense of his presence nearby. He seemed highly amused by my question, although I knew he had come to be with me in the event he was needed. Because it is quite common for a student to grieve deeply at the passing of a Master Teacher, I assumed that he probably visited a number of those who loved him. He was a kind man and would have wanted to insure that those remaining on Earth did not sorrow too deeply. At the same time, Professor seemed to be somewhat amused over the fact that I was taking his departure with great cheerfulness, and once he knew that I was aware of his presence, he materialized a bent arm and suggested that we go for a walk on the beach. Although his gesture was lovingly received, I did not accept the proffered arm because of a number of matters that was of deep concern, one was another change of location. Nevertheless, I have regretted this decision ever since.

The following day Cheryl and I bid our hosts farewell, but there was absolutely no idea about where we should go. The funds from teaching in Phoenix were rapidly dwindling and it was necessary for us to get to work as soon as possible, particularly since there was at least a six-week interim between my arrival and my first appearance. Also, there was no longer just myself to think about; I had to consider Cheryl.

It was time to have one of those serious talks with God. Looking up at the sky, which one often does when they think of Heaven, I said, "God, you need to tell me where I should go next. We have very little money; therefore I cannot afford to make a mistake."

Immediately, I heard the words, "Go to Tampa, Florida."

"Tampa, Florida," I argued, as usual, "You can't get any further from Maine than that."

He said again, "Tampa, Florida."

Looking over at Cheryl, wondering what she would think when she heard, I said, "Cheryl, we are supposed to go to Tampa, Florida."

If Cheryl was surprised, she did not show it. As we turned the Seagull Too toward Florida, I shook my head. The instructions were quite surprising, considering the distance between Maine and our assigned destination. While I did not understand God's reasoning, I knew that I would in time. By now I had learned that to follow His will meant that things would work out. This concept would certainly prove itself again in Florida, for our work throughout the state went very well. Cheryl proved to be a superb public relations spokesperson and succeeded in getting me interviews with almost every newspaper in the Florida, as well as appearances on almost every television and radio station, including those in more fundamental Christian areas.

During this time, as with much of the remainder of my life, what had now become the Dark Night of the Spirit placed a heavy hand on me. Although it differed in some ways from the purgation of the senses, it was still that same powerful force of God. He continued to work on every aspect of my soul and, with the assistance of my Angelic Teacher, He insured that I make atonement for any wrong to others and the process to purify my feelings, emotions, and actions, as well as in the mental and subconscious layers of my soul continued.

The purpose of this particular phase of the dark night is well defined in St. John's book. "These proficients who have reached the Dark Night of the Spirit have two kinds of imperfection: the one kind is habitual; the other actual. The habitual imperfections are the imperfect habits and affections, which have remained all the time in the spirit, and are like roots, to which the purgation of the senses has been unable to penetrate."

To me, the following words sum up the agony of this purgation best: "To this end God is pleased to strip them of this old man (lesser nature with its old desires and aspirations) and clothe them with the new man who is created according to God. He strips their faculties, affections and feelings, both spiritual and sensual, both outward and inward, leaving the understanding dark, the will dry, the memory empty and the affections in the deepest affliction, bitterness and constraint, taking from the soul the pleasure and experience of spiritual blessings."

Although I knew that my suffering was caused by the purgation of all my senses and that this was leading me to a happier life and oneness with God, I sometimes wept and begged Him to remove the crown. All was to no avail and He persevered in His disciplines.

When the holidays arrived, Cheryl and I traveled to Costa Rica in support of the Professor's wife, Norma, who was going to conduct her first seminar following the Professor's departure from his Earth form. She was still grieving deeply over her loss and I felt that this first Christmas might be especially difficult for her. It seemed that we, as students on the path, should give up our personal Christmas to help someone else. I contacted those who had studied with me in Arizona and invited them to join us in beautiful Orissi Valley, Costa Rica for the holidays. A number of them agreed, and later the Costa Rican airport at San Jose became a joyful place of reunion with many hugs and much excitement.

There were enough of us to collectively rent a private bus to take us on the two-hour journey from San Jose to Orissi Valley and its overview of several volcanoes. Our guide and bus driver could speak some English, which would prove to be a great blessing before the night was over. Having traveled extensively by this time I had learned that kindness and a lot of smiles carry a language all their own, so communication with our driver, Juan, progressed without too many complications. Wrapped in a cocoon of excitement we set off on the two and one-half hour drive from San Jose to Orissi Valley, first asking our guide to locate a suitable restaurant for us.

After eating, we left the metropolis of San Jose behind, eager to see what we could of Costa Rica's beautiful countryside. We were certainly not disappointed in this republic, which rests between the Caribbean Sea and Pacific Ocean and reputed to have been named by Christopher Columbus on his fourth and last voyage to America.

Professor Bordeaux had chosen Costa Rica, once called Nujeva Cartago, for retirement because it was a country of neutrality and peace. He felt a need to continue his work in an environment free from war. Having accepted the vow of poverty under the Order of the Franciscan Monks, Professor lived a very simple lifestyle. The main base of his operation existed in the form of a small house at the top of a long 45% incline overlooking four volcanoes. It had always been Professor's opinion that people did not get enough exercise and that if they walked; it should be uphill at an angle of approximately forty-five degrees. Therefore, anyone visiting him was compelled to get a measure of exercise first.

As we traveled along the elevated tableland rising 3,000 to 6,000 feet above the sea, we talked and occasionally broke out in song. The fact that it was also the day before Christmas cast a special aura over our journey. Here we were, a group of travelers, wandering in a strange land on Christmas Eve. Our reservations had been made at the one and only inn situated near the Professor's home and they had been confirmed. Before the night was over, however, we would share in a most unusual holiday adventure. I like to think of it as "no room at the inn."

It was dark when we arrived at our destination, and by this time some of our earlier excitement had worn off and we had relegated ourselves to quiet discussion. Most of us were very tired, for we had flown at different hours from different parts of the States. Now it was getting late. As we drove up to the entrance leading to the inn, however, we found the gate was locked. A few moments of silence passed while our driver seemed to contemplate our dilemma. Apparently in an attempt to alleviate our concerns Juan's voice had a decidedly cheerful tone when he spoke, saying that he would take care of everything. At least I think that is what he said. As Juan jumped over the gate and disappeared into the night, I am certain that each of us must have had a brief moment when we wondered what we would do if he did not come back.

Although Juan was gone for quite some time, eventually we saw him coming through the night wearing the smile of someone who had just won a marathon. He opened the gate, climbed onto the bus, and started the motor. Soon we began bouncing up and down on what was a rather rough road or lane. In limited English, Juan was able to convey the fact that the inn was not prepared for us but that they would hurry to get some rooms ready. In the meantime, we were to be taken to the only restaurant in the valley, which also happened to be adjacent to the inn. We were to wait there until we could take occupancy of our rooms.

It was now eleven P.M. As we sat in a dining room without

walls (I have no other terms to describe it), we could not help remembering another night when there was no room at the inn. I do not believe any Christmas will ever match the magical feeling of being in a foreign country and having no immediate place to stay. It was as though a miracle had descended upon us, presenting each of us with this special gift because we had given up our personal life and personal Christmas to give to another.

Eventually, the discussion worked its way around to my writing. At the time, I was about two-thirds through my first book, "Pathway of the Immortal." It was designed to serve as a textbook for my beginning classes, although there was little expectation on my part that it would ever become part of any best-seller list. Nonetheless, I was proud of my first work and relished the satisfaction that I would actually finish it. During my youth, I had seldom finished writing anything because I found that it took too long. The fact that I now was actually in the process of completing an entire book seemed miraculous.

While we sat listening to the rain falling on the over-hanging metal roof, someone asked me what I was going to write next. I replied that I really did not know, but it would probably have to be a health food book. At the same time I explained that this was not necessarily my preference. Judy, who had flown in from Phoenix with her husband, Benjamin, spoke up and suggested, "Why don't you do Revelation?"

For a moment I did not answer her, because who was I to interpret Revelation? At the same time, it certainly sounded like a much more exciting project than writing about health food. After a moment of thought I spoke the words that would open the doorway to one of the greatest adventures ever to befall me, "Yes, I think I will."

Shortly before midnight, we were notified that we could move into our rooms. Each unit could comfortably house several students, so I shared mine with Cheryl and Suzanne, an aspiring artist. To say that no more difficulties plagued us during our trip would not be quite true. Before an hour had passed, our unit was flooded with water from some unknown source. Rolling up our pant legs and removing our shoes, we prepared to mop up. It was two o'clock in the morning before we completed the task. In order not to succumb to poor dispositions, and having discovered long ago that a positive attitude creates a positive outcome, our group decided to name our particular unit Noah's Ark. Neither did we lift any of the mattresses to look under them during our stay in the Ark. I was afraid of what we might find, and what one does not know does not hurt.

Each day for the following week, we departed from the inn in the morning and walked up the steep incline leading to the Professor's small house. Our classroom was an open porch overlooking the beautiful Orissi Valley and its volcanoes. Unfortunately, it rained almost every day, and sometimes we became quite chilled as we sat and listened to the Professor's wife conduct her first seminar.

The highlight for me was seeing the countenance of the Professor once more. He always stood in the doorway and greeted us as we finished our climb. My students (and most of those attending were my students) had not yet developed inner sight, so they could not see him. Neither could his wife, although she could sense his presence. I will never forget that first day when we stepped onto the porch and I saw him standing there in his old familiar blue slacks and white shirt. Of course, he was aware of the fact that I could see him, and he smiled as he always did each time we met.

CHAPTER XVI

Appearance of
St. John The Beloved

Cooler weather had descended upon Florida by the time we returned from Costa Rica, freeing Cheryl and me from the heat and terrible humidity that had plagued us through the summer. We had also remained free of cockroaches for some time because of the bitter war I had waged on them when we first arrived. Over the weeks the cockroaches decided that the dozen or so other available apartments were more conducive for their steady encroachment on human society. The war had been fought without mercy, and although I acknowledged they were God's creatures, and perhaps I apologized to Him, I had spared neither the spray nor the cockroach motels.

Once our work in Florida was completed, a new door opened for Cheryl and me: We were given an opportunity to go to Hawaii. Having never been to the Hawaiian Islands, we eagerly accepted the invitation and prepared to return to Seattle where we would store the van. We packed everything in the apartment, loaded the van camper, and began our drive cross-country.

Immediately upon our arrival in Seattle, we stored the *Seagull Too* and proceeded to the airport to catch a flight to the island of Oahu. Our gracious host and hostess, Mr. and Mrs. Ing were Chinese and lived in the more aristocratic area of Alewa Heights. Upon the death of Mrs. Ing's mother and father, the property had passed on to her and her husband and now stood empty. Mr. Ing was a wealthy land investor who had become a client during my years at the school. It was he who had warmly invited us to come and experience Hawaii.

Cheryl and I took up residency in the large home—located just seven houses below the one occupied by the Ings. Nothing could have been more perfect, for the weather in Hawaii can be sublime. The house stood high on a hill overlooking Diamond Head and Waikiki, and the rooms that Cheryl and I primarily occupied were on the view side. Everyday we could look out over the beautiful panorama of the sea. Shortly after we settled in, an automobile appeared in our garage, courtesy of the Ings. This ensured that we would have transportation during our seven-month stay.

A few days after our arrival, I looked up to see a gentle Asian woman standing on the stairway. My immediate thought was that it was Mrs. Ing's mother, the original owner the property. She did not say anything, although she looked somewhat puzzled. At the time, I perceived that she wondered who we were and what we were doing in her house. Since she was not of solid human substance but encased in a semi-material body, I sought to mentally assure her that we would take good care of her home. She then graciously left us to enjoy our quiet surroundings and wonderful view. I did not see her again during the entire time we remained in Hawaii, but as always, I marveled over the remarkable vibratory shield that separates our world from that which is without dense form.

The seven months we lived in Hawaii and mingled with its people are among my most cherished memories. It was a period when God seemed to pour His special magic upon us, helping us in everything we did. My appearances drew large audiences, and these produced enough students to encourage me to remain for a few months and teach. Before long, I was once again enveloped in teaching. Our classroom was a large glassed-in living room overlooking Diamond Head, the famous Hawaiian volcano.

At the end of each month, I conducted two-day seminars, which also drew more and more people as time passed. My in-house workload was minimal because three more women, all students, came to live with Cheryl and me. Marilyn was from New York. Mary was from the island of Hawaii, and her sister, Verna, was from the Midwest. My all-woman ashram, as I fondly referred to our living quarters, freed me from much of the mundane daily chores, such as cleaning and much of the cooking.

The bedrooms that Cheryl and I occupied were upstairs. Between us was a private sitting room. This, too, overlooked the panorama of Oahu and presented an ideal ambiance for writing. Each of us had set up make shift offices in our bedrooms, and before long, the rat-a-tat-tat of clicking typewriters could be heard throughout the building. Computers had not yet become a way of life, at least not for us, and so Cheryl and I worked the old-fashioned way. At the time, it seemed natural enough, but when I think back on it now, I wondered how writers endured before the computer age.

The classes in Hawaii had barely begun when I decided that it was time to send Cheryl to Swami Chinmayananda to learn some of the ways of the East. Like most Westerners, Cheryl was somewhat casual regarding spiritual matters, which, in fact, require a fair amount of dedication in order to succeed. Therefore, I thought some Eastern-style discipline would be good for her. At the time, Swami was in southern California, where he had scheduled a month-long retreat at one of the colleges. It was a good time for Cheryl to leave, because "Pathway" would soon be finished, and plans for my next writing projects were not yet formulated. I felt also that the break would be good for her, since we had been in close quarters for quite some time. Therefore I wrote to Swami and told him that I was sending Cheryl.

While Cheryl was reluctant to go because she had been with me every day for over a year, and had shared in every experience, I insisted. She was gone only a week when I received an urgent telephone call from her, begging me to allow her to return. Apparently, where she was staying had several dorms, each one housing a number of people and she couldn't get any sleep. Some talked into the night, and others apparently indulged in all night meditative practices. All of this seemed to bother Cheryl a great deal. At the same time, Swami was also giving her special attention, meaning that he was doing a bit of pruning on her ego. Believing that the ego usually needs a bit of extra attention now and then, I merely laughed when she called, and said, "Cheryl, don't allow Swami to get the best of you. Stand up and fight." I doubted that she ever regretted her time with Swami, despite her initial difficulties.

While Cheryl was spending the month in California with Swami, I not only turned my attention to those students now gathered around me in Hawaii, but continued working on "Pathway of the Immortal." At the same time I started writing a little allegorical and visionary fiction book called "Maya Sangh," meaning *illusion talk*. A wise man had once said that "even to talk was half a truth," and I agreed with him. The book was a charming story about an infant taken to the Valley of the Sun to be raised by a Brotherhood, who knew the secrets of the universe but not how to raise a human child. Actually, much of the material in Maya Sangh was derived from my own personal experience with Okaji. Although I finished writing the shell of the book during our stay in Hawaii, twenty years would pass before I actually finished it.

At the end of April, Cheryl returned from California. By this time, I had finally completed the last pages of "Pathway." During the process, I kept an earlier promise I had made to God, that I would include a chapter on both natural foods and healing — if He would allow me to escape the doldrums of writing a health food book. Of necessity, therefore, these two chapters received very special attention. Otherwise my fear was that He might insist that I attend to people's digestive systems, rather than being allowed to write the book which had over-shadowed me since Costa Rica: *St. John's Revelation.*

Finally, Pathway of the Immortal, my first book, was turned over to a publisher. After the manuscript had been dropped off, my attention turned toward what I considered a more serious work. While thinking about writing "Revelation," a voice from the Angelic Kingdom spoke, saying, "There is a surprise in store for you."

The sun would rise and set only a few more times before the meaning of those words would touch my heart and soul, and launch me on an odyssey that could one day help change the understanding of the world.

The dawns of Hawaii are always magnificent, and thanks to Okaji's persistency I had finally developed a fondness for getting up early and greeting the sunrise. This particular day was, as usual, a glorious day, and Diamond Head stood in a distance like a silent sentinel. In the foreground I could see Hawaii's beautiful and opalescent waters, kissed by a touch of blue-gray and magenta. I knew the time had finally come to begin work on St. John's Revelation. Picking up my King James edition of the Holy Bible, I immediately turned to the apocalypse and began reading. Horror engulfed me, for it was the most complicated work I had ever tried to decipher. A few verses later, I laid the Bible down and shook my head, saying to myself, "Elizabeth, you must be kidding. How can you do what religious scholars for 2,000 years have not been able to do?"

When something seems impossible, my habit has been to set the matter aside for a brief time and take another look at it the following day. The consciousness of God has a remarkable way of overcoming the vagrancies of the mind during its non-involvement with matter, meaning during sleep. Sometimes what appears impossible at sunset is radiantly clear at dawn. For want of a better description, it is as though God downloads information during the hours the conscious self is asleep from the great computer in the sky to the small computer of the mind. On awakening, one suddenly seems filled with a knowledge and understanding that did not previously exist. It became obvious to me, if this book were ever to be written I would have to allow St. John's beasts and dragons to reveal themselves in their own time.

The next morning, I was awakened somewhat earlier than normal by a power beyond my own. Shortly after opening my eyes, I sat up and saw a wondrous light entering my room, a light not born from sunrises and sunsets, but from a world beyond mortal boundaries. In its center stood a beautiful countenance of a man whom I had never met. He introduced himself as John the Beloved, the original author of Revelation.

Despite my initial surprise, there was little time to marvel over John's appearance, for he was ready to begin work on the book. The consciousness of such an ascended master, meaning a master without embodiment, usually puts one at immediate ease. A visit from such a one is similar to the feeling one gets when being visited by an old, but revered friend. As St. John stood before me I felt, as though I had known him all of my life, and any awe I might have felt did not have time to manifest. Once more, I opened the Bible to Revelation and we began, taking each scripture in sequential order.

As the months passed, St. John revealed every mystery of his profound work to me. This included some of the more intimate details of his life, which lead me into areas that broadened my scope of understanding. Very soon, it became obvious that John was much more than a martyred saint who had been exiled on the Isle of Patmos; he was a Master, one who had successfully maneuvered, what is referred too in Christianity, as the Resurrection of the Dead. In the end, that was what his Revelation was, and is, all about: not a battle that takes place on land, but the battle of the soul as it fights for supremacy over its human nature.

By this time, my inner hearing had developed well enough to hear John's words as well as those of any human being, although I could not see him as easily. For him to appear in more solid form would have required him to lower his vibration, and I did not ask this of him. I was content to bask in the world of his conscious-ness and the mysteries he revealed to me. Admittedly, I enjoyed talking to him, however, and he became the special event in my life every morning for the next seven months. Without fail, he came at 6:15 a.m. and stayed until 9:30 or 10:00 a.m. As soon as he had departed, I found myself utterly incapable of interpreting the next scripture.

John, and I will refer to him in that manner, is not the tor-tured shell we often weave in our images of saints and martyrs, but he was a brilliant man. He possessed an amazing sense of quiet humor; one I feel the passing generations of theologians should have detected as they perused the mysteries of Revelation. His beasts and dragons match the images produced by some of the greatest writers of mythology. To have created such symbolism took not only great imagination, but also tremendous intelligence capable of obscuring the mighty secrets of spiritual of transformation within his creatures. Being in the throes of the dark night actually helped a great deal, and sometimes I found myself laughing at his beastly descriptions pertaining to the purification of the body, the mind, and the soul.

As we worked together, John would occasionally reveal per-sonal details surrounding his life, although this was not his pri-mary focus. I found his stay on the Isle of Patmos to be particu-larly intriguing, and much of it is historically verifiable if one studies his life. Apparently, John was forced into exile after narrowly es-caping being boiled in oil by Caesar. Later, he was placed on a boat with other prisoners and sent to the sparse island of Patmos, which was set apart for political offenders. His primary disciple, Proculus, had also been relegated to share the austerities of imprisonment, so John had a measure of companionship. Not only did this great man convert those aboard the ship to the teachings of Christ, he also converted the governor's daughter shortly after his arrival on the island.

While much of the forgoing material can be verified, John's optimistic outlook pertaining to his imprisonment cannot. It was here that his Revelation took root, not in a single downpour of transcendental experience, but rather as an author weaving a remarkable autobiography of his own journey through the transformation from human to divine. As John created his dragons and beasts, he tried to paint the glory of this reformation in enchanting allegory and leave its vision for mankind. He knew that every human would one-day pass through the resurrection and that our world would become a planet of peace.

Many people may wonder why John wrote in allegory and why he was so secretive. There were actually several reasons. First, John was a man of great wisdom, and like many other illumined people before him, he revealed the sacred mysteries thoroughly, but not openly. In other words, the truth was always there for everyone to read, but only those who had studied higher mysticism and were ready to approach the entry to transformation could actually interpret it.

Obviously, John was also a fine writer and this is personified through his numerous manuscripts, such as the "Lost Jesus Scroll," "Acts of John" and the "Gospel of John. He enjoyed creating beasts and dragons, each one representing some aspect of the mysterious transformation. Some signified the body, others the mind, and still others represented the purgation of the soul. Each dragon and beast was created absolutely perfect, in that each was mystically accurate.

Thirdly, allegory was a means of preserving his teachings.

At the time John wrote his Revelation, the followers of Jesus were being tortured and killed. Therefore, it was necessary to find a method to ensure long-term preservation of the apocalyptic secrets. To this end John was successful, for his work did survive, showing that he was clever as well as brilliant. Not even the Roman Vatican, which was once the greatest Christian Mystery School the world has ever known, was able to penetrate all of its secrets. Nonetheless, a whisper of its truth flowed down through the ages and took root in the Knights of the Round Table and organizations such as the Masons and the Order of the Rose Cross.

By now the twentieth century was coming to a close, and as my work with John unfolded I wondered about his appearances to me. Did this mean that the world was finally ready for the great truth of the Resurrection? Why had he chosen someone like me to reveal the interpretation of his mysterious writings instead of some great theologian?

To this day, I can provide but meager answers. Perhaps it was necessary for John to provide an extension of his original writings in a manner compatible with the modern mind. Insofar as "Why me?" I have very few answers. It is my hope, however, that this remarkable Master found my brain intoxicated with curiosity, my heart open to truth, and my intuition a sufficiently developed receptacle.

Reflecting on the months that John and I worked together, I cannot say that he gave all of the material to me easily. He did not dictate the book as many might think, but he taught in the process.

One day, I came across Revelation 12:14 and reached one of those impasses I frequently experienced when working on the *Apocalypse*, with the words "time," "times," "and half a time."

"And to the woman were given two wings of a great eagle, that she might fly into the wilderness, into her place, where she is nourished for a time, and times, and half a time, from the face of the serpent."

Realizing that I was greatly perplexed, John asked, "Now, Elizabeth, what is time?"

"Time," I replied, "signifies singular, or one."

"And times?" he asked.

"Times represents plural, or two."

"And half-time?"

"Half-time signifies that part of the day which occurs between the sunrise and high noon." I answered.

Then, as always, a light dawned, and I muttered, "Of course! When the two selves, the soul and the indwelling Christ, become one, then the Christ shall stand resplendent as the sun at high noon (1-2)."

After completing a complex scripture such as this, we would immediately go on to the next. One morning while attempting to decipher another one of John's numerous beasts, I shook my head and said, "Oh John, you have done it to me again!"

Revelation 13:2: "And the beast which I saw was like unto a leopard, and his feet were as the feet of a bear, and his mouth as the mouth of a lion: and the dragon gave him his power and his seat, and great authority."

With a smile, (for I believe this always amused him), John instructed, "Now Elizabeth, get a sheet of paper."

When I was ready, he said, "First, what does a leopard symbolize?"

I responded, "A leopard has spots and signifies the treachery of mankind's lower nature (black spots) opposing that which is divine in him."

Next, he told me to draw some bear paws and asked me what they meant. So I drew bear paws and told him how I defined them, knowing that he would correct me if I interpreted anything wrong. After that, he had me continue in the same manner with a mouth of a lion, after which the dragon gave this beast his power.

As the sheet of paper lay in my lap, a light dawned, and I joyously announced, "Of course! The deceits of man's ego, or lesser nature, are like spots on a leopard and must be rend, as a bear rends its carcass. Through this process, the ego is destroyed, in a manner likened to a lion (symbolizing the Christ nature in every human) tearing at the flesh of its kill. The impurities of the mind are therefore sustained by the ego's (dragon, or mankind's lesser nature) participation in the world of sensory enticements."

The weeks passed, as this wonderful Angelic Master led me through his Revelation scripture by scripture. By October, we had completed the entire work, for every single symbol contained in John's ancient writing had now been broken.

When it was finished, an Angelic voice spoke to me and said, "This book will still be read a thousand years from now."

After the voice had finished speaking, a vision of the future was shown to me. This work had indeed lived and was apparently being used by scholars in the future as a master key for deciphering Revelation.

Tears came to my eyes.

CHAPTER XVII

Pork & Beans & Africa

*I*t was fall again and time for me to return to England for another public appearance tour. The seven magic months in Hawaii had passed by quickly as though on the wings of the wind, and it was hard to leave. Our host and hostess encouraged me to remain, an idea that was very appealing to me. However, when I seriously entertained this delightful odyssey in my mind, I was told that I would miss an important appointment if I stayed and that I must return to Seattle after my tour in England was finished.

By that time, Cheryl had entered into the early stages of the dark night of the senses. Although I did not realize it at the time, I would soon discover that her spiritual work lay in a different direction. Obviously, however, the Angelic Kingdom was aware of this and told me that she was not to go to England with me this time. Sadly, I bid her farewell, although our paths would cross a number of times throughout the ensuing years. Cheryl went on to establish an alcoholic awareness institute in Phoenix, Arizona, and her work with youth alcohol and drug addiction training programs has ultimately become known worldwide.

Packing everything except what I needed abroad, I shipped a number of boxes back to Seattle and caught a plane to England. After England, I planned to go on to Ghana, West Africa and visit with my few students there. At the time, I little dreamed that I would never return to beautiful Hawaii or swim once more in God's bathtub at Waikiki.

As my third tour in the United Kingdom neared its conclusion, I turned my attention toward West Africa. Despite the fact that there were but a mere handful of students there, I decided that a visit was necessary anyway. I had been shown that Africa would one day become a great and powerful united nation. It was my hope that when this time came, some thread of the deeper spiritual truths would have survived, and that they would become a part of creating a greater Africa. So, with suitcase in hand, I boarded the plane that would take me from London to Accra, Ghana, West Africa, and yet another great adventure.

Ghana is home to some 75 different tribes; the most numerous are the Akan, followed by the Mole-Dabani, all of which are predominately English speaking. It is not only an independent nation of over 18 million people, but its primary religion is Christianity; mostly divided between Protestantism and Roman Catholic. The remarkable Volta River basin dominates the flatlands of Ghana, while grassland plains garnish the north and heavily laden forests adorn the south. The southern coastal plain, known as the famous Gold Coast, extends inland for thirty to fifty miles, and is home to lions, leopards and elephants. However, it is also home to something else – painful memories of human abasement. The country was once a major center for slave trade and a faint memory of those times still linger in the minds and hearts of Ghana's people.

The capital is Accra, seaport and largest city of the Gold Coast. The climate is wonderfully moderate and dry, with temperatures between 73-86F. Its name seems to be a European version of *nkran*, meaning *black ant*, applied by the Akan speaking peoples, who in the 16th century arrived from Nigerian to settle on the Accra plain.

From Accra, tarred arterial roads lead westward along the coast to Cape Coast and Takoradi, eastward to Togoland, north Kumasi and beyond. It is a haunting land, touched by mystery, intrigue and simplicity. At the same time, it possesses a quiet simple beauty that soon captivates its visitors.

From the moment my plane touched down on the runway in Africa, I fell in love with both the country and its people. We landed during the early evening, the most enchanting period of the African day. The soft breeze, which I would find magically appears at sunset, greeted me when I landed. A short distance away, a small retinue of students was waiting for me to disembark. It was not necessary for me to stand in line to take my luggage through customs, as almost immediately, one of the waiting students took charge of the matter and whisked my luggage away. Soon he came back smiling and said it had all been taken care of.

It somewhat surprised me to discover that all of the students spoke excellent English, and that most of them had college educations. Here was a country whose people dwelled in utter poverty by the standards of American culture, yet they were well educated. At that time, and it may still be so, it seemed that the African government provided its people with an opportunity to attend college and the government paid for it. I had difficulty not comparing Africa to America in this instance. The cost of attending a university in America had long been a thorn in my side because they are too expensive for many worthy students to attend. I wish that the educational system in the United States operated in the same fashion as Africa, for as I observed these relatively poor but well-educated African people, I felt that they had riches beyond compare.

As soon as I had been cleared through customs, I was whisked away to a Christian school where accommodations for my residency had been arranged. Although I did not wish to offend my African hosts in any way, one look at the open food on the table, and later, what I considered to be an unclean bed, left me deeply concerned for my health. As in India, I was afraid that I might be carried off by unseen creatures, some of them previously relegated to the pages of science fiction. However, my greatest fear was picking up a disease.

Unfortunately, I had not renewed my shots before coming to Africa. Even though my doctor had written a letter stating that the vaccinations would be harmful to me, the African Consulate had refused to grant me amnesty from them. Remembering the aftermath of my cholera inoculation and feeling that I could not go through that illness again, I took the health papers I had used for India, and changed the apparent dates of the injections. My ruse worked, and I received clearance from the Consulate to enter Africa. Now I had to face the possible repercussions.

After sleeping with the light on the first night, I talked with my sponsors and told them how much I appreciated all that they had done. Then I explained to them that because of possible health complications, it would be necessary for them to find me a motel or hotel that was a bit more isolated from public contact than the school. Certainly I did not want to offend my gracious hosts, but what is clean to those who live in undeveloped countries is not necessarily clean to a Westerner.

Although I spent the next night in a hotel, in truth it was not much better than the Christian school. The room had no window and was therefore quite dark and dreary. Confident that strange creatures lurked in the hidden corners of the room, I again slept with the light on — not because I was afraid of the dark, but more because I hoped that light would prohibit strange and mysterious nocturnal creatures from prowling the night. Of course, I do not mean to infer that America does not also have its tenements, pollution and garbage-strewn roadways. Nonetheless, Western culture provides certain conveniences not available in poverty-ridden countries, such as high power vacuum cleaners and laundry facilities.

By the third night the matter was finally resolved, and I settled into a hotel sufficiently clean to prevent any possible reprisals from my lack of inoculations. Also, the wife of my host was now preparing my evening meals, and she delivered them to me carefully covered with a napkin. Our combined efforts kept me free from illness for the duration of my visit.

The slight inconveniences of Africa did not stop me from enjoying its people, its culture and its amazing ability to find happiness amidst the poverty. Neither did the poorness of its nation bother me, because I too had been poor when I was growing up in Idaho. Since then, I had also spent many months living in a tent during my travels. I understood why African people looked upon Americans as being wealthy, for what is so common to us, such as washers and dryers, refrigerators and dishwashers are not within the reach of the common masses of Africa. Some of the African people were surprised when I told them that many Americans could not afford hospitalization or go to college, or buy food for their children.

Africa had truly captivated me, and I believe it will do the same for anyone who visits it. Never have I seen such beautiful children any place in the world, nor can I forget the soft evening breezes or the sound of distant drums and chanting. Even more amazing to me, was the perfection with which things were accomplished. Every one of my appearances had not only been setup in advance, but also run perfectly. The students had never arranged such appearances, yet they seemed to intuitively sense what had to be done. Every task was accomplished in a most precise and orderly fashion.

Each morning as I departed from the hotel and prepared to travel to the Christian school, I found one of the male students standing outside my door. Whoever was assigned to me that day never left my side during shopping or any other exposure I might have to the outside world. Whenever I wanted to buy something, my escort negotiated the price for me, explaining that the students were afraid I would pay more than I should because those operating the kiosks sold their wares by bargaining. Of course I could not resist bringing home some African treasures for future Christmas gifts, and I had to add a piece or two to my ever-growing school museum.

When I arrived at the Christian school, my work began immediately and continued far into the night. People stood in line and waited hours to see me, asking that I remove some curse, or help them with some health problem, or encourage them with a glimpse into their lives. It was easy to create what appeared to be miracles, for the people believed that I could. Actually, nothing that I did was a miracle in my own mind, although I suppose seeing into their future and describing their ailments might have appeared so to them. By simply visiting with me for a few moments, anyone who believed that they were cursed immediately believed the curse had been removed, and they departed from me radiant and joyous. As I watched them leave I felt a deep sense of compassion. How I wished I could have conveyed to them the magnificence of a world yet to come, and the vision of their country as it would be 5,000 years into the future. But that would have to wait. The African people would grow into it and create it in time, but until them they would have to toil.

One morning upon my arrival I noticed a teenage girl waiting for me. When I inquired regarding her, I learned that she had refused to go home until she saw me, and that she had waited patiently all night. I put my arm around her and took her inside, saddened by the fact that she had waited so long. After she told me of her problem, it became apparent that she had a tapeworm. This was not uncommon, nor was venereal disease, for Africa was and is without many of the amenities of Western culture. How I wished I had brought some herbs and homeopathic medications to ease the suffering of these people. However, this was my first visit to Africa and I had been afraid to do so, lest their Customs Inspectors believe that I was trying to bring in drugs.

Sadly, I found myself ill equipped to do anything for the girl, since many of the substances that might kill the tapeworm could also prove harmful to a person. Surgery is, of course, another way, but that was not an option at that moment. Therefore, I could do little but recommend that the girl be given medical help. It was logical to assume that the doctors in Africa had dealt with this many times. However, I swore then that should I ever return to Africa I would not only insist on bringing a doctor with me, but I would also bring some simple homeopathic and herbal remedies.

Natural methods of healing were very important to this country so far from the Western world. The African people suffered a great deal, and too many were unable to afford proper medical treatment. Therefore, my first discourse in Ghana was on the topic of natural healing.

Arrangements had been made for my talk to take place in a large tented area. This was not a surprise, for many schools and other facilities in Ghana did not have walls. I found this situation quite pleasant, for walls seemed unnecessary in such a warm climate. What did surprise me was the large attendance, which consisted primarily of medical doctors who had come from all over Ghana. When I begin speaking on the attributes and techniques of natural and spiritual healing, my audience proved to be most receptive as well as curious.

Spiritual healing is free to everyone, and all benefit from it. Combined with medical knowledge, this form of healing transcends even homeopathic treatment, primarily because the vibratory frequency of spiritual healing is more refined than anything having solid form. Like homeopathy, the pure energy force of the Creator does not destroy the disease, but rather refines it. In time, occasionally almost instantly, the disease is restored to its true state, that of non-disease. With practice, anyone can learn to mingle with the consciousness of God and eventually learn to allow His power to flow unhindered by the human mind into the seat of the illness. That is where and when the miracles occur.

The laying on of hands is one of more common forms of spiritual healing. This allows a focal point for the energy of the universe to flow into the patient, as well as an opportunity to free the mind sufficiently to merge into a higher consciousness. A person does not actually possess the power to heal as a mere mortal, but prayer, meditation and concentration are all tools, which enable the mind to mingle with the creative energy of the universe. As I explained to those attending my lecture, one must develop the ability to submerge one's own consciousness into that of God. A person should never try to heal another with the finite mind, primarily because one is dealing with subtle, but impressionable cells. The finite mind of a person without medical knowledge can send the wrong *message* to the cellular structure of the body, such as energy to a growth, rather than restoring the growth to its original non-existent state. Therefore, the ability to surrender the human mind to Divine Will is of paramount importance.

Following my talk, the audience asked many questions. On leaving the tent with my escort I felt that I had been able to give something of value back to these people who proved to be such wonderful hosts.

My next appearance was scheduled at the Christian school, and was one of the most unusual speaking experiences I would ever encounter. My speaking platform was a raised area without a roof. It was early evening and the soft African breeze I had come to love so much once again lent itself to the magic of the moment. The sky was clear, but dusk was consuming day. My students, along with members of the school, had hooked up a loudspeaker and a fan. The latter not only ensured that I remained cool, but it also kept flying insects from becoming a distraction. It seemed that the longer my voice flowed out through the evening, the more people took their seats in the open pavilion below. I do not know if all of them could understand me, but that did not seem to make any difference. To them, this was a special event, and they merged into it as smoothly as they danced to the beat of the drums.

In the Western world, one often forgets simplicity in their search for some measure of peace. Here in this amazing country so far from America, I found a people who thrived on a simple lifestyle, and in doing so they shared a different kind of wealth. Unfortunately, that is now beginning to change, for Western civilization is having a direct influence on Africa. The African people are beginning to desire the conveniences they see and hear about through the media, and inner peace has departed from them. They cannot be blamed for having these desires, for they also want full stomachs and nice homes for their families.

Little did I know at the time that Ghana, West Africa would one day become our largest associate, and would host over three thousand students before the beginning of the new millennium. In 1998, I received a letter from our Bishop, saying, "The work you came here to do has been done. We are the only peaceful nation in all of Africa."

Adventures into the unknown always have their humorous moments also, and a series of such incidents occurred during my stay in Africa. As in India, these had to do with food.

Before my arrival, my hostess had written and asked me if I liked pork and beans. Although I had been fond of them as a child, I had declined them in recent years because of my involvement with natural foods. Nevertheless, I responded to their inquiry by writing that, yes, I liked pork and beans just fine. Now, each time my dinner was served, a part of it consisted of pork and beans. No matter how hard I tried to get my hostess to understand that I would be satisfied with plantain and rice, Africa's primary diet, it was to no avail. Gratefully, I found that I still liked pork and beans, and came to the conclusion that they were less hazardous than coming to Africa without my shots. So I ate them.

To this day, however, I am particularly amused when I remember the very last meal I ate during my visit. It turned out to be the ultimate climax of the pork and bean saga. One of my students mentioned that she wanted to cook a special dinner for me and that she would like to host it at her brother's place. Apparently, he was a school principal and had a nice home. I remember looking up at the sky, as I always did when I talked to God, and thanked Him profusely for my timely rescue from pork and beans on this final night of my visit.

The next evening when I arrived at the spacious home of my student's brother, I received a warm greeting. As we sat talking, I saw a young servant girl pass by carrying a silver can. I was certain that I knew what was in it. Suffice to say that as we sat down to eat a delightful meal, I noticed that it included pork and beans. "Oh! Pork and beans," I commented, trying to present a cheerful countenance.

"Oh, yes," my hostess said, "I asked your minister's wife what you liked to eat."

At that moment, I promised myself faithfully that when I returned to the States, I would eat a salad as large as the airplane. I kept that promise. Now, whenever I tell this story about my nightly rendezvous with the pork and beans in Africa to my students, I always end by saying, "On my return home, for a period of three days I consumed a salad as large as the airplane. On the third day, I resurrected."

All too quickly the time for my departure from Africa arrived. The students insisted on going to the airport with me, and I shall never forget that night. As I walked across the airstrip to the plane, the black and white African shawl the students had given me was thrown across my shoulders. The soft familiar breeze swirled the shawl around me, and in those moments there was a feeling of oneness with this country so far from the United States. Before climbing the steps to board the plane I turned to wave goodbye, for what would be the last time. The students had walked out on the flat roof of the terminal and stood, in single file, around the edge of the porch-like structure waving against the dusk of approaching night.

The wonderful people of Africa have never been forgotten, for I carry them in my heart. Neither have I lost contact with them, but have continued to help whenever possible by sending tapes and books. A few years after my visit to Ghana, the students had grown to over a thousand strong, and together they had built the Elizabeth M. Burrows Peace Center. When someone asked me for a picture of myself so that they could put it on the altar by Jesus' picture, I grinned up at the heavens and said, "Watch out Jesus, here I come."

After flying back to the Midwest and completing some pre-arranged appearances in that section of the United States, I returned to Seattle. Mr. Ing, who had hosted Cheryl and me in Hawaii, also owned a number of apartment complexes in the Emerald City. He and his associate were now kind enough to provide a nice apartment. Although Cheryl had returned to Phoenix to begin her work in youth alcohol and drug addiction, Judy and Benjamin had moved to Seattle and were waiting for my arrival. Within a few hours after retrieving the van camper from the storage garage, I settled into the apartment. Before long Judy and I were hard at work re-establishing the school that had been left behind two and half years earlier.

CHAPTER XVIII

Writer's Nemesis

The first thing Judy, Benjamin and I had to do after my arrival from Africa was to find a place large enough to conduct classes. This led us to one of the more amusing situation associated with what would turn out to be a series of buildings.

On a Sunday morning, as the three of combed the city in an effort to find a place we could afford; we stumbled on a run-down uninhabited house. It was not only uninhabited, but it was also completely unsuitable for anything other than spiders, bugs, and rats. We entered through an unlocked door and worked our way through two stories of rooms. The smell reminded me of a garbage dump. Naturally, we immediately turned thumbs down on the idea of trying to convert it into a school.

One thing frightened me about the house, however, and that was the fact that the very large living room had a fireplace and yellow walls. A few days earlier, I had been given a vision that we would take a very unkempt place with yellow walls and a white painted fireplace. During the vision, I seemed to be scrubbing and cleaning yellow walls similar to these with impassioned vengeance. Now this vision seemed to manifest before me in living color and situated right in front of my eyes. I looked at the dirty white fireplace framed with yellow walls, which were just as dirty, and raised my eyes to Heaven, muttering, "Oh, God, please don't tell me this place is in my destiny!"

The next day, as Judy and I were about to begin another day of searching, I looked over at her and asked, "What do you think, Judy? Do you think we can make that place work?"

She did not ask me what place.

"I think so," she replied.

Off we went to sign a lease.

Subsequently we signed an eighteen-month lease with an option to buy, and hastened back to tell Benjamin the great news. A look of disbelief crossed his face. His expression and words summed up the situation well. When we told him that we had taken the place we had all turned down the day before, he let out a terrible moan, which sounded like something between a death rattle and someone who just got thrown out of an airplane without a parachute. He cried out, "Oh, my God, no!"

When the three of us began the work on the uninhabitable building, we were in fairly good spirits; but as the long hard days wore on, we sometimes wondered if we had taken on more than we could handle. One day, while scrubbing yellow walls, I said, "God, I wonder what I will be doing five years from now?"

Pausing for a moment, I added, "Oh, I know I will be teaching, but one wonders what kind of a building we will be in."

Suddenly, a scene unfolded before me. I seemed to be standing in a large foyer, and hanging overhead was a beautiful crystal chandelier. Shaking my head at Him, I said, "God, I believe everything you tell me. However, I want you to know that with the allowance you give me, we cannot afford a crystal chandelier."

Having made my comments, I faithfully returned to scrubbing the yellow walls. Had the vision continued I would have seen 25 students, now painters, sitting in a beautiful foyer awaiting the lighting of a glorious crystal chandelier. Five years would pass before this vision bore its fruit.

Once the renovation on the property had been completed I returned to the South. While traveling, most of my nights were spent in the van camper. By this time God and my Angelic Teacher allowed me to watch occasional television, but it was necessary to be quite selective in what shows I watched. So, for Christmas Judy and Benjamin gave me a small five-inch set. Now it would be possible to hook up to a campground cable and enjoy a few moments of respite from the long grueling days of driving and negotiating with the media. My writing also proceeded, although I was still not computer literate. Eventually, my manual typewriter was traded for a word processor, which had a small screen capable of displaying two sentences at once. It seemed like a touch of Heaven after working on manual and electric machines for so many years.

Writing was a nemesis for me. The publishing world was, and still is, based upon what sells. While this is understandable, it did not enhance my popularity, for it seemed to be a common rule for many publishers at that time to accept nothing which combined evolutionism and creationism. The problem was not so much that my work did not have some merit, but I could not separate the two factions of creationism and evolutionism in my writing. Of course, this was not the only drawback. I also taught a reality without Satan, and could adequately prove that he did not exist, at least as he is generally conceived. I believe that some publishing houses may have thought that my work would prove to be as dangerous to them as a hydrogen bomb, although a number of my rejects were quite glowing.

If discarding Satan was not sufficient to hamper the sale of my writing, the concept that one might have to re-enter a series of embodiments in order to progress was also considered heretic, Eastern, or at best relegated to New Age advocates, who were looked upon as cults. To conceive such a reality threatened the foundation of Western beliefs. After my merger into the consciousness of God, however, I saw that His Divine Plan created all people with equal potentiality. Only through successive re-entry into embodiment for the purpose of soul progression could God provide a fair, equitable means by which all people could have their moment of greatness in the winds of destiny.

If reality was really as many believe, it would be necessary to accept a universe governed by a biased God. Fortunately, the laws of the universe express through all life forms, and a seed of greatness dwells in every soul in spite of corporeal sense vagrancies that attract it to matter. This is not a new concept, but one that has been taught by every enlightened religionist, philosopher, scientist, poet, musician, and writer throughout the ages.

One aspect of the Dark Night of the Spirit is that it brings a conscious awareness of everything which the soul has undergone since it began human existence. It also helps it to work out every unlearned lesson, even as it purifies the body and the mind. Nothing has been hidden from God, and every transgression of the soul stands revealed when the indwelling Light is raised from its tomb of unknowingness.

Throughout Revelation, John the Beloved discusses the soul's pain as it struggles to overcome its darkness and unknowingness and to set itself free from corporeal attraction. However, he also speaks of the glory of the soul and its ultimate victory. It is this influence that enabled his Apocalypse to survive through two thousand years of illiteracy, and the promise that helped me to face my own vagrancies and indiscretions.

The Apocalypse now stood resplendent in all its glory, with every symbol broken, but the publishing media seemed to find it unacceptable. Although hundreds, even thousands of books had been written on the subject, none of them completely revealed the fact that St. John's writings did not pertain to the end of the world. Some of the greater and more enlightened writers alluded to it, but they did not fully disclose it. Here I was — not some preacher or rabbi, but a simple woman who could not possibly be qualified to discuss such profound wisdom. Every publishing house rejected my work, and "The Hidden Secret of the Apocalypse" was ultimately shelved in despair.

With enough rejects on St. John's Revelation to start a wallpapering business, I decided to turn my attention to Jesus' life. As I mentioned earlier, I wanted to write a book about him unlike any book that had ever been written. Primarily, I wanted to introduce him to the world as a Master and at the same time reveal his lost teachings. Therefore, while I traveled I began working on "Jesus, The True Story."

The title, in part, came from a meeting I had with Reverend Don Jacobs during my sojourn in Hawaii. Reverend Jacobs, who became known as Moby Dick after the name of the great white whale, was a large, rotund person with short, dark beard and a wonderful personality. A graduate of Southern Methodist University, Don had served as a Methodist minister from 1945 to 1955, specializing in ancient Biblical history. He had read the entire Bible in several translations, including the New Testament in early Greek.

Like many people, Don became obsessed with the truth of Jesus' life, particularly his birth date. This led him into the research work of several astronomers. He became particularly captivated by the discrepancies existing between the Kepler calculations, those of Schnabel, and the calendar events that covered the last three years of Jesus' life. The dates these astronomers presented apparently could not have produced a genius of Jesus' magnitude.

For eight years Reverend Jacobs sought another date. By this time, modern technology had devised new ways to determine the exact placements of heavenly bodies during certain important historical events. Using a computer, Don diligently worked forwards and backwards over the configurations to find a period when planetary influences were sufficiently exacting to bring forth a person of such extraordinary genius. He gave particular attention to Kepler's calculations, but they were weak on two points: first, the configurations did not follow Biblical chronology; and second, the astronomer's calculations would not have signaled the birth of a soul of Jesus' magnitude. Then, when Don least expected it, a five planetary conjunction showed up on his equipment. He was amazed to find that it not only coincided perfectly with the scriptures, but also indicated the birth of someone who would possess a genius greater than the common person.

In time Reverend Jacobs left the ministry and became an astrologer, calling himself Moby Dick. To carry on with the theme of his new name, he wore white shirts and slacks, or white suits for dress. His book "Astrology's Pew in Church" is a remarkable piece of writing, although now out of print. However, I was fortunate to receive an autographed copy during my visit with him many years ago. His book contains the configurations of Jesus' birthday and consists of numerous trines, or three point configurations. These overlap each other, forming into a giant harp.

When I began to work on an outline for the book, Jesus appeared to me and asked that no miracles be included. He did not explain his reasons, but unspoken words often reveal the consciousness behind them. It was clear that Jesus wanted the world to have his lost teachings. He also wanted the world to cease worshipping him for his miracles and live as he taught, so that every person might ignite their own Divine Flame and express their true greatness.

As the work proceeded on "Jesus, The True Story," I hoped that Jesus might come to me each day as John had done. However, the work about his life took a different course. As I had once been united with the Professor's consciousness, my mind now seemed linked to Jesus' consciousness. While writing, I sensed and felt every detail of the book, just as he had lived and experienced them in his life. If I started to write something that had shadowed tinges of unreality, a crushing heaviness fell over me and my writing was not allowed to continue until the subject matter was corrected.

To further enhance the details of the book on Jesus' life and offer a realistic view of the topography where he grew up, I decided that it would be necessary to travel to Israel. By this time fall had taken over and, as autumn gave birth to its myriad of glowing colors, preparations began for my annual tour to England. As usual, my teaching schedule was full. Therefore, it seemed feasible to go to Israel after completing my work in England, now my second home.

At this time, I teased my students by telling them I had a date with a man in Israel and that it was long overdue. They were aghast over the idea that their teacher might condescend to date a flesh and blood human. After having a bit of fun at their expense, however, I finally revealed that my date was by no means human.

Like most people, the holy lands had beckoned to me throughout much of my life. Now, at last, I would finally walk with Jesus, at least in memory, along the shores of Galilee. My assistants, Judy and Benjamin were not to be left behind, and they, with their older daughter, Jeanine, made the decision to travel with me. In October, just as the early chill of autumn embraced the Seattle area, the four of us boarded a plane for England.

At the end of my public appearance tour in England, we departed for Israel. Because of my long overdue date with the Master, I wondered if he might meet the plane, although there was no real expectation that he would do so. Since he held one and a half billion followers in his heart I knew his time was restricted, and I usually tried not to increase his burden. This was my gift to him. Nonetheless, there was still a faint tinge of human desire, a hope that he might come. At the same time there was little doubt, but that he would make his presence known some time during our stay.

The plane was about ten minutes away from landing in Tel Aviv when Jesus came. He came not just for me, but for everyone, and for a few magic moments he held the entire plane in the embrace of his heart. Most people were probably not aware of the special feeling that must have flowed through them; and if they were, they probably believed that it was merely the excitement of arriving in the Holy Land. Nonetheless, I knew. Even though he departed prior to our landing, I was overjoyed that he had come, as he always had, in a surprising and an unexpected manner.

The home of three great religions, Christianity, Islam, and Judaism, Israel did not openly display the bloody wars that had taken place within its borders. As we traveled through this mystical land, I felt a deep sadness over the fact that man, the crowning achievement of creation on Earth and of one God, should fight because of religious differences. For me, it seemed almost impossible to conceptualize that religion had been a major cause of dissension among people for hundreds of years. Even now, it still is.

There was also a sense of loss and it touched me deeply as we visited Jerusalem. I would have preferred that everything had remained as it had been 2,000 years ago. But, things change, and many places had succumbed to the natural movement of progress. Part of the Old City was now covered with modern housing. Temples, mosques, and cathedrals overshadowed the holy places where the Master had once taught. Even the Via Dolorosa, the path of sorrow, where Jesus had carried his cross, was lined with merchants trying to sell their wares. I resented their harsh intrusion on my thoughts and feelings, as we were pushed and jostled by busy crowds going about their daily shopping. Therefore, I sought a quiet solace as we traveled through the surrounding deserts, which as yet remained unscathed by the touch of human hands.

According to my research, Capernaum and the Garden of Gethsemane had been Jesus' two favorite places to teach. Of the two, it was Capernaum that captured my heart. Sitting on the steps of the ruins of an old temple some 680 feet below the level of the Mediterranean Sea and looking out over the beautiful Sea of Galilee, I could almost imagine that we had stepped aboard a time machine and traveled back through the ages. It was easy to understand why Jesus had chosen this site as one of his retreats, for it seemed to be an oasis of solitude against a backdrop of metropolitan influence. I could imagine Jesus sitting with his disciples on the shore of this beautiful sea, once called the Lake of Gennesaret, through which flows the famous Jordan River.

Unfortunately, all things must end. Our reverie was broken by the announcement that our tour bus was departing. Looking over the beautiful blue water one more time, I did not bid just farewell to this sacred place, but also farewell to those special moments I had shared with the Master in my heart. There was no foreknowledge that I would return to this land one day and that when I did, my journey would transcend all human expectations and would be overshadowed by both the power and love of the great Angelic Kingdom.

While touring along the Jordan River, I asked the bus driver if he would stop long enough to allow me to baptize Benjamin and Judy. Earlier, they had both expressed a wish to do this; and of course, I wanted to have what I so often refer to as, the "John experience." To our delight, our driver and guide kept announcing to everyone that we were going to stop on the banks of the Jordan for a *baptismo*. This charming phraseology stuck in my mind long after I had returned to the United States. Later, I often found myself having some difficulty saying the word baptism.

When we arrived, at what our guide considered a suitable site along the riverbank, the bus was brought to a halt. Everyone got out and stretched, while I led Benjamin and Judy into the warm waters of the Jordan to receive baptism. As I performed the rite according to the ancient customs, I had a great deal of difficulty maintaining calm fortitude, for hundreds of little fish were nibbling at my feet. It was necessary to keep shuffling them to ward the fish off, at the same time not appearing to do so. This was supposed to be a solemn occasion, and I tried to make it so for

Judy and Benjamin. At the same time, one had to wonder how John the Baptist fared under such circumstances 2,000 years earlier, or if there had been fish in those days to munch on his toes.

On the last day of our visit, I informed Judy and Benjamin that I must return to the Via Dolorosa. So far we had only walked a portion of it. However, during the preceding night, the Angelic Kingdom had instructed me that this task had to be accomplished in its entirety before leaving Israel. Although there was no necessity to have company, I was glad when my three traveling companions expressed their desire to join me. Before long, we reached the beginning of the "Path of Sorrow" and began our walk. I do not know exactly what I expected, if anything. It was not long, however, before an agonizing pain affected my thighs, making it difficult to walk and even more difficult to climb. This unusual but excruciating pain puzzled me, and when I mentioned it to Judy, she said, "Elizabeth, I believe that it is the same pain which Jesus experienced as he walked the Via Dolorosa during his final hours."

There was in me a sense that her words were probably true: I was indeed experiencing the pain Jesus had felt when he carried his cross to Golgotha. How else could I describe the last period of his life in "Jesus, The True Story"? Consequently, by the time we reached the designated site of the cross and the end of our destination, I was in serious discomfort. Yet, the four of us each had the satisfaction that we had persevered until the end. By the time we boarded our plane that night to return to the United States, the painful influence of the Via Dolorosa had dissipated.

Once Israel was behind me, much of my attention became focused on writing "Jesus, The True Story." This experience would exceed any and all expectations. Books and translations of books with unknown, but valid information came into my hands. Before long, it became relatively easy to determine which were fraudulent and which were not. The main obstacle remaining was that of surmounting the rigid and long-established pre-conceived ideas surrounding the Master's life. It often seemed that one had to believe within the parameters of common precepts, or else included amongst the names of a long line of accused heretics. I was not the first to stretch beyond the boundaries of acceptable standards, for the list was long and was comprised of some of the greatest Christian philosophers the world has ever known. My consolation while I wrote was in knowing that my feet were walking the same uncharted waters as many greats before me.

During the months while the book gathered meat on its skeleton, each of Jesus' followers who were included in the book appeared to me. One of my favorite moments occurred when I met John the Baptist, although it was certainly in a very unique, but quite humorous manner.

While sitting cross-legged on the bed one night and having just turned out the light in order to meditate, I saw a silver platter floating by me. John's head was on it. As I watched the platter cross in front of me, I made an effort to capture every detail, and remember saying, "John, you were very good-looking, even without your body."

For several days thereafter, an image of a torso without a head kept appearing before me. Finally, one day I realized the significance of the apparition and broke out laughing. John was obviously now sending his torso to go along with the head that he had sent earlier. That, of course, was the end of the episode, but my love for John the Baptist has lived as a light in my heart ever since. At the same time, this experience also presented a good physical description of him, particularly as to his size and coloring.

One night shortly thereafter, members of the Angelic Kingdom came to take me to meet with Jesus. Once again, I was on my way to meet with him in his world. Such incidents were very precious to me. As I mentioned earlier, when one is taken to the Angelic Regions, it is possible to visit someone for a longer period of time.

When I arrived, Jesus was standing some distance away and talking to a group of people. Immediately on seeing me, he left them, came over, and sat down by me, crossing his legs in the customary manner of the East. We talked about several things, briefly mentioning John the Baptist. Sitting there side-by-side was almost like visiting with some next-door neighbor and having an afternoon chat. It seemed natural, as if it were something that happened all the time. I still marvel that anyone as great as Jesus can take the time to be so unassuming, yet never lessen his power or authority. He was, and is, a Master among Masters.

Finally, I asked him if he could stay. He replied quietly that he could not, but he instructed me to tell all my friends that he would see them. I knew that he meant he would come to those who sought to walk a dedicated spiritual path. Then, as suddenly as I had come, my soul was returned to its flesh counterpart to continue with the struggles and lessons of human life.

As "Jesus, The True Story" continued to unfold, I was caught between two worlds. One was the historical account of Jesus' life, and the other was the Biblical story. There were many variances between the two, although the historical accounts offered a more complete spectrum of both his life and teachings. Had I followed the path carved by pre-established ideas, I would have written nothing original and my years of research would have been in vain. It would have been much easier to choose the path that the man in the scarlet robe (scarlet-sacrifice) laid before me, if I had not known that I would have to combat centuries of pre-established concepts.

For a time, my research created considerable conflict within my soul. This was further complicated by the growing problem of presenting the lost teachings of Jesus in a manner acceptable to the human senses. However, the powerful empathic link connecting myself to the consciousness of the Master was too strong to be broken. In the end, I knew that I must offer what I considered to be the true story of his life and teachings without modifying it to meet traditional theological standards.

With Professor's Bordeaux's translation of 'The Lost Jesus Scroll," the Apocryphal account of Jesus' birth, Lentulus' description of Jesus at the time of the crucifixion, and a transcript of his court trial, I was able to offer a deeper insight into the man, the Master, and his Lost teachings. This was further enhanced by the writings in the *Gospel of Thomas,* and the *Pali Scrolls,* which described Jesus' sojourn in India.

As I neared completion of the book on Jesus' life, I was perplexed on how to end it. The historical accounts again varied from the Biblical. The historical records indicated that Jesus lived for a short time after the crucifixion, while the Biblical account indicated that he died while on the cross. To go either way was to discredit the other. As the Christmas Holidays again cast their magic over the country, and Christmas Day approached, I remained perplexed about the final scene.

Although I had a number of invitations to dine out on Christmas Day, I did not wish to accept any of them. Instead I preferred to spend the day quietly and work on "Jesus, The True Story." Sitting down, I made the decision to review the last chapter, hoping that it might stimulate some new creative impulse. As I held the manuscript in my lap, suddenly, there it was: the perfect ending. They were the words of Jesus, as they had been written in "The Lost Jesus Scroll," and they reflected the one great truth that he had lived and died for: "There shall be no peace among people till there is one garden of the brotherhood over the Earth."

On that Christmas Day, as the completed manuscript lay in my lap, a voice from the Angelic Kingdom spoke to me and said, "This book is one the most accurate books ever written on the life of Jesus the Christ."

On hearing those words, I realized that true greatness does not come through the sacrifice of one's ideals and principles. Even Jesus had been considered a heretic in his time, but he did not relinquish his ideals because of this. On the contrary, he gave his life for them; and because he did, his work has lived, and will live, through the ages. My research had spanned almost two decades, and I had done my best. Although I do not necessarily expect my work to live through the centuries, right or wrong, I can face both Jesus and my own conscience. I rejoice that Jesus' strength gave me the courage to write his greater story.

At first, the book of Jesus' life seemed destined for the same fate as the Apocalypse. Publishing houses did not wish to accept it. Once again, my work did not follow the pattern of accepted theological doctrine. Yet, I was still somewhat surprised when the rejections began coming, for I knew that "Jesus, The True Story" was a good book. Those who had reviewed the manuscript before it was sent out to editors and publishing houses told me that it was like going back in time and actually walking with the Master. They felt that I had brought Jesus to life in such a manner that anyone who read the book would experience the living consciousness of the man who walked the shores of Galilee.

Over twenty years of research had gone into the discovery about the truth about Jesus' life. Ten years of writing and rewriting had been spent on what would ultimately become a trilogy, with little or no opportunity to share this wealth of knowledge with mass consciousness. This deeply puzzled me, for people by the thousands will buy unusual and controversial, as well as good spiritual books. Best sellers like *The Prophet* and *Jonathan Livingston Seagull* have proven this.

In spite of the rejection letters, I decided to go on to the third book of the trilogy, "Covenant at Sinai," the Life and Secret Teachings of Moses. To date, however, this book is only a draft, a hulk gathering dust, in the room where I do much of my writing. One reason for the delay is because I obtained a translation of the original Hebrew covering the first five books of the Old Testament. The original Hebrew and the accepted interpretation of theology are radically different, as well as extraordinarily complex. Therefore, to date I have been unable to develop a suitable form of presentation.

Putting "Covenant of Sinai" aside, I decided to do another rewrite on both the "The Hidden Secret of the Apocalypse" and "Jesus, The True Story." I discussed one of the problems that I was having pertaining to *Odyssey* with a fellow author who had several published books on psychology. We agreed that the primary obstacle to the smooth flow of the material was my inclusion of numerous author notes. Unfortunately, I have always had a distinct aversion to footnotes because I feel that many people do not read them. Therefore, periodic author's commentary had been inserted at various places to reduce the encyclopedic amount of footnotes required. Now it was painfully obvious that these were more of a nuisance than footnotes.

After a great deal of discussion, we decided that a preliminary introduction to each chapter should be done. These would give a summary of the chapter's subsequent context. Whatever could not be included in the introduction could then be relegated to footnotes. In the end, this produced a beautiful and concise book that could more easily be comprehended by mass consciousness. Nonetheless, at the time, this did not seem to make the book more publishable.

Eventually, I made the decision to develop both books into cable TV series. They have aired many times over the years. After the cable company had begun to show the programs, the station told me that "The Life and Secret Teachings of Jesus" drew more viewers than any cable series of its kind.

In time, my perseverance paid off and both books were ultimately published. Only the ghost of Moses' book still continues to rests its shadowed hand across my mind. In February of 1998, I boarded a bus and crossed the desolate, but beautiful, Sinai Desert in pursuit of Moses' vision of the Promised Land.

CHAPTER XIX

Inroads
of the Self

A number of years had now passed since my first United States tour in the old rebuilt taxi. I had become tired of driving and relished the idea of having a more permanent center. At the same time, I hoped for a more suitable space than previously occupied.

Before returning to Washington, with intent of moving the school, I stopped to visit Judy and Benjamin, who were now living in Montana and running a health food restaurant. During my visit, they told me that they did not wish to run a restaurant for the rest of their lives. They had decided to sell and were ready to join me once more in the resurrection of another piece of property. Financially, little had changed for us. We were still in no position to buy property, at least a place that would be satisfactory for the school. For this reason, it was necessary to turn to my Hawaiian benefactors once more.

Searching for a new place was no easier than it had been before. One thing about God is that unless something *is* right, it doesn't work out; and when something is right, He seems to maneuver people and events together with the speed of the wind. I remembered the crystal chandelier, but my allowance was no larger now than it had been before. Also, should we find a place; I was not certain how we would afford to renovate it, although there was a very small estate pending which would have belonged to my great-grandfather. Since he had been deceased for some time his part of the estate was supposed to pass on to me. This had taken such a long time to settle that I had almost forgotten about it. Yet it was a possibility, as well as a possible solution, so we began our search for a new school location.

Another Christmas passed, and New Year's Day arrived amid tooting horns, skyrockets, and whistles. Judy and Benjamin took a much-needed vacation, for they were very tired after the arduous work in their restaurant. This had been further compounded by the renovation of the small house they had recently moved into. At the time they left, we felt we had probably found the right location and that it was only a matter of waiting for our benefactors to consummate the sale.

For various reasons, the sale simply did not work out. It soon became obvious that we had not selected the right place. Still, there was no doubt in my mind that a move was immanent. At Christmas, as He had done every year, God appeared to me and gave me a Christmas present. This year He presented a wrapped gift a few days before the holiday began. It occurred one morning, as I sat quietly meditating. As He sometimes did at Christmas He was attired in a Santa Claus suit and His materialized hands held a strangely shaped package wrapped in red paper. The package was flat on one side and had a raised lump on the other. It definitely looked like a piece of property, with some kind of a building on it. Nonetheless, He was quite secretive and placed the wrapped package in a metal safe. I assumed this meant that the gift was not to be opened yet and that He had also put it in the safe to signify protection and security. It was destined.

Shortly after our failure to secure the earlier piece of property, a delightful young real estate woman called and wanted to show me a few places. At the beginning of our tour, she mentioned that she had exactly the place for us, but she was going to show it to me last. After looking at a couple of rather impossible possibilities, I said, "Let's forget about the next few places, and look at the one you are saving for last."

When we drove up in front of a massive derelict, I knew that this was it. There was a fountain with a lady pouring water, symbolizing the forthcoming Aquarian age, as well as my ruling sign Aquarius. On each side of the steps leading up to the main door were two lions, long a Christian symbol signifying Guardians to the Throne of God. When I walked into the foyer, I saw a chandelier, although it was not crystal. However, it was the same foyer I had been shown five years earlier while scrubbing the yellow walls.

This large 7,100 square foot house seemed to reach out and embrace me as though I were its long-lost owner. It had fallen into great disrepair, but its lengthy thirty-two foot living room was adorned with beautifully carved wooden pillars and stood resplendent in spite of the ugly purple, pink, and green rooms surrounding it. It was a love affair at first sight. This time, when negotiations began, there were no breakdowns; and within days, the property was essentially mine. Although I did not own it outright, I was given a lifetime estate, insuring that I could remain there for the rest of my life. At the end of that time, my benefactors could sell Gethsemane and retrieve their investment.

Restoration of Gethsemane, so named because it reminded me of Jesus' Garden of Gethsemane, would be extensive. It sat on a third of an acre and was surrounded by trees and shrubs. On the southwest corner stood a small guest cottage, also in sad need of restoration. There was no doubt in my mind that this was the right place for a school, for there was plenty of room for offices, a very large classroom, and the house included all of the other nice amenities that would give every student who studied with us an isolated and quiet environment. At the time, the place seemed massive, and I felt almost dwarfed as I wandered from room to room, particularly upstairs.

When Judy and Benjamin returned from their vacation, I could barely contain my enthusiasm. As they rambled about the empty rooms they became as excited about the property as I was, and we began immediate plans for restoration. Miraculously, at that same time the impending estate was settled and I received my great-grandfather's share the same day the sale on Gethsemane closed. Once more, the wisdom of God had overshadowed the events of the human world, and the timing too perfect to be considered the fortuitous act of fate. Nevertheless, the project before us also seemed mountainous; this was the third large building we had done within five years.

As we worked, I remembered the vision five years earlier. The foyer was exactly like the vision, but the chandelier was not crystal. I decided that this would not do, for the vision that God had given to me had to be fulfilled. So I set about finding a crystal chandelier. To accomplish this purpose, I contacted some of my former students who were in the antique business. After driving to Bellingham, a beautiful oasis near the Canadian border, I stopped at the home of my student, who lived in a huge home known as Wardner's Castle. Together we went to an old school on the outskirts of town to hunt for a crystal chandelier. Shortly after our arrival, we found, gleaming amid the pile of things to be sold, the object of our search. My heart was joyous over this find; now I had a suitable gift for God, who had given me my beloved Gethsemane.

None of us will ever forget the day of the great "Lighting." Twenty-two students, who were now twenty-two painters, sat in a circle in the foyer. We were eating lunch. Benjamin brought a ladder in to finish hooking up our chandelier to the world of electrical energy. In one blinding moment, the foyer stood resplendent, as overhead the crystal shone like the light of the sun. In spite of this wondrous moment, I looked up at the top of the ceiling and took a moment say, "God, you did not tell me that I would have to buy it."

It was the most interesting building we had ever tackled, for it loved us, and it loved being restored. Even though it had been a derelict and vacant for a long time, it still bore a shadow of its former glory. The place bent magically under our will, and everything we did seemed to make it joyous. I know now that it was because the presence of God had moved within its walls; I had come home, for I would live in Gethsemane the remainder of my life. Once, when thinking about selling it because it was so expensive to maintain, God came to me and said, "This has always been my home." I knew then that it was not to be sold.

At first, I was gone from Gethsemane as much as I was there; but as the years passed, I found that maintaining the expense of traveling, as well as the support of the school was too costly. Finally, I returned home for good. When I did, a new phase in my destiny began. It is considered inner plane work, or development of inner peace and inner powers. Everyone does some of this during his or her life in the form of forgiveness, positive thinking, and trying to be a better person. For the most part, however, there is a tendency to blame others for many things that happen and a desire to run as fast as one can from anything that appears as a personal inadequacy. For me, running was not an option. There was no escape but to painfully plod through the mire of the subconscious mind.

As with all things of God, the inner purgation of the Dark Night of the Spirit was interspersed with both extensive study and bearing the consciousness of my students. As I had been linked to the consciousness of my teachers (seen and unseen), I was now linked through His Spirit to those I taught. For the first few years, I found this to be quite disturbing, and words Professor Bordeaux had once said to me came back to haunt me again and again: "I told you I would help you, and I have been paying for it ever since."

While I have never fully adjusted to this link of consciousness between a student and myself, it did become more habitual. My Angelic Master, who has guided and taught me through the years, told me that I would one day become more accustomed to it. And it seems that there has always been one student or another dwelling in my mind since. If I ever did any wrong to a student, I had to right it. This was somewhat difficult at times because a teacher is supposed to be an example. How many times I heard the voice of my Okaji telling me that these were lessons in humility, perseverance, dedication, compassion, and atonement.

There were periods when I was compelled to spend several days going over some situation of unrest and error. I say compelled, because most human have difficulty thinking about one single thing for even a few minutes. Now there was occasion for me to think about some individual for hours. Even more painful, was the fact I was taken to task over every inadequacy and driven to straighten matters out, while others were not.

The purification of the senses had lasted about five years, but the Dark Night of the Spirit seemed to stretch out before me like a relentless wind blowing across a barren desert. There were two consolations that brought a measure of solace during these years. First, my summer tours continued for a few seasons. This allowed a bit of a reprieve from the constant mental indigestion of my students for a period of several weeks. Second, I had to keep developing new classes. Some of my students remained under my tutelage for six to seven years; and in meeting their needs, it was necessary to increase my own comprehension and understanding. This resulted in quite a remarkable series of classes. We tackled any subject, and saturated ourselves in the deep studies of philosophy, music, religion, the mathematics of Pythagoras and the original Zend Avesta of the Persian sage, Zarathustra.

As we learned about the mysteries of the pyramids the students and I traveled by film to the land of Egypt. Then we walked the streets of Jerusalem with Jews, Muslims, and Christians. From the fiery pits of Earth's beginning to the far reaches of the universe, we perused the mysteries of science, while the lives and music of classical composers soothed our struggling senses. I will never forget the day I walked into the school's rather selective library and realized that my consciousness had become as large as it was, for now I could teach anything written in the books it contained.

By this time I had begun to wonder if I were really just a Christian Mystic, for the years of teaching had taught me that every study has the same source. Even the terms science, religion, and philosophy are mere man-made, and created in an attempt to explain what appears to be different but is not. However, when I questioned the title of Christian Mystic, which had been allowed me in the beginning of transformation, the Angelic Masters told me that it was "Christian Mystic, or death."

Upon hearing this rather abrupt and penetrating statement, I knew that the Angelic Kingdom meant death to the work that had done and the work that had yet to be done. In my enthusiasm for teaching, my assignment with destiny and my commitment to help reveal the deeper mysteries of Christianity, I had occasionally stepped beyond the boundaries of even Christian Mysticism. Yet, those whom I taught still signified an integral part of developing others and doing my part to help to bring forth an enlightened people to carry on the great teachings, each in their own unique way. At another level, I continued my personal development through the never-ending purification of the soul. No one is capable of raising the consciousness of another higher than his or her own. There is always someone greater, just as a solar system must respond to the movement of the galaxy.

This world of knowledge brought a slim hope that someday I might become wise like the giants before me. It was as though the words of these great wisdoms stirred within me, and as their consciousness played through my soul I wanted to dance to their music.

Never will I forget a series of classes on ancient Persian culture, for Okaji had lived during those times. He would pronounce, as well as clarify, words that we might never have understood. Many times it seemed that he was the teacher of this particular class and I was the student. By this time some of the students could partially see him, although they did not always hear him. I, on the other hand, could always see him by extending my inner sight, but I could hear him even more clearly. If there was a question over the pronunciation of some word, he would say it, and then he would explain it. In turn, I would then pass the information on to the class. The students came to adore him, for they knew that he was present at every class and that he was our link to a world beyond the limitations of the human senses.

Although we ultimately explored many different subjects, the Christian Mysteries remained closest to my heart. Jesus remained my ideal, although God was my goal. Therefore, the secrets of creation, the inner powers of mankind, and the mystic transformation of the soul remained my primary course for beginners. Once, when I complained about giving the students such sublime mysteries so easily because some seemed to place so little value on what they were learning, the voice of my teacher spoke, saying, "you have been given much." On hearing these words, I realized that he meant that I had received, and now I must pass on what had given.

In time, the original Hebrew rendition of Genesis and the life of Moses, St. John's Apocalypse, and the books on the life and teachings of Jesus became the central core of the school's curriculum. We taught at least one course in the Christian Mysteries every semester. Usually, I cherished those hours when I was able to share these mystical secrets and instill in the student an understanding that had long been locked away from the masses of humanity; yet this sharing had a bittersweet quality, for the impact of what I had earned through long years of spiritual rebirth and what I now shared so freely depended upon my students' ability to understand.

Jesus once taught that some seeds fall on barren ground, while others take root. I had to remind myself of this statement many times. After partaking of spiritual nourishment, the ego of some of those whom I taught decided they had achieved such knowledge strictly on their own. Clement, Bishop of Alexandria once warned of this situation in his "Stromateis": "that he cannot explain the mysteries because he should thereby, according to an old proverb, put a sword into the hands of child."

One of the church fathers, Tertullian, who died about A.D. 216, said something similar in his "Apology": "None are admitted to the religious mysteries without an oath of secrecy. We are especially bound to this caution, because if we prove faithless, we shall not only provoke Heaven, but draw upon our heads the utmost rigor of human displeasure."

In view of the secrecy of the early church, although I understood its reasons, I felt that what had been given belonged not only to my students, but also to the world. Having received, it thus seemed logical to give my knowledge to the masses that were no longer illiterate and unlearned in the ways of science and philosophy. If I taught as the world thought I should teach, then I would offer nothing beyond what it already had, separation, segregation and war.

There was very little concern on my part when I made the decision to step beyond the lesser, more popular teaching, and openly teach all that had been revealed to me. In considering this rather bold move, I took into consideration the lives of those students who had gone on to make their mark on the world; such as the thousands of young teens around the world who had been helped because of Cheryl's programs in alcohol and drug abuse, or the unwanted children, cast off by their parents, who became adoptable through the work of Benjamin and Judy.

Those whose lives had been changed because of my teaching had become a greater asset to themselves and to the universe than the hundreds who turned away because the path was too hard. I never condemned anyone because they sought teachers who were more popular and who taught a less demanding path. I understood; and knew that whatever path a person traveled, that the spark of greatness would be ignited in them someday. Then they too would go on to do great works. In the meantime, there was a measure of peace in knowing that I had helped each of my students take at least a small step up the ladder of transformation. Nevertheless, I fear that I was always somewhat astounded to learn, that those who had departed for other paths imagined that they had reached their newly-found enlightenment all by themselves.

Another disconcerting thing, although it also brought a bit of humor in my life; when a student entered into the transformation of soul they blamed me for their agitation. Of course I really had little to do with the chaos that began to envelope them. It was the Spirit in them, which brought unrest as the doorways of the subconscious opened and the soul was prepared for entry into the sacred halls of divine metamorphosis. In times like this, some words in Mabel Collin's book, "Light on the Path," reminded me of what this journey is all about. She writes, "You shall not stand in the presence of Masters until your feet have been washed in the blood of your own heart. You shall not speak in the presence of Masters until your tongue has lost the power to wound."

During the period in which the divine spark is raised in the soul, the ego does seem to reach its greatest height. In St. John's Revelation this is referred to as the great beast rising out of the bottomless pit. Thus, whatever patience I had during these times was derived from a remembrance of those who had helped me on the path, and of the Angelic Master who has stood by me during the long years of my own inner battle.

As I progressed deeper into the mysteries of life, my study of people became more in-depth, and my counseling practice flourished. In order to understand why people did what they did and the intricate chain of cause and effect, which wove their current existence, my search took me into the very depths of their souls. Nothing was hidden if I took the time to both study and to understand. Extreme emphasis was placed on the latter, for God does not reveal intimate things to a heart that refuses compassion and to a heart that condemns.

From sexual addiction, drug addiction, and broken marriages, to depression and even schizophrenia, I was to learn about it all. As I once had been taught the deepest mysteries of mankind's outer world, I was now taught the mysteries of man's inner world. While God condemns no one, nothing is hidden from Him. He taught me to rise beyond the corporeal lessons that each human was learning through their current experiences, and see instead what these lessons would ultimately accomplish.

The story of mankind is a beautiful one, and its destiny is magnificent. To be allowed to work, even in a small way, on the same team with those who are helping to bring a greater world into existence was, and still is, a wondrous adventure for me.

What amazed me most, as I continued to study these secrets handed down through the ages, was the brilliant heritage of enlightened people from the past, such as Plato, Pythagoras, Da Vinci, Beethoven, and Lao Tsu. These and many others had weathered the storms of ridicule, controversy, and hardships, and had risen victorious from the deserts of human existence to create the foundation of education in our modern world. In their times, the world was basically illiterate and remained primarily that way until the Twentieth Century. Knowledge was once thought to be a gift of the Holy Spirit, and our world was believed to be the center of the universe. Still, from ignorance and superstition, these Masters of the past found the doorway to reality and became the educators of today's world.

Many times students attended classes, who did not possess a great deal of formal education. They were often afraid that they would not progress as well as those who were educated. Then I reminded them that neither God, nor Moses, nor Plato, nor Jesus, had gone to formal colleges, and that God was still the direct source of all knowledge. Next I explained that He had co-authored all of the important works in music, poetry, science, philosophy, psychology, and religion. It was not uncommon for me to say, "You are in good company, but success or failure in life is not limited to academia alone, but on the faith and belief in oneself."

When the soul of any individual fuses with the consciousness of God, that person enters a college of learning that never ends. This transcends the general scope of academics, for it encompasses all learning and does not isolate itself into a single specialty. It is the secret behind the knowledge and wisdom of many great geniuses and saints throughout the ages. Even my own endless training has covered everything from the origin of the universe to the inroads of the psyche. It has reached back six thousand years into religion, philosophy, and history. At the same time it is wonderful to know that this same doorway is open to all walks of life, regardless of whether people are rich or poor, fat or thin, educated or uneducated.

Naturally, science has not always accepted my theorems; religion, my theology; nor psychology, my consensus of opinion, although I have dissected the human mind and psyche with the skill of a surgeon. Because of my own experiences, it has always seemed wise to warn the students that they might not be accepted for hundreds of years, or even a thousand years, but this should not dishearten them. Every individual has a choice: to explore new frontiers and carve new trails, or to remain on the routine and crowded freeways.

One of my favorite quotes pertaining to success comes from the wisdom of Theodore Roosevelt.

> It is not the critic who counts, not the man who points out how the strong man stumbled, or where the doer of deeds could have done them better. The credit belongs to

the man who is actually in the arena; whose face is marred
by dust and sweat and blood; who strives valiantly; who
errs and comes short again and again; who knows the great
enthusiasms, the great devotions, and spends himself in a
worthy cause; who at best, knows in the end the triumph
of high achievement; and who, at the worst, if he fails, at
least fails while daring greatly, so that his place shall never
be with those cold and timid souls who know neither victory nor defeat.

When I think back upon some of the progenies of the light
whom I taught, and who entered that mysterious doorway leading to the unseen world of learning beyond mortality, I must think
of Miguel. I was teaching a seminar in Austin, Texas, when Miguel
first entered my life. He was a young Mexican lad about twenty
years old. During the seminar there was little time to pay any
more attention to him than the others. My main concern was
focused on giving each student the best instruction possible during our brief sojourn together. At the end of the seminar I put
away the affairs of the day, and returning to my motel room began to pack for my departure the next day.

Some weeks later, while preparing to teach again in Phoenix,
Arizona, there was a knock on the door. To my surprise I saw
Miguel standing there when I opened it. He had given up whatever sort of home and possessions he owned, and had come to
study with me. "My-oh-my," I thought to myself, "This poor
young man needs a cleanup outside and inside."

Immediately Miguel set about finding a part-time job, sufficient to allow him to live meagerly and still have time for his
studies. It was obvious that the opportunity to study was very
serious to him, and I could not help thinking how much better
off the world would be if every human being was this willing to
sacrifice so much to find God. That is the price that I have imposed upon myself and that is the price that people like Cheryl,

and Judy and Benjamin had also been willing to pay. None of us, or others yet to come, ever regretted this decision, for each found that God gives back a hundred, even a thousand times more than any of us can give to Him, or the world.

When classes started in Phoenix that fall, Miguel was one of my most dedicated students. He not only attended every class, but also came on every retreat. By January he had entered into the early phases of transformation. His direct connection with God enabled him to write wonderful music for the guitar and exquisite poetry. His poetry had both the elegance and sophistication of the most accomplished poets, and his music was sweet to the ear. Unfortunately, because of my extensive traveling, I lost contact with Miguel, but he is ever a reminder of the potentiality in every soul.

There are other wonderful stories about the progenies of the light who came to study over the years. I cannot give myself credit for any success they achieve, for I was but someone who simply opened a doorway to their greater self. It is the individual who brings such changes within themselves through dedication and perseverance. However, sharing in some of these magic moments has always brought a satisfaction and joy that no amount of wealth can ever supply.

One of these special stories is about David. David worked part-time in a small bookstore in the northern part of the state of Washington. He lived with a wonderful free-spirited group of people in the community. For the most part the group was comprised of free-lance artists and musicians, as well as health food enthusiasts and organic food growers. One thing I loved about the group, their hearts were as big as the world. Several of them became an intricate part of the group who studied with me. Even when much of the city was immobilized by winter storms and snow was piled high, they trudged through the snowdrifts in order to come to class.

One day David came to me for counseling, and as we sat down together I was shown that he had the potentiality to become a Naturopathic Doctor. This was a world far away from working in the small bookstore. To achieve such a goal would require extreme effort on his part. Not long thereafter, however, David said goodbye and told me that he was on his way to Portland, Oregon. Taking a job as a caregiver to pay his expenses, he entered one of the highly respected Naturopathic colleges. From time-to-time he contacted me to let me know his progress, and on occasion, he sought guidance. His biggest concern was financial and sometimes he was afraid that he might not be able to finish.

Remembering my own days in tents, inexpensive motels, cockroaches and scorpions, I told him what I have told so many over the years, "David, when we reach a road that seems impassible we must look at it as we would a beaver dam. If we rush in and frantically try to tear such a dam asunder, we will be defeated. On the other hand, if we begin to move the debris from the dam's foundation one stick at a time, it must ultimately collapse. Therefore, do what you can today to remove any obstacles; even if is but a tiny step. Eventually that obstacle must surrender under the assault."

Six years passed, and one day I received a letter from David, along with a very special invitation to his graduation. He had become a Naturopathic Doctor. He was not there to see the tears of joy that fell down my cheeks.

Another time one my students, a housewife, came for a consultation. She felt completely unfulfilled in her housewifely duties and wanted some understanding of her destiny. As we proceeded with our appointment, I was shown that Carol should work with the blind and that if she did so, her life would be changed forever. Because she was sighted and had no experience with the blind, it seemed best that she start by doing some volunteer work for one of the special organizations established to help people without sight.

Carol did not believe in wasting time. Within a matter of days she had found a place for her services. Some months later Carol opened the Louis Braille Institute for the Blind. Although it was said that sighted people could not read Braille, she had not only learned to do so, but was also tutoring. The last time I heard from Carol, her work had started to expand into other countries and international recognition had opened its doors. I still read about her in the newspapers from time-to-time.

The classes and counseling also touched the young. God not only provided me with inner knowledge into the younger mind, but my own reckless years in the desert of ignorance had given me a deep understanding of the vagrancies of youth. One of the remarkable things about God, or Cosmic Consciousness, is that the individual becomes one with what is here and now. Therefore, when teenagers came to be counseled, they did not come into a reserved and clinical environment, nor were they met with the usual clinic-like reception.

My office, called *Star Base*, is much like walking into a Captain's ready room aboard a starship. I designed it this way to remember that I am not confined to an office, or even the world, but rather we are all part of a great universe. Therefore, when a member of the younger generation comes aboard, they find this starship environment quite to their taste. Also, they come because they want to. When any parent asks me to help one of their teenage children, I insist that they first make certain that their teenager wants to come. It is never a completely compatible situation when a child, or a teenager, is forced into counseling by his or her parents. Because there is good in everyone, every teenager has an inner desire to become a better person. However, many times drugs, alcohol and dysfunctional homes blind them, and they cannot see their inner potential.

The parents also have to give me carte blanche. I do not allow them to sit in on the counseling, because I know their presence may inhibit the openness of my client. Neither is anything that takes place within the room ever discussed with the parents unless my client gives their permission. Absolute trust between the youth and counselor is paramount, and I strive to never betray this trust. After we have discussed starships, the fact that the recording tape we will be doing belongs to them, and that I will not discuss their personal affairs with their parents, the session usually starts off in somewhat the following manner,

"Have you met anyone like me before?" I ask.

Perhaps they answer yes, perhaps no, or perhaps they are seeing a regular counselor.

"Well, I ask nothing from you except absolute honesty. Don't try to deceive me, because I was born with the ability to see the future, and I will know if you are not telling the truth."

I pause. "You may not believe this, but I was your age once."

Then I tell them a story. Sometimes it is about driving the old family thirty-two Chevrolet into a ditch and breaking off the bumper. I tell them about driving it home and parking it under a barbed wire fence. Next I tell them, "The next day my mother backed up, and off came the bumper. Later, I heard her telling my father that she could not understand it, because she had simply backed up and nothing more."

At this point, I inform my client that I never really confessed until I grew up and moved away from home. Of course, I have a repertoire of stories, so I may tell another one, like the time a group of us pushed a neighbor's car down the street and put a sign on it, Stolen Car for Sale.

After a story or two, my young clients are usually much more relaxed and more willing to discuss serious matters like drugs and home life.

It would be hard to forget a young fifteen-year old girl, named Mary, who came to my office one day. She had dropped out of school, was living with an older boy friend and, like many teenagers, she was also using drugs. We went into detail about her relationship, family and what she wanted to become. Although I did not see Mary again for two years, she returned when she was seventeen. She said, "I came because I want you to know what I have done with my life since I saw you two years ago."

Miraculously, she had managed to leave her relationship and

was living at home again. During this time she had returned to
school, gotten a part time job that required her to work with people,
and had made some firm decisions regarding her future.

She had accomplished what every teenager really wants to accomplish, if they looked deeply into their heart. More importantly, she said, "I do not know how people can stand to be on
drugs. Life is so exciting."

These contacts with teenagers did not always bring about miraculous changes. Sometimes they find it impossible to remain
drug free, particularly when they started using at a very early age,
such as nine, or ten. They still have dreams and hopes, but the
patterns of the past often sink their tentacles into them so deeply
that they find it too difficult to remove them. Such youth need
day-to-day guidance and support, and because of the nature of
my work it was impossible to fill this need.

Since my particular assignment was to teach, there was not
time to give the intense day-to-day follow-up that some teenagers
required. More than once I thought that it might be nice to be
two people, because I really cared if these teens made it back to
the pathway of success. And because of my own dysfunctional
teenage years, a doorway was never closed to any of them.

Others, who came to Gethsemane to study, or have counseling,
were already successes in their own right. Yet, some were not following the dictates of their heart and came to me to find their dream. It
is often more difficult for these people to achieve transformation because they are deeply rooted in one of the many comfort zones. Their
current lifestyles may not actually be a hindrance to the spiritual path,
but sometimes there is a conflict within the soul because of a desire to
do something else, or to be something else. It is only when the familiar comes into conflict with a new desire that a soul finds unrest and
lack of satisfaction. However, for those who seek a spiritual path,
regardless of whether they express it through music, art, or science, or
religion, it is also necessary to come into harmony within themselves,
as well as the ever-changing cosmic order of things.

Once I was teaching a group of eighteen men and two women. Several members of this group were college professors. There was one among these who did not wish to remain in his current professorship. He wanted to become a storyteller. We talked it over and I suggested that he should begin by using weekends to start his new career. He could do his story telling at weekend parties and in the evenings. After doing this part-time, he could then determine if this was really the path he wanted to take and whether he would be successful enough to supply his physical needs.

Within a year he had left his position as a professor and was working full time as a storyteller. He was so good that one evening, while I was watching the evening news, I saw the Mayor of Seattle present my former student with the key to the city. He was being named the city's official storyteller. Later, he went on to become very famous.

The students who have passed through the many classes in the school number into the thousands. Some went on to great success, both spiritually and physically, but there were also those who simply could not change. True spiritual transformation requires deep introspection and hard work. Some people are simply too comfortable to reshape their world, to reprogram their subconscious mind, and to work at guarding their thoughts and actions. And why should they? They have already achieved the American dream, though the American dream is temporal and will carry little weight when the soul removes its earthly clothes. Jesus once said, "And again I say unto you, it is easier for a camel to go through the eye of a needle, than for a rich man to enter into the kingdom of God." (Matt. 19:24)

Nonetheless, the people of Earth are good people; and each in his or her own way tries to do the best that he or she can. Having seen mankind's glorious destiny, I simply teach those who come; help those who wish to change; and allow the remainder to go peacefully. These too will one day pick up the magic burden of their destiny, for their magnificence has been carried in the Master Plan since before the worlds began. In the meantime, they are co-creators in the slower but necessary recasting our planet must make. I am ever grateful to them, for they package my groceries, bake my bread, serve me in restaurants, and give their lives in battle so that I might live in a free world. I well understand the opaque skies that may cloud their vision. Here on Earth, we are, after all, but shadows of the eternal; and until we have sought the inroads of the Greater Self, we little understand the fantastic voyage that awaits us.

Having pierced these planes beyond mortal boundaries, life has become a passing panorama of human development. If the world had always known the things it is only now discovering, it would not have been satisfied to be human. Skyscrapers would not have risen against the distant horizon; and while man might have flown, he would never have experienced the joys of creation and success. The wonder of discovery, the strength that comes from failure, and the layers of collective experiences that make each individual unique, would have been lessened. Only in not knowing does every human struggle to overcome the almost insurmountable odds that affect day-to-day living. One day, as God did for me, the veil will be lifted and the past will drift away. Then all eyes will see clearly; that it is the past that creates today.

As I journeyed these inner-planes, I ceased to hate the ignorance that once ruled over my own senseless acts and thoughts; and as I could not hate them in myself, I could not hate them in others. The inner senses see the uniqueness of every individual and the chains that made them what they are, as well as the glorious destiny that will one day awaken in them. Sometimes I am impatient, for we all hunger for the world that is yet to be. However, my hunger does not come because I seek personal peace, for I have found that. My hunger is to see the happiness in every human face, when the hand that wove the veil of night has pierced human blindness.

CHAPTER XX

Return to Israel

n January of 1998, I returned to Israel, this time with twelve students. I had started out with thirteen, but one became ill from bad drinking water before we reached London; and upon landing, she wanted to return to the States. After assuring ourselves that she was in no real danger, the rest of us boarded the plane for Tel Aviv. This second trip to the birthplace of Jesus would take a most remarkable and surprising turn.

Before we departed from the Seattle-Tacoma Airport, my Angelic Teacher told me that this would be my last trip to the Holy Lands. I had been working very hard and had not had a vacation for a number of years. Perhaps this was the reason the Angelic Kingdom decided to give me a trip of a lifetime. The surprises that were planned for all of us came from the hearts of these wonderful presences living in the semi-light, semi-material world beyond matter. None of us who went on this trip shall ever forget it, or them.

When we arrived in Israel and disembarked from the plane we made our way to the terminal gates, where we were met by an official tour-guide who worked for the company that had planned our trip. This part of the tour package proved very helpful to us, for most of our group had never been to Israel, and some had never even been abroad. The miracle of this trip started almost immediately. From the moment our plane landed in Tel Aviv, a heightened state of consciousness seemed to fall over all of us. Suddenly we were enveloped by an intense state of unity and one-ness not previously there. This unseen force holding us in its embrace not only affected us as a group but also enabled us to be one with the country. It was as though some great light held us in its arms and elevated our souls, minds, and feelings.

The magic of this journey traveled with us as we passed through the gates and met Jan, our tour guide.

It soon became apparent that we had been allocated one of the best tour guides in Israel. She was a remarkable person, and as the days passed, we found that she was strong enough to make us toe the mark, yet so delightful that we did not seem to mind. With her, it was early to rise and late to bed. At the end of each day, we returned to our hotel, resembling a pack of homeless waifs rather than secretaries, publishers, and computer analysts.

It is said that with every ray of sun, a bit of rain must fall. This adage certainly proved applicable as we toured throughout Israel, for it was January. Our days did not begin with warm, beautiful sunrises over Galilee, but rather with a wet drizzle, a great deal of dampness, and cold weather. I am confident that none of us have forgotten the bright, multi-colored Fuji umbrellas we purchased to ward off the constant rain. These not only became an intricate part of our daily attire, but we saw them everywhere. A common statement among us was, "There goes Fuji." Nevertheless, we did not allow the cooler weather to dampen our enthusiasm. With Fujis in tow, we greeted each morning with a measure of groans, stiff muscles, and sleep-laden eyes.

Our tour had been arranged by an organization specializing in religious groups, so we were matched with other like travelers. Some of these turned out to be ministers and their wives. When I heard this, I instructed my students to live the teachings of Jesus and not to get involved in religious discussions. That way, we could peacefully co-exist and abolish any potential dissension with those whom we traveled with, for I knew that our opinions might differ greatly from theirs.

The students took my instruction seriously and seemed to consider it a privilege to put on happy faces each day. This proved quite humorous, actually. Some people cannot tolerate joyous behavior, particularly early in the morning. Sometimes I think that our cheerfulness irritated our fellow travelers more than the fact that we dressed in white. However, white had become a tradition in our school and followed in the path of the great philosophical and religious schools of antiquity. White also emulated the attire Jesus wore during his sojourn on Earth. Nevertheless, this did not seem to endear us to some of our fellow travelers.

Our guide, Jan, was Jewish, and as most Jewish people, deeply revered Moses. Since I had perused Moses' life with my customary intensity at the time I wrote my first draft of The Life and secret Teachings of Moses, I was able to share in many of Jan's beliefs. To have studied Moses, was to love Moses. For this reason, I could honor Jan and her faith. Perhaps it was because of this, or perhaps it was because our group remained joyous, giving, and mannerly, that she never forgot us and still corresponds on rare occasion.

Once the initial excitement had worn off, our Angelic Escorts began to introduce themselves. The wonder of their presence filled us with a pervading sense of suspended time and magic. We could almost believe that we were indeed not of Earth but dwelled beyond those portals of human senses and walked in the presence of Masters. For a brief time, the curtain separating our two worlds had been lifted, and because of this a greater sun, than the one behind the clouds lit our travels through Palestine, and later Egypt.

Always I sensed that The Master was somehow behind this wondrous welcoming committee. It was as though he had given instructions that we were to be cared for during the days and nights of our stay. One thing that lent evidence to this miraculous chain of events was that many of the angelic beings came from the "Christ Consciousness." In using this term, I refer not only to those who lived during The Master's time, but also to those who later encompassed his teachings and transcended the necessity to live in embodiment because of them.

The first night following our arrival, we were taken to a hotel just north of Netanya. I doubt that any of us had difficulty getting up, although we were still influenced by Seattle time. This meant that most of us had periods of being very much awake in the middle of the night. Although I do not remember counting sheep, I do remember letting out a groan or two when I looked over at the clock and saw that it was one or two in the morning. In spite of this, we left our rooms that first morning fired with enthusiasm and ready to begin our adventure. After eating breakfast, Jan and Juseff, our driver, came to whisk us away for the day. Within minutes, we were boarding the tour bus that would take us along the Mediterranean Sea.

The first stop was Caesarea; an ancient city built by Herod the Great in honor of Caesar, and once the capital of the Romans in the Holy Land. I found it fascinating, not only because it had been a great city and a crusader's fortress, but also because it had been one of the places that Paul, the apostle, had frequented. It was from Caesarea that he had embarked on his journey to Rome.

Interesting things pass through one's mind when one travels where the ancients once lived. For me, it was a feeling that I had walked many times in these symmetrical hills with their contoured and austere terrain. There was no sense of separation between those events of two thousand years ago and what was happening at the moment. It did not seem that the day existed, at least as time is normally conceived, only an infinite timelessness without beginning and without end. It was like boarding a time machine and going back – back – until the present merged with the undulating waves of the past. I knew that His Spirit within me made this possible, so the joy I experienced was greatly magnified. Like the wide-angle lens on a camera, I was able to capture every detail and imprint them on the inroads of my heart and mind.

Our first day's itinerary also featured a drive to the crest of the 1500-foot Mount Carmel where the Prophet Elijah brought Israel back into allegiance with Jehovah and killed the prophets of the foreign and false God. It was reputed that there had once been an Essene monastic school in the vicinity and that Jesus had studied there during the years that the Biblical scripture does not cover. However, it was the beauty and ruggedness of Mount Carmel that captured my fancy; and as I looked out over the distant hills, the Prophets of the past lived once more.

Alas! All too soon we were called back to reality, and boarded the bus to semi-jog our way toward Megiddo.

This was a moment of triumph. At last I would stand on the site where the final battle on Earth with all of St. John's beasts and dragons would be fought. I smiled inwardly, for I was taken back to a conversation I had with one of my doctors. (I believe he was Muslim.) The discussion had come around to the end times, at least as it is perceived through the eyes of the Christian world. He said, "You Christians believe that the final battle and end of time will take place at Megiddo."

I will not forget the stunned look on his face when I replied, "You know, I have a problem trying to reconcile that. I simply cannot imagine an all-out nuclear war taking place on eleven acres of land."

It is true that Megiddo was once a famous battlefield, for it was here that Barak gained a notable victory over the king of Hazor. However, the chief historical interest in this site is concentrated in the death of Josiah, for here Josiah endeavored to stop Pharaoh Neco of Egypt, while the Egyptian was passing through the glens of Carmel into the plain of Megiddo. However, Josiah was defeated; as he fled, he was shot by the Egyptian archers and died on the road to Jerusalem.

On departing from Megiddo, I became aware of the watchful eyes of one of the heavenly emissaries that had been sent to watch over us.

Professor Bordeaux, who had done the translation of "The Lost Jesus Scroll," was the first of our Angelic Host to make contact with us. While I had met him several times in the subtle ether regions where we dwell when our body is asleep, I had not seen him under these circumstances since Cheryl and I had been in Costa Rica. Therefore, it was a delight to bask in his conscious presence once more for he has always been as a father: kind and firm, possessing a mind as expansive as the sea, yet keeping his feet planted firmly on Earth. No one I have ever met since has merged the angelic and human worlds together more perfectly. Still, I wished that the others could have seen and heard him as well so that they could directly experience this Great Teacher of mine.

On Wednesday, January 23rd, we were supposed to witness a sunrise on the Sea of Galilee. Unfortunately, it was still winter in Israel, and a sunrise was a rare ingredient, particularly on this day. We had no alternative but to enjoy the beauty of a silver mist, spawned by a constant drizzle of rain. The only visible bright spots one could see were our Fuji umbrellas as day began to slowly creep across the shadowed hills.

During the preceding night, following dinner at the hotel, my devilish side escaped from its cage of self imposed dignity for a brief time. This simply occurs during unexpected times of extreme humanness. I do not make excuses for it, but rather allowances, primarily because my Angelic Teacher is always present to remind me of my inadequacies and imperfections.

On this particular evening, I glanced over and saw the ministers and their wives sitting near by. Because I expected to be conducting a baptism service in the Jordan River the next day, I thought it would be nice if I were baptized also. Thus, I turned to those ministers who were traveling in our tour group. I approached them as they finished dinner to ask if they were going to do any baptisms the next day, explaining that I was looking for someone to baptize me. After having glowered at us from time to time during our early morning smiles and exuberant enthusiasm, I thought they might jump at the chance to save my soul. Apparently, I wasn't enough of a temptation, and they informed me that they were not going to do any baptisms.

At the time, I could not resist asking one of the minister's wives if she was going to be baptized. Looking at me with some measure of contempt, she responded coldly that she had already been baptized. Her disdainful look was too much of a temptation for me, and I replied, "Well, so have I. Actually I have been baptized twice, but not in the Jordan River." Then I walked away.

In fact, this was not a joke, for I had been baptized twice before. The first time was when, at the age of twelve years old, I had accepted Jesus as my savior. That was when I had signed my vow to live by the standards of the Methodist church, which included not drinking, smoking, and not taking the Lord's name in vain. My subsequent baptism had been just prior to my illumination, when I felt it necessary to formally commit my life to God. Now I had returned to Israel, and to be baptized in the Jordan was very important to me. If the Master could humbly walk into the river to be immersed by John the Baptist, I felt I could hardly do less.

Though it had been arranged for me to baptize any of my students who desired it, I was, for the moment, lacking someone to baptize me. This privilege had also evaded me during my preceding trip to the Holy Lands. Therefore, I had promised myself that I would change this if I ever returned. As this would be my last trip to Israel, I knew that this must take place now. It was obvious that our fellow tour ministers were not going to be of any assistance. Therefore, I could only hope that some other minister would be with his or her group when we arrived. If so, I could take advantage of that person's willingness to save my soul, and I was quite certain that someone would think my soul needed saving.

Our first scheduled stop on the following day was Capernaum. When we arrived, I went over to sit on the same steps where I had sat several years before. As I looked out over the water, I was once more caught in the past, wishing that I could sit at the feet of the Master, if only for a brief moment. I loved Jesus passionately, so passionately, in fact that I seldom talked about it. There are no adequate words to define a relationship that causes one to wander the land, live in tents, and sleep with cockroaches. It is a transcendental love that reaches beyond the barrier of finite love, devotion, and human emotion. One does not laugh or cry, but rather expresses it through word, deed, and thought, struggling to live in a manner that shames neither the teacher nor one's own soul.

Memories are like an instant time machine, for we travel where they go. Today, as I sat on the temple steps, my thoughts took me back to the time when Matthew, Peter, Andrew, John, and James sat listening to our "Teacher" on this shore and had witnessed his miracles. Off in the distance, the Sea of Galilee was darkened by an over-hanging gray sky, lending an almost silver sheen to the gentle waves. It is said that there is a sound in the silence of the night, and now this silence moved through me like a muted whisper in this solitary moment between what once was and what is.

Because Capernaum had been one of Jesus' two favorite places, it was also one of mine, and I was loath to depart from the warmth of its past. However, on tours such as this, one must shake the dust from his or her feet and quickly move on to the next scheduled rendezvous.

Before long, Jan was rounding us up for a boat ride across the Sea of Galilee. Most of our group took seats toward the back of the boat, while I occupied the one closest to the stern. Only in the aloneness of one's thoughts can one really share in something that has been. Amidst the cold, the gaiety, and the picture taking, I wondered how Jesus had stilled the winds and walked on water. The sea was now dark and calm; but the high hills surrounding the below sea-level water, combined with abrupt temperature changes, often contributed to sudden and violent storms. For a moment, I sought to ride the wind and waves with those who cried for help in an ancient past. I realized that oneness with God gave Jesus his power. He had said, "These things I do, ye shall do and greater." Would we then, who had landed on the moon, also one day tame the seas?

Following lunch, we traveled through the lower Jordan Valley to the designated baptism site located on the Jordan River. It is said that to pass the Jordan was like figuratively crossing the Rubicon. Many of the most remarkable names and events of Scripture are associated with this river: Joshua leading Israel into the Promised Land, the parting of Elijah and Elisha, Naaman healed in its waters, David crossing to escape from the rebellious Absalom, and of course, the baptism of Jesus by John.

When we arrived at our destination, we found that everything had been nicely set up to handle tourists, as well as those who sought baptism by immersion. There was a small souvenir shop as well as a bathhouse with showers. Soon, those of us who were planning to be baptized were given baptism garments. After we had donned the long, white cotton gowns, we made our way to the river's edge with bare feet. The day showed no mercy, for it was cold and wet, and the rain had made the Jordan River muddy and dirty. Because the water was so unclean, I decided that I would not immerse my students but that they would wade out to the waist, and I would baptize them with a sprinkling of water and the laying on of hands.

The day was quite cold. Therefore, I did not see any other group willing to accept the challenge of the river. This meant that my own baptism would have to be handled by one of my students. I picked Rene, who was a newly ordained minister.

As I made my way down the steps and entered the river, I found the water extremely frigid. Each step became a matter of will. The cold numbed my toes and pierced my body like some icy fragment born from the distant hills, bathed in winter's mist.

Not only was the water chilly, the rocks were slippery and cut into the bareness of my feet. However, even if the river had been colder, it would not have deterred me, for this was my dedication to the white-robed man who had once walked the shores of Galilee. There would be no other chance for me, so I braved the dirty and cold river to fulfill the calling in my heart. As I made my way into a deeper section of the river, the ministers stood on the bank watching. Under no circumstances would I allow them to see the difficulty I was undergoing, and sought to maintain an impassive countenance.

When I finally found a place with secure footing, the water was up to my waist. Pausing, I knew that each student would have to endure this same ordeal. As I looked up, I saw them standing in single file on the shore in thin, white cotton garments in the chilling wind and for a moment my love for them was as if my heart was as deep and as wide as the Jordan itself.

The oneness that had penetrated our consciousnesses since our arrival became even more apparent now, for an unspoken understanding passed between us. None would, in any way, allow the frigid circumstances of the weather or the water to dishonor their commitment and the solemn rite of the occasion. One by one they entered the water; and sometimes as they came near me, I saw their chins quivering from the chill, even as they struggled valiantly to subdue any outward expression of their discomfort. Only one broke the chain of unspoken words. When Kerry came and stood in front of me, he spoke in a very low voice with great stoicism, his lips barely moving. "Oh, it's cold."

Due to my own chill, I had difficulty maintaining a measure of dignity as he spoke. Only Kerry could put into words the feelings of himself and others without any expression marring his placid countenance.

While I was baptizing the students, my St. John of Revelation joined me. As always, it is difficult to find words to explain what it means to share even a few precious moments with such Great

Beings. There is magnificence in their comings, and for a brief time, Earth almost takes on the persona of heaven. There had been little contact with John after we had finished the original draft of "The Hidden Secret of the Apocalypse." Now, his presence brought back the many wonderful months I had been allowed to share with him in Hawaii, and I was joyous over his arrival.

After two or three of the students had been baptized, one of the ministers standing on the bank and watching decided to extend a hand of friendship. Stepping forward, he came to the top of the stairs and helped each one as they climbed the steps leading out of the water. Upon seeing this, I knew that this was the way things were meant to be. There should be no religious separation, for all denominations were one denomination and loved the same Master.

As I neared the moment of my own baptism, I somewhat hoped that John the Baptist might come to help in the rite. This did not occur, although he did make his presence known during our later visit to the Essene community at Qumran.

Rene was last to enter the water, and after she had been baptized, she remained in the water in order to perform the ceremony on me. It was not only one of Rene's first official duties, but she was also about to perform this rite on her Teacher. By this time, I was numb with the cold; and to complicate things, I had decided on a full immersion in spite of the unclean water. This made it more difficult for her, as she had not witnessed the process of immersion. I could see that she was very nervous and was having difficulty organizing her thoughts. However, we finally got underway, albeit in a decidedly awkward manner. As the minutes passed, and Rene stood with her hand on my head, I became afraid that she was too concerned to push me under. To help her, I finally took a deep breath and ducked.

As I sank below the water, the best I could hope for was that God's Holy Angels would give me their blessing because I had heroically braved the elements to honor the Master. At least I could not get much colder than I already was, although my hair was now wet also. When I surfaced, the damp cold reached out to embrace me with tentacles of unpleasantness. I don't remember much about making my way to the shore except that I was glad to be leaving the river and was looking forward to dry clothing. My prayer for Angelic benediction, however, had not been in vain. As I left the water, one of the Angelic Messengers brought me a message from Jesus. It said, "Come to me later. I will baptize you with an even greater fire. I await you in heaven." The message thrilled me and made my subsequent bout with a cold virus worthwhile.

The students waited for me on the shore in spite of the chilling wind blowing through their wet garments. As we made our way toward warm showers, there was a sense of satisfaction, peace, and joy, which the cold and rain could not diminish. We had accomplished our purpose and had braved the elements; we would never have to look back with regret over a missed opportunity.

After warm showers and dry clothing, we felt completely renewed and ready to continue our tour. First, of course, was a visit to the gift shop, where I was given certificates to fill out for everyone to commemorate our baptism. While there, I decided to purchase a small vial of water that had been drawn from the Jordan River, so that I could use it later. It was good that I did so, for one of the two members who had decided not to get baptized because of the cold weather and unclean water later regretted this decision. The rest of us had shared a very special time, made even more so by our discomfort. We felt as though we had won a certain kind of victory over ourselves.

CHAPTER XXI

Miracle of the Via Dolorosa

The scenery the next day following our baptism was wondrous. We traveled to Jerusalem via the Jordanian Border and began our day with a stop at Gergesa. Next, we headed south through Beth-Shan, the Jordan Valley, to Jericho and the Mount of Temptation. This was the first time I had seen the Bedouin camps other than in documentary films. I found them fascinating, perhaps because there is a touch of gypsy blood in all our souls, and also because they had been responsible for the discovery of the original *Dead Sea Scrolls*.

As a scholar, I had spent considerable time on whatever translations of the scrolls I had been able to obtain. The *Hymn of the Initiates* from the *Manual of Discipline*, as well as that which is often referred to as the *War Scroll*, depicting the engagement of the *Sons of Light* against the *Sons of Darkness* was of particular interest to me. Since Armageddon is not only the death of mortality, but is also a spiritual rebirth, it carries with it the initiations the soul must undergo in order to transform. The *Hymn of the*

Initiates, although pertaining to the practices of the Essenes, lent itself well by expressing many of the attributes that must eventually be developed in every soul. The following phrase from the *Hymn of the Initiates* beautifully defines this spiritual rebirth of the soul.

> And when he comes to birth (the indwelling divine consciousness) all those pangs of travail that rack the world's great womb – that crucible of conception – will take a sudden turn; what has been conceived with all the bale of a viper (lower nature of man) will end, at the moment of (divine) birth.

It was thrilling to see these nomadic Bedouin camps with my own eyes. I had both read and heard much about them during my years of research on Jesus' life. Now, as I looked at their camps, they seemed to lose their past. Unfortunately, however, it seemed that their future was in jeopardy. According to the 1996 Statistical Abstract of Israel, 50% of Negev Bedouins were under the age of 14.

The Bedouins are reputed to be a hospitable people. Their tents are customarily divided into two sections by a woven curtain known as a ma'nad. One section, reserved for the men and for the reception of most guests, is called the mag'ad, or sitting place. The other, in which the women cook and receive female guests, is called the maharama, or place of the women. It is said that once you have been welcomed into a Bedouin tent as a guest, you are honored, respected, and nourished, frequently with copious amounts of fresh, cardamon-spiced coffee. Guests also provide cause for some festivity, including music, poetry, and on special occasions, even dance.

During one's travels, I fear that fancy takes over now and then. It was impossible for me not to wonder what it might be like to spend time with the Bedouins, for in many ways their lifestyle had remained unchanged over the past 2,000 years. I also wondered if they had found a sense of peace in raising their sheep, goats, and camels, a peace that escaped those of us who dwelled amid a city's maddening roar.

When we arrived in Bethlehem, we followed the traditional pattern of most tour groups, with a visit to the Church of Nativity followed by a bit of shopping. Then we were taken to our hotel in Bethlehem. This was to be our base for the next few days. The ministers, along with a couple of other people attached to our tour group, were housed in Jerusalem, so we no longer saw them in the evenings.

Exhausted, and most of us suffering the miseries of a cold from our exposure in the Jordan, we piled gratefully into the hotel with our luggage. I looked forward to a bit of rest, for it was still early to rise and late to bed for us, and my illness increased my exhaustion. Our accommodations were superb, not because they were very elegant, for we were traveling lower middle class, but because those who operated the hotel made us feel so welcome. They rather spoiled us by bringing us cake from a wedding, or some tasty little delicacy to introduce us to their culinary delights. By this time, as vegetarians, we were also rapidly becoming addicted to savory falafels, Israel-style soup, bread, and hummus, a pate-like mix usually made with garbanzo beans.

The weather was still inclement; and because the virus cold had made its rounds and affected almost everyone in our group, our tour of the Old City the next day was sandwiched in between sniffles, Kleenex, and familiar Fuji umbrellas. Still, we managed to walk the Via Dolorosa and shop in the Old City bazaars.

With Jan as our guide, shopping was a rare ingredient. We usually found it necessary to quickly purchase whatever we wanted to take back to the States in the few rare hours she allowed us to wander. This was probably good for our budgets, but we had two shop-o-holics with us, and every time we turned around, they were gone. This meant that we often had to wait, whether it was in hotels, airports, or near street vendors. I found this rather enchanted me in some ways, because the two of them could find shopping places where I thought none existed.

The highlight of the day came toward evening. We were taken to visit the Garden Tomb and Golgotha, also referred to as the Place of the Skull. I was possessed with a sense of mystical wonder as I walked along Golgotha and drank in its beauty, for the winter had produced an abundance of green plants not visible most of the year. When we reached the end, we descended into an open grotto, which brought us almost directly in front of the Garden Tomb. Taking advantage of the time allocated for private services, I had the students take their seats and led them in a silent meditation. Here amid such hushed seclusion and beauty, I felt that they could best experience the wonder through the privacy of their own hearts.

There was and still is controversy as to the actual burial place of Jesus: that which was maintained in the Church of the Holy Sepulcher; or the more recent, acclaimed site known as the Garden Tomb. The British maintained the latter; therefore, a church building did not violate the natural beauty of the land. While I realized that people wanted to worship Jesus because they loved him, it was still refreshing to honor him among the flowers and trees of his homeland. I remembered my previous visit to the traditional tomb, when Jesus had given me the message that he wanted people to stop worshiping his crucifixion and walk with him as a world family amid the beauties of nature. Perhaps this was the reason that I found the Garden Tomb the more appealing of the two sites.

There was far too much detective living in me to not concern myself over which one was the real tomb. I had spent over twenty years of research pertaining to the events surrounding Jesus' time, but this was my first contact with the Garden.

Even as Drucilla's beautiful voice rang out over the grotto with the words of the *Holy City*, my favorite spiritual song, my mind swirled around and around, assimilating facts, trying to remember every detail of the crucifixion. In the eye of my mind, I removed the church from the traditional gravesite and envisioned only its tomb. Next I tried to visualize the execution site, as it might have been 2,000 years before a church had been built over it.

During our walk from the Old City past Golgotha and subsequent descent into the grotto, that special feeling I always had when doing intense research enveloped me. Our British guide had given a very logical presentation supporting the Garden Tomb as the original burial place of Jesus. However, if this were true, I wondered how it affected the thousands of pilgrimages made to the Holy Land each year for the right to worship at the traditional site. At last I made the same decision I had made when I wrote the end of the book on Jesus' life, *Jesus, The True Story,* and also as I concluded of my findings regarding the Shroud of Turin. I decided that each person would interpret as they chose and worship what they believed in. My conclusions pertaining to worship, however, in no way lessened my own insatiable desire for the truth.

When it came to Jesus, I doubt Sherlock Holmes would have been any match. I, who had always lacked patience in my youth, had found myself immersed in detailed and methodical research over the years. Nonetheless, I did not approach my pursuit of truth in a stuffy and scholarly way. Perhaps that is why research has always been so exciting to me. It is like being an armchair detective, for I never know exactly what I will find on the next page of some rare manuscript. Most of the time, therefore, I did not feel as though I was actually researching, but chasing after clues. Over the years God seems to enjoy when a game is afoot as much as I, for He has taken me down many strange streets and has protected me from closed-mindedness and preconceived ideas.

When I think back on my great curiosity of that day, I know why the tomb was so important. Truth was, and remains, a way of life for me, and no stone was left unturned in my pursuit of it. I like discovering things that others are prone to overlook, although my findings may not conform to pre-established concepts, at least at the time. Knowing where Jesus was actually buried was simply a part of my research adventure into the life of Christ, although I wasn't quite certain what it would contribute.

As we sat in the Garden Tomb in the silence of the early evening, Jesus came to me like a soft, summer wind, bringing with him the pervading sense of love that accompanies all his visits. When he appears, I am often overcome with emotion and start crying, or my mind becomes a tornado of turbulent thoughts as I try to figure out what I should say to him. Sometimes he disappears again before the proper words can even formulate in my mind.

On this occasion, Jesus' visit was very brief. I am sure that everyone in the grotto at the time must have felt something different, like the soft touch of a summer mist, the glory of the sunrise, or the gentle lap of waves upon the shore at sunset. His words are not only etched in my heart, but I wrote them down, lest I forget one single word. Although many people would like to know the words he spoke, I will only say that he answered the question I had regarding where he had been buried.

Now I was faced with a decision, for I had questioned which burial place was the real one, the Garden Tomb or Church of the Holy Sepulcher. In the end I realized that each individual would form his or her own conclusion, and that each would walk the Via Dolorosa surrounded by the passion of his or her own heart. However, which site is real is something that Theology can argue in the centuries ahead. For me, I love both tombs and find him in both places, for one holds the devotion of thousands of people, and the other portrays the freedom he enjoyed as he wandered the hills of Galilee.

Leaving the grotto, we again made our way toward the Old City. It had been a long day, and for a brief time we had been able to put the umbrellas away. John the Beloved also journeyed with us, for he had remained one of our primary protectors since the baptism ceremony, leaving us only when we boarded the bus for our hotel. As we walked in the peace of the descending twilight, Jesus' brief words traveled with me, as did the memory of his presence.

The next day, we headed south toward the Dead Sea, 1300 feet below sea level and the lowest spot on Earth. How strangely brilliant and still it was in its isolation. The shore consisted of a low graveled beach, varied by marl or salt marsh. Twice on the west side, the mountain cliffs came down to the water's edge; and on the east coast, there was a curious peninsula somewhat resembling a spurred boot. I believe this is referred to as El-Lisan, or The Tongue. Ancient beaches were visible all around the sea, while steep terraces of stained and greasy marl haunted its coast. The mountains rose precipitous and barren behind the terraces on either side.

A number of our group donned their swimsuits and went into the water to experience its wonder, but I resisted. For one thing, I was still sniffling from immersion in the Jordan, and besides, I had spent considerable time near the Great Salt Lake in Utah. The salt water, therefore, did not hold much fascination for me, so I stood on the shore wrapped in the solitude of my thoughts.

This famous body of salt water brought Ezekiel's wonderful vision to mind. In his vision, he saw a stream of water issuing from the Holy Temple of Jerusalem. Its volume began to increase as it swept down toward the Dead Sea to heal its bitterness, teaching "that there is nothing too sunken, too useless, too doomed, but by the grace of God it may be redeemed, lifted, and made rich with life." (Ezekiel 47:8-9)

The shores of the Dead Sea were now dotted with people, who had descended from the Holy City to seek healing and solace and to partake of the water's remote beauty. Perhaps Ezekiel's vision had been fulfilled after all and the Sea had been made rich with life. Certainly my students seemed to be enjoying themselves, although their ability to swim proved of little worth against the sea's salty influence.

After lunch our guide, Jan, managed to assemble all of us once more; and we boarded the bus to continue the day's activities, including a visit to the Qumran Caves, where the Dead Sea Scrolls had been found. Although we had seen the Bedouin camps, we had not yet visited the caves. These were of particular interest to me because Professor Bordeaux had mentioned them many times, and of course there was also considerable controversy concerning them. For one thing, all the scrolls had not been translated; and for another, scholars and theologians were fearful that the scrolls might contradict the Bible. Of course, I had intensely studied what had already been translated into the English language. From what I could ascertain, scholars and theologians had little to worry about. For the most part, I thought the Dead Sea Scriptures added to, rather than contradicted, what has been traditionally accepted as biblical text.

While we traveled, we were again honored by Professor Bordeaux's consciousness. Actually, he had been with us a great deal during our trip. I assumed, from this, that the responsibility of our group fell primarily to him and my Angelic Teacher. Therefore, it seemed natural for the Professor to be our escort at Qumran. He was very knowledgeable on the subject of the Dead Sea Scrolls and was one of the foremost authorities on the Essenes, who had once inhabited this monastic community by the Dead Sea.

The openings to the caves were located high in the granite-like hills surrounding the monastery. According to Flavius Josephus, the Jewish historian, some of the residents of the monastic community at Qumran had been considered prophets. Thus, they probably had foreknowledge of the coming political encroachment on Israel, as well as the desecration of their land and sacred religion. A number of their members were also apparently scribes and it was these scribes who carefully recorded the scriptures so as to preserve them for mankind.

Records of the Essene way of life have come down to us from the writings of their contemporaries. Pliny, the Roman naturalist;

Philo, the Alexandrian philosopher; Josephus, the Roman historian; Solanius; and others also spoke of them in various ways as "a race by themselves, more remarkable than any other in the world."

There is nothing in the Essene writings about Jesus, but that would not be unusual because they had begun their movement almost three hundred years before his birth and had completely disbanded by 50 A.D. An Alexandrian manuscript, discovered by a member of the Abyssinian Mercantile Company, describes an eyewitness account of the crucifixion and confirms Jesus' association with the Essenes between the ages of twelve and nineteen. Again, this is a debatable subject with theologians. Although I have some reservations about the Alexandrian manuscript, I had none pertaining to Jesus' probable affiliation with the sect, the *Lost Jesus Scroll* by John the Beloved had dissolved any doubts that I might have had by this time, for Jesus taught his disciples the mysteries behind Essene angelology as an intricate part of his private discourses.

As I looked at the remnants peaking out of the rubble of archeological excavation I could almost see the white-robed figures moving silently through the corridors of the monastery like misty shadows of an ancient time. A quiet peace prevailed in spite of the tourists, and in a distance were dark entry ways leading deeply into the cliffs that had so carefully guarded the Essene secrets for two thousand years.

As always, time passed swiftly, and once again, our guide was sounding the general call to assembly. We would have to leave the wonder of the Dead Sea and the remains of the Essene monastery for the comfort of our more modern hotel in Bethlehem. It was with a measure of sadness that we watched the day fade away, for we knew that our journey was now almost over. We were scheduled to fly to Cairo the next day. All that remained before we embarked on our late evening flight to Egypt was one final morning to visit the Old City and to bid Israel farewell. For me this was a final farewell, for I knew that I would never return.

As the bus wound its way from Jerusalem to Bethlehem we sang the *Holy City* once more. This was a ritual we had started several days earlier and continued to do each evening when returning to our hotel. I am not certain whether the other passengers enjoyed this as much as we did, although Jan, our guide, participated with a measure of robustness. When we sang this time, it was with a sense of loss, for we had become one with this land so far away from our own. I am certain that we all felt we would like to live within the embrace of Israel forever. As we sang, I little realized that something was about to occur which would become some of the most treasured moments I would ever encountered.

While our voices were lifted in song, an Angelic Messenger came. He told me to assemble my students at the St. Stephen's Gate at 11 o'clock the following morning, as Jesus planned to walk with us for one hour.

It was hard to believe what I was hearing. Before, when the Master had appeared to me on Earth, he remained for but a very short time. On the two occasions when I had been taken to him, I was allowed a longer visit because the higher realms are of a less dense vibration than Earth and therefore less restrictive for our great angelic hosts. Now I was being told that he had decided to circumnavigate the bridge between our two worlds and walk the Via Dolorosa with us.

The next day, we donned our best apparel and took the motor coach to the Old City. Juseff drove us, as he had throughout our stay. This was above and beyond the call of duty, for the official part of our tour in Israel had actually ended. Nonetheless, we were grateful for his helping hand, as we had come to love him dearly and this gave us one more opportunity to say goodbye.

The weather was still inclement, and as we gathered just inside the gate, we again felt the chill of Israel's winter. We had arrived early, primarily because we did not wish to dishonor this sacred time by being one second late. As we stood quietly waiting, a number of presences from the Angelic Kingdom also came. They were apparently going to walk with us, although not for our sakes, but to be with the Master. Shortly before eleven o'clock, I received instructions from the Angelic Kingdom to tell the students to line up in single file. Okaji explained that Jesus planned to lead us; and when he came, we were to follow behind him in this manner. He also told us that we were not to talk during our time with him but should instead maintain complete silence.

The events that followed will be forever etched in my heart and mind. Jesus arrived two minutes before eleven. As usual, tears began to flow down my face, and my voice shook when I spoke what were probably completely unnecessary words: "He is here." I am confident that everyone felt his presence. However, I spoke knowing that the inner-sight in some of the students was not sufficiently developed to see him.

Everyone was already standing in line and waiting in the order in which we had been instructed to walk. Without speaking, we got behind Jesus, and our journey began. My own teacher walked in front with Jesus, who guided us from the invisible ether of his world. I sensed, rather than saw the entourage of angels that had apparently joined us. They seemed to spread out ahead in an inverted V formation. I assumed that this was done to form a protective barrier between the Master and the outside masses, which had no realization of what was taking place. Certainly this reminded me of the Great Angelic presence who had sealed my entry into Cosmic Consciousness, and the necessity at the time of using music to raise the vibratory frequency of my surroundings. Therefore, I knew that these Angelic forces were necessary in order to heighten our current vibratory frequency and make the Master's trip easier.

Jesus' face was surrounded by soft white light. This light seemed to flow downward, blending into a pale gold, and encased his loose, flowing white robes. He walked before us, a semi-light, semi-material body, created from the ether substance of a higher world. Because of this he remained unrevealed to the masses that crowded the byways of the Holy City. In some ways, I remember every detail of that hour; and in others, I remember little. There was a sense of numbness and a vacancy of thought, except that he had come and he was with us.

Within a short time, Jesus led us out of the Old City and began moving in the direction of the Garden Tomb. For a moment, a bit of mental indigestion filled my mind, for I thought that we were going to walk the traditional route of the Dolorosa. Although I was not concerned about where we went, I momentarily wondered about the seeming change of plans. Then Jesus spoke to me quietly and very gently, saying, "My hour is not yet up."

Soon I realized that the Master had brought us this direction in order to escape the wall-to-wall people who crowded, pushed, and jostled one another on the main route. In overthrowing the moneychangers in the temple, he had clearly shown his displeasure over the material desecration of any holy place. Now, and through the centuries, he must have sensed that merchants violated this same sanctity by imposing their wares upon those who came to worship him as they walked the Via Dolorosa. Unfortunately, only Christians behold the "Path of Tears" as an artery of holy pilgrimage. It is of little interest to the Jews or Muslims, and they think nothing of trying to sell their wares to the moving masses that come each year. Therefore, I could understand why the Master had selected an alternate route.

We walked along quietly; and as we exited from the Old City, a sense of freedom, humbleness, and peace surrounded us. It was easy to maintain silence, for we were enveloped by Jesus' consciousness, and its magnitude left us in an almost suspended state of timelessness. He did not speak, either. It was as though, for a moment, he too was enjoying this momentary respite from the mountainous demands made on him by his over one billion followers. For me, a dream had come true. I was finally walking the hills of Galilee with Jesus of Nazareth.

A few minutes before twelve, Jesus led us back within the walls of the Old City to the Church of the Holy Sepulcher. As we entered, another unusual thing happened. Quickly, one of the church guides came to us. He motioned the crowd of people back that we might be allowed to enter the Tomb of the Holy Sepulcher before them. Signaling us to follow him, he took us ahead of the waiting worshippers and up the back stairs. Then he motioned for us to enter, treating us as though he were tending to some special group of holy people who might have just stepped from the pages of the ancient past.

It was not difficult to understand why we were being given this preferential treatment. At the moment, we were the Master's special guests. It was readily apparent that he wanted us to arrive at the tomb precisely at twelve o'clock. This is the hour, which is symbolized in the Christian mysteries as the marriage of the Indwelling Christ with the soul. (1-2=12, when the two have become one, or the Lion and Lamb lay down together). When this holy union has been completed in every living soul, the world will become one, and peace will descend over the whole of Earth.

Thus, just as the clock prepared to strike high noon, the Master preceded us into the Tomb of the Holy Sepulcher. We entered after him in single file, following as we had done throughout our walk. Then, one by one, he bid each of us goodbye. Even some students whose inner-sight was not yet fully developed were rewarded with a vision of him. During these final minutes, not one single outsider came near the entrance of the grotto. It was as though his mind had reached beyond the walls of hewn stone and held the people away from the boundaries of this secret world that we had shared for one enchanted hour.

Then Jesus was gone. We departed silently from the Church of the Holy Sepulcher, each wrapped in the solitude and wonder of what taken place.

Shortly thereafter we boarded the bus and returned to our hotel in Bethlehem to pick up our luggage. While we were traveling,

I looked out and saw a tree standing on a knoll overlooking the city of Bethlehem. I asked Juseff if he would stop so that we could have one last look at the holy city and bid Israel goodbye, each in our own private way. We descended from the bus and gathered under the tree. After a few moments of silence, we sang a little song that I had written at one of the stops. It was a promise to Jan, to Juseff, to the people of Israel, and most of all, to the "Master," that peace would come to Earth.

> *Israel – Israel – Weep no more today.*
> *For God will shine and build anew your city in the sun.*

Avenu Shalom Aleichem. We brought peace to you.

When I look back over those magic days in Israel, I do so with deep gratitude. This universe is full of things we have not yet discovered or even dreamed of. For most people, the concepts of infinity, living forever, and timelessness are like a foreign language; yet all of it is true, for everything in this vast sea of stars reveals the wonder of centuries past and of centuries in the future. I relish thinking of that time when all people will walk with the angels and live in a world no longer divided by the differences of human thought.

CHAPTER XXII

Exodus to Egypt

*L*ater in the afternoon, following those final hours of our miraculous sojourn in Israel, we boarded a plane for Egypt.

During my extensive research on Jesus' life, I had ascertained that the rumors of his sojourn in the Land of the Nile were most likely true. There were too many references, although subtle, that spoke about his relationship with the great learning centers at Karnak and Luxor. Because of this I knew that I must ride a camel to the pyramids one day, for I hungered to touch the sands of the ancients.

As a researcher, I had long known that I could never fully understand the real Jesus if I did not travel where he had traveled, study what he had studied and taught, and follow in the footsteps he had carved to the best of my ability. Egypt had been on my priority list for quite some time and was the last of what I call my Jesus journeys. At the same time, I still hoped to continue my work on the life and secret teachings of Moses one day. It would be more difficult to describe his exodus if I did not travel to the land where it all began and cross the barren sands where he had once walked. Therefore, I eagerly looked forward to my camel ride, as well as the return trip across the Sinai Desert by bus.

The visit to Egypt would be brief and we would be denied an opportunity to visit many historical places. However, large cities packed with people held little appeal to me and my personal trip there was intended to complete a final phase of my soul's longing.

Egypt forms the northeastern extremity of Africa. It is bounded on the north by the Mediterranean, on the northeast by Israel, on the east by the Red Sea, on the south by the Sudan, and on the west by Libya. It was once a land of multi-gods, as well as the former home of my Angelic Master Teacher. Therefore, Okaji became both guide and mentor during our stay, and from time to time he divulged some of the stories of his life there.

Had Egypt been the Egypt of Jesus' time, I would have loved it; but its' capital, Cairo, was a very populous city. I was not prepared for its lack of cleanliness, although I had found a similar situation in a number of the countries I had traveled. Wherever there is a great increase in population, there is also an increase in tenements, homelessness, and poverty. Even when driving in the United States, one has but to look out of the car window to see garbage strewn by the side of the road for miles. To understand the danger in this we have but to travel to some of the countries that face over-population, lack of sanitation and contaminated water, and witness their sorrow and suffering.

Not only was Cairo densely inhabited, but our hotel also reflected the overall run-down condition of the city, and it was very dirty. While I am very comfortable with simple living, I am not comfortable in a situation where one is afraid to sit down in a chair or to sleep in a bed because they may be filled with lice, bed bugs, or other indescribable creatures. Give me the clean Earth anytime for sitting and for sleeping. Nevertheless, I believe that I would have learned to love Egypt as I do all lands, if I could have extended my stay and traveled beyond the parameters of city life. That, of course, was impossible. On the brighter side, by day, the weather was more hospitable than it had been Israel.

As my research had included the works of some of the greatest philosophers in the known history of mankind, I found myself enthused about the possibility of visiting Heliopolis, Memphis, Luxor, and Karnak. These are reported to have been the sites of some of the most remarkable philosophical schools throughout the ages. It was written, that to survive the initiations of these schools was to raise immortal over Earth. Such giants as Hermes, Moses, and Pythagoras once carved their footprints in the sands of Egypt and they had left monuments of learning that would change the world. Among these great schools rose the colossal pyramid of Gizeh, built during the Fourth Dynasty.

When one is seeking truth, scholarly research can and should go beyond the boundaries of history and geography. One can pierce deeply into the greatest mysteries of the universe only if their knowledge is released from its predefined and narrow definition. The word scholar means to learn, and to learn is to approach all things with a dedication and desire to know its underlying truth, whatever that may be and wherever it may lead one. No scholar should ever be confined by the discoveries of their predecessors. Prior discoveries are but tools to the true explorer, just as a rope and a pick are to a mountain climber. Tools help one get to the top; but in the end, it is the perseverance of the climber that allows him to arrive victorious on the summit. In this instance, as I sojourned in this land of the Pharaohs, only exploration and research could pierce the secret of the Great Pyramid.

According to historical accounts, Khufu, founder of the Fourth Dynasty, was responsible for the building of Gizeh. In early records, there was some discussion pertaining to the possibility that the pyramid was something other than a burial chamber. The theory advanced by Herodotus, and the one now generally accepted, however, is that the Pyramid was the tomb of the Pharaoh Cheops.

Nonetheless this cannot be substantiated. Manetho, Eratosthenes, and Diodorus Siculus all differ from Herodotus, as well as from each other. Those who followed after them held opinions that differed from their predecessors and from each other. Such is the dissection of discovery.

Whether or not Gizeh was the tomb of Cheops makes little difference. The fact remains, that mathematically, even by modern day standards, the pyramid reveals the entire process of mankind's transformation from human to divine. This metamorphosis is also substantiated in the mathematical statistics of the Tabernacle in the Wilderness and, subsequently, of Solomon's Temple. The pyramid is reputed to be 486 feet high, if the capstone were in place. This symbolizes that the soul must rise from its sense attraction to the four elements (4), or earth. Next the soul, which has been bound to earth (4), must purify and unite with its indwelling Divine counterpart, which has also been bound by the four elements (4+4=8). This frees the soul and its Divine counterpart from the bondage of human life (6), or the sixth epoch of creation.

Certainly, each room from the queen's chamber to the subterranean, and then to the Kings chamber is equally symbolic and fascinating. For instance, the King's chamber is 39 feet long, 17 feet wide and 19 feet high, and reveals the forthcoming transformation of mankind from human to divine. The soul and its Divine counterpart (2) unite and become (1), thereby heralding rebirth, or nine (9) periods of the gestation in the spiritual womb of creation. Now it enters into the seventh and final epoch of earth's progression (1-7). The soul, united (1), has completed rebirth (9).

It is said that the modern world may know a million secrets, but the ancient world knew but one. That one secret was greater than the million, for the million secrets bred death, disaster, sorrow, selfishness, lust, and avarice, while the ancient secret conferred life, light, and truth. The unfolding saga of man's spiritual nature is an exact science, as much so as astronomy, medicine, or law. The world of exploration has produced science, philosophy, and logic as methods whereby mankind's journey through matter, and subsequent transformation, may be understood.

The pyramid speaks of a time yet to come when every soul will unite with its indwelling God-self and raise the capstone of the pyramid from its tomb. Casting aside dogma and tenet, the human race will seek Truth and be satisfied with neither substitute nor counterfeit.

Here, at last, I, as well as those students who traveled with me, would behold these mighty monuments that had cast their shadows and mystery over the teachings of the greats. If Jesus did travel to Egypt during his lost years, and there is much evidence to indicate that he did, then he would have come to Karnak and Luxuor. Although I, and those with me, could not behold the same pristine beauty that had existed two thousand years earlier, we could at least remember that we, like the ancients of old, had come to the great pyramid to view an ancient culture.

Even our camel ride would be short, for the encroachment of civilization had reached its choking tentacles almost to the base of the pyramids themselves. Only in consciousness could we roll back the hours of the clock and close off the city's noisy penetration. In doing so, it was again possible for the mind to capture the wonder and magic of the ancient days.

Sitting high aloft and swaying from side-to-side as the camel made its way to the Great Pyramid, I thought about the fact that this was what I had come to Egypt to do. The circle was now almost complete, and there was but one thing left: to cross the Sinai Desert.

My perspective of the Master had been remodeled through the years, for I could no longer perceive him in the same manner as the churches saw him. He was in so many ways more than they could ever imagine. He was a master to all people, all races, and all countries, for in his day Christianity did not exist. Rather it was born because he had lived. My search for the real Jesus had now covered the span of a quarter of a century. Although I would never know every single detail of his life, neither would I ever completely close the doorway on my exploration. I would marvel over his genius and his mastership forever; and above all, I now knew what had made him what he was.

As I made my way toward the great pyramid, I felt that I had walked in those huge boots Jesus had presented to me so many years before. They were still too large and had caused me to stumble many times as I journeyed after him. Yet every time I fell because of my humanness I got back up, even though the sword of the dark night of the soul had sometimes pierced me bitterly and deeply. To me, failure is only failure when one is afraid to try something or when one refuses to try again when one has fallen. Most of all we do not have to pick ourselves up by human will alone, for our world is one of God, Angels, and Masters. The doorway between Earth and Heaven stands open, and those who watch over this world are ready to help anyone who asks.

Even as these thoughts floated through my mind, the camel came to a halt and kneeled. I dismounted. Before me rose the enormous monument dedicated to the coming greatness of the human race.

In the days of old, those who sought the secret of divine metamorphosis would have entered through a long, hidden underground entrance, quite possibly hidden beneath the mighty sphinx, a symbol of mankind rising from its beastly nature. From there, the student, called an initiate, meaning someone seeking initiation into the mysteries of God and creation, traveled up a long corridor leading to the Queen's tomb. Upon arrival in the queen's tomb, the initiate received the mysteries of divine birth. From this chamber, they descended down a narrow passageway into a dark subterranean chamber, signifying a mother (soul) giving birth to the indwelling, divine light. The time in the subterranean chamber was relegated to comprehending the soul's passage through the dark night of the soul and subsequent rise from the shadows of death.

As the initiates made their way upward along a steep corridor, they reached the connecting point that led to the Grand Gallery. Had they failed their trial in the subterranean chamber, they were told they must exit. Otherwise, they were allowed to enter into the Grand Gallery with its seven overlapping stones, signifying the seven epochs of Earth's progression. These elect then made their way toward the King's chamber, marking victory over the first six periods of creation (known as man, or the bondage of the body, soul and its Divine nature to its corporeal senses). Eventually the initiates, who had succeeded in the earlier trials, entered the King's chamber and received a crown symbolizing immortality. It is then said that they raised the capstone of the pyramid to stand resplendent beneath the heavens as the sun at high noon.

The illumined greats, who left their remarkable work for mankind, knew that this transformation would one day embrace the whole of Earth and touch every human. When this ancient prophecy comes to pass, the pyramid will no longer represent an unborn world. Instead, its ruins will become a silent reminder of the struggles and trials of a noble race that once walked in the sands of mortality.

The story was all there, engraved in the measurements of the great pyramid and its chambers. The ancients had revealed it in hidden allegory, as John has done in his Revelation. Always it is the same story, promising all people that they will one day finish their lessons upon the Earth in a triumphant blaze of glory. That promise is more certain than the world's rotation around the sun, and more inevitable than the movement of the stars in the night sky; for the Earth, the sun, and the stars may pass away, but the soul of mankind – never! It alone is more powerful than the wind and mightier than the tallest mountain.

Standing and looking at the mass of stones rising before me, the revelation of mankind's destiny, as it had been given to me that day in June so long ago, now merged with the vision of the ancients. They were the same. How joyful I was to be a link in the continuity and promise to humanity that peace would one day come to Earth.

When we took our departure from the pyramids, I turned for one last look. I like to think that that these colossal giants of the past, which now cast their shadows over the desert, held other shadows, those of the greats who had left their footprints in the sands of Egypt. For a brief moment, I felt my heart touch theirs, a touch more solid than that of a human and more enduring than the endlessly shifting sands of the desert.

As the bus departed, I wanted to reach out and stop time. I wanted to bathe in what had been, even as reality wrapped its tentacles tightly around my soul. However, no one can stop the passing of the hours or halt the forward thrust of universal progression.

Early the next morning we boarded our coach, returning to Israel across the Sinai desert. Like most people, when I think of the Sinai, I think of the Sinai mastiff where Moses received the Will of God and etched it on stone tablets for the people. However, beyond the mastiff there exists a wilderness, commonly referred to as the Sinaitic Peninsula. The northern part of this bears witness to the ancient oft-trod road between Egypt and Palestine, one of the most famous in all history.

To me, it seems fitting that Moses received the Ten Commandments on the highest peak of the desolate, post-volcanic mountain district known as Mount Sinai. Just as the pyramids rose tall upon the sands of Egypt to signify mankind's desolation and unknowingness, so Mount Sinai, the tallest peak in the Sinai mastiff (Antiquities of the Jews, III: V, Josephus), rises against the sky as a stark reminder of our desolation without God's Law to set straight the path of the human race.

Although I would not elect to live in the wilderness by choice because I had been raised amid the sagebrush and desolation of the Idaho desert, I truly enjoyed the quietude of the land now stretching out before us. Though the winds of time had long ago covered the footprints of Moses, it had never been able to abolish his teachings. These rise higher than the tallest mountains in the world and stretch their boundaries into all nations. The stark beauty of this land was more enhanced by the fact that I knew that I would never pass this way again.

As we rumbled along on the dusty road leading from Egypt to Israel, I put thoughts of Jesus out of my mind and placed my attention on Moses. He was one of the greatest Spiritual Masters the world has ever known. Many have underestimated him and claimed that he was not allowed to enter the Promised Land because he had been twice married and had killed a man.

However, the Jewish historian, Flavius Josephus writes that Moses was appointed General over the Egyptian army and that he served brilliantly in this capacity. His marriage to the princess of Ethiopia had a condition attached to it. She was to turn Ethiopia over to him and stop the war. Josephus also writes that the man whom Moses killed was an assassin sent by the Pharaoh to slay him, because the ruler was afraid that the General would usurp his power. Although Moses was successful in defending his life, he knew that the Pharaoh would not rest until he was dead; thus, he was forced into exile. (Flavius Josephus, *Antiquities of the Jews*, Book II, Chapters X & XI.)

While the historical material about Moses was fascinating, I was more enthralled with his illumination on Mount Sinai, for I knew what Moses had experienced that day long ago when he had taken his herds to feed near the volcanic mastiff. I could close my eyes and stand with him as he watched the burning bush. He had seen the consciousness of the Creator flowing through all life as the flame flowed through the thorn bush and he witnessed His Divine Plan. It had to be that way; for in the original Hebrew text Moses laid out this plan without flaw. His revelation not only correlates with the ancient writings, but also perfectly with the discoveries by today's astronomers.

As I thought about his journey across this same desert I was now traveling, I hungered to become a part of the Israelites who had followed him through this barren wilderness for two generations. How awed he must have felt on that final day of his life when he went up from the plains of Moab to the top of Pisgah, and God showed him the land of his people. His work on Earth was done, but he had reached the Promised Land long before when he had entered illumination on Mt. Sinai.

There was a pain in my heart when I thought about the majesty of Moses juxtaposed with his humanness. There was so much to write about him; so much I wanted the world to know. The works of Josephus and the translation of the original Hebrew texts by Fabre de O'livet were two of my most important reference books. Although they had been written for different times and different ages, they made it difficult to view Moses other than one of the greatest masters who had ever lived.

Even as the bus rumbled over the dusty terrain, the angelic presence of Professor Bordeaux joined us once more. I was pleasantly surprised, for I thought that we had bid him farewell at Qumran. When I mentioned my surprise, as well as my delight over visiting with him again, he said that he would not have missed our journey together across this historical land. Neither did he wish to leave us until we had safely boarded our plane for London.

As the bus moved through the desert, Professor and I rode together quietly. How wonderful to share such a sacred journey with this great teacher who had helped plant my feet solidly on the pathway where the great ones had once walked. I knew that he, too, had referred to Moses numerous times in his books and that he loved him as I loved him. For me, the circle was complete. Although I regretted the brevity of our stay in Egypt, I was now sorry that our journey across the desert was passing so swiftly.

Our exodus finally came to an end, as must all things. When we boarded our plane for London, the Angelic Force, which had lifted our consciousness and held us suspended for twelve days, now withdrew. We all felt its' passing, for the world returned to what it had been before we began our journey. By comparison, everything seemed stark and desolate, and we felt as if all of the rocks of Mount Sinai had fallen upon us in a gigantic volcanic upheaval. However, I knew this terrible heaviness would pass away as we once more became accustomed to human existence and adjusted to the vibration of dense matter. I could not help but wonder how we endure this world and its heavy sheath and how we remain so oblivious to our home beyond mortal boundaries.

CHAPTER XXIII

The Final Voyage

fter my voyage to Israel and Egypt, I prepared to settle down at Gethsemane and continue teaching. I had walked where Jesus walked, seen the land that raised the ancients, and had crossed the sacred soil where Moses led the Israelites. Having experienced these things, I waited with anticipation for the next doorway to open on this vast adventure of life and to see where it would lead. I did not have long to wait.

The incident took place one day, as the sun was just rising in the east. A beautiful angelic presence awakened me, saying, that my time on earth had been shortened and that I must prepare to set sail to another unknown world, on a voyage that each of us must take someday. For this journey, there are no airplanes, ships, or automobiles.

Apparently, the time had come again to leave my comfortzone and experience what very few on Earth have been allowed to experience. I was being given the opportunity to observe the period of my final voyage on Earth with eyes and mind no longer bound by the limitation of human senses. I was also being given a chance to develop a deeper understanding of death through the conscious awareness of my own inevitable departure from life. Unlike many people, who would perhaps look upon the process of witnessing their own death as terrifying, I have found the transformation both fascinating and beautiful.

To step beyond these portals of darkness that bind the soul into a world of unknowing is as natural as the falling leaves and the autumn wind. It should be a wondrous time, a time of knowledge and understanding, and a time full of happiness because one's human struggles have almost ended.

Kahlil Gibran wrote:

If you would indeed behold the spirit of death, open your heart wide unto the body of life. For life and death are one, even as the river and the sea are one. Only when you drink from the river of silence shall you indeed sing. And when you have reached the mountaintop, then you shall begin to climb. And when the Earth shall claim your limbs, then shall you truly dance.

During my pilgrimage on Earth, I have come to realize that everything here is but a shadow or a reflection of that which we call God. I am not the first person to have made this discovery, for it is a truth that has been understood by all enlightened prophets and philosophers through the ages. It seems that no matter how high we climb, how many thousand books we peruse, or how many angel wings we grow, we still remain just that: a shadow and an expression of the Divine. As we ascend, however, this reflection will become more like He who created us.

If only I could paint a picture of this pathway that leads to God, for it is both within and without: within, for His Spirit transforms our humanness into angelic beings; and outer, for He creates a new world, one where miracles are commonplace and fear dissolves in the challenge of exploration. Once His world and ours unite, the soul never again experiences loneliness or lack of self-worth, and has no need to question its rightful place in the universe. The Master Weaver has woven each human being into His tapestry of life and has endowed them with His qualities, that all might be equal when His light in them has been brought forth. And when this time has come to pass, every human being shall ascend out of this human night of dark shadows.

For me the circle of life has almost completed itself. Should I laugh at those who laughed at me, or should I pity the darkness that covered their eyes? Should I seek revenge and allow myself to be filled with hatred because poverty was the spoon that fed me, or should I rejoice because ridicule, poverty, and loneliness enabled me to possess a deeper understanding and compassion for the human race? Should I begrudge the unrest of my earlier years, which taught me the depths of other's despair? Those things, which once hurt me, are now the things I bless, as each person will one day bless the rocks in life that mold their own greatness.

All life is continuity without cessation. For this reason if for no other, I wish that the word death could be removed from human vocabulary, or at least redefined as that moment when the soul ceases to exist in embodiment. Perhaps the terrible connotations woven into its fabric would then disappear on the outgoing tides of forgetfulness.

Cessation of physical form is a beneficent act of nature. It takes away the burden of old age and endows one with the breeze of youth. Gone are the pains, illnesses, and depressions. Yet, this does not mean one should take his or her life in order to escape the mountainous climb of human struggle. The perfect law of cause and effect is relentless and still prevails in word, deed, and thought. Those who take their life will sometime, someplace, in the future movement of God's cosmic order, lose their life.

I have begun to see living on earth differently. The importance, necessity, and opportunity to exist on this planet are more defined than ever. No one can progress and grow without existing in matter. If we were allowed to remain without deterioration of

the body, this earth upon which we live would become more stag-
nant than an inert cesspool. There would be more than diseases in
the body; there would also be diseases in the upward climb of
human progression and evolution. Therefore, death, as it is all too
often called, is part of the adventure of life which enables the soul
to cast away the old and build anew its glory in the sun.

Certainly I have found that this world of angels, which has
guided not only me, but also the planet Earth for so long, is not
far away on some distant star. It is here now, a dimension of consciousness beyond mortal boundaries. I know that we live in their
world, even as we live here on Earth. The refined ethereal Light
bodies of the immortals and the subtle ether of their Kingdom
interpenetrate our planet, just as the sunlight fills our day. By
raising our own consciousness while on Earth we can walk in the
footprints of Jesus and live in this world, yet share another world
unseen and once unknown.

Death has long ago lost its sting, for in dealing with the reality
of life, I have experienced both worlds. They are similar yet different. We do not suddenly appear with angel wings and fly around
singing sweet songs for the billions and billions of years of eternity. Rather, we co-exist in cities with loved ones; continue to
study the religions of our choice, and work to help others. One
thing that is different in this realm beyond the human senses is
that there is no death or robbery, murder, war, sickness, or old
age. Certainly, we must consider this a more heavenly estate than
that of Earth, where we struggle to survive the rugged pinnacles
of human progression.

After departure from this Earthly plain, there is much to learn,
not just for me but also for all people. Each in the same unique
fashion, as on Earth, will continue with their soul development
through kind thoughts, kind words, and kind deeds. My own
personal commitment to God has not been for this life alone, but
for the duration of my soul, and I suspect that this might encom-
pass millions of years. I promised Him that I would go anywhere

at any time I was needed and teach. As Jesus, his disciples, and so many great beings have continued to work with humanity; I have had to ask myself if I can do less.

It is all so clear now, this transition from life into more subtle form. I wonder why we grieve so when we say goodbye to some loved one who has entered a world we cannot see. They are well; they are beyond pain and are no longer embraced by the fetters of old age. More importantly, they are not dead. Somehow I believe that we have always known this, for we have prayed to those beyond for help. We have also believed that we will live with the angels someday and abide in Jesus' kingdom forever, without war, violence, or hurt. These thoughts could not exist if humanity really believed only in its mortality.

At the moment, I am being taught to live in mortality, to wonder about the portals of immortality, and to create a certain measure of comfort in both worlds. For the first time, these seem so integrated that there is little sense of separateness. I know that this is the way mankind was intended to live: free from fear, joyous in adventure, elegant in old age.

Many times I wish that I could reach out to all people on Earth and help them discover the wonder and miracle of what they really are. It is for this reason that I have written this book, not to exploit my own experiences, but to help everyone who may read it. My life is their lives yet to be, and their lives were once my life; and as my pain has passed away, so will theirs. I want my experiences to serve as a guide to people, lest they miss the greatest adventure of all, *a Journey beyond the Portals of Mortality*, the journey home.

Our God is not a religious figurehead, icon, or a person. He encompasses the universe, and because a part of Him lives in each soul we are an expression of all of his attributes. Thus, He is the wisest of the wise, the most knowledgeable of the knowledgeable, the most humorous, personal, loving, kind, gentle, understanding, and compassionate, along with a lot of other adjectives all at the same time. For over thirty years He has disciplined me, taught me, and not only introduced me to, but also enabled me to experience, worlds few humans have ever known. There is no sadness when I think of leaving the worldly state of dense existence. Earth has given me an opportunity to live and learn, but Heaven presents an opportunity for new exploration.

It is my request that my ashes be taken to Burrows Inlet, a body of water that peacefully surrounds a game reserve known as Burrows Island. Although the island does not belong to me, it is home to a tiny light station. I feel akin to it because I have been but a small light also. As I once laid my first United State tour at the feet of the Statue of Liberty in New York Harbor, it somehow seems fitting to lay the remains of my worldly pilgrimage at the base of this tiny light. Just as the light station has sent its beacon into the night to guide oncoming ships, I too have tried to guide those lost in the shadows of human life to see the light of another world.

Because the sea has always given me a sense of God's power, I have asked my students to take my tiny bit of remaining human existence to the inlet and ride the winds with me once more. I have also asked them to include a large supply of golden sparkles in the ashes. Then, as we bid farewell, I would that they remember me, and that the Light is in all of us. It is that part in each of us which is as a rainbow against a gray sky, the golden hues of a morning dawn, and a droplet in the evening mist.

In the words of Pierre Teilhard de Chardin:

> *Someday after mastering the winds,*
> *The Waves, the tides and gravity,*
> *We shall Harness for God the energies of love.*
> *And then for the second time in the history of*
> *The world, man will have discovered fire.*

CPSIA information can be obtained at www.ICGtesting.com
Printed in the USA
LVOW042017230512

283028LV00002B/43/P